WYANF

SCOTLAND'S BEST SMALL MOUNTAINS

About the Author

Kirstie Shirra is a freelance writer and environmental campaigner. Climbing mountains since she could walk, she has travelled throughout Europe and the Americas, but always ends up back in the wonderful mountains of north-west Scotland where she now lives with her partner Pete.

Scotland's Best Small Mountains is Kirstie's second Cicerone guide. The first, with Michelle Lowe, was the first guide to the GR7 in Andalucia, a 1200km route in southern Spain. Kirstie also writes regularly for *Trail* magazine.

SCOTLAND'S BEST SMALL MOUNTAINS

by

Kirstie Shirra

Dorset County Library	
Askews	2010
796.522094	£12.95

UMBRIA LA7 7PY

© Kirstie Shirra 2010
First edition 2010
ISBN 978 1 85284 578 0

Printed by MCC Graphics, Spain

A catalogue record for this book is available from the British Library.

All photographs are by the author unless otherwise stated.

Ordnance Survey This product includes mapping data licensed from Ordnance Survey® with the permission of the Controller of Her Majesty's Stationery Office. © Crown copyright 2010. All rights reserved. Licence number PU100012932.

Acknowledgements

Huge thanks to the wonderful friends who accompanied me on the different walks and subjected themselves to my constant photographs: Michelle, Karen, Annie, Rachel, Stephen, Jill, Jeremy, Steph, Kristin, Oran, Natasha, Robert, Janice, Canna and Torran, and to Lou for trying to come. A special thanks to Pete, for coming up many of the hills, coping with me while writing and doing the scree on Glamaig when my legs turned to jelly – you are my hero.

Finally, I'd like to thank my parents for introducing me to so many of the hills that were to become 'best small mountains' – I only wish you could still carry me when I get tired!

Advice to Readers

Readers are advised that, while every effort is made by our authors to ensure the accuracy of guidebooks as they go to print, changes can occur during the lifetime of an edition. Please check Updates on this book's page on the Cicerone website (www.cicerone.co.uk) before planning your trip. We would also advise that you check information about such things as transport, accommodation and shops locally. Even rights of way can be altered over time. We are always grateful for information about any discrepancies between a guidebook and the facts on the ground, sent by email to info@cicerone.co.uk or by post to Cicerone, 2 Police Square, Milnthorpe LA7 7PY, United Kingdom.

Front cover: Rocky pinnacle crowning the summit of The Cobbler

CONTENTS

INTRODUCTION 11
Walking in Scotland 12
Wildlife 13
The History of Scotland 14
Getting there 15
Getting around 15
Accommodation 16
Weather 16
When to go 16
Winter walking 18
Mountain safety 18
Access 19
Using this guide 21

Sutherland and the Far North 24
1 Ben Loyal 26
2 Quinag 30
3 Suilven 34
4 Cul Mor 40
5 Stac Pollaidh 45
6 Ben More Coigach and Sgurr an Fhidhleir 48

Torridon and the Northwest 54
7 Beinn Ghobhlach 56
8 Beinn Airigh Charr 60
9 Baosbheinn 65
10 Sgurr Dubh 72
11 Beinn Damh 77

Lochaber and the West 82
12 Sgurr Coire Choinnichean 84
13 Streap 88
14 Rois-bheinn, An Stac, Sgurr na Ba Glaise and Druim Fiaclach 94
15 Sgurr Dhomhnuill 101
16 Beinn Resipol 107
17 Ben Hiant 112

The Great Glen to the Cairngorms 118
18 Creagan a'Chaise and the Hills of Cromdale 120
19 Meall Fuar-mhonaidh 125
20 Meall a'Bhuachaille 129
21 Creag Dhubh and the Argyll Stone 134
22 Creag Dhubh (Newtonmore) 139
23 Morrone (or Morven) 144

Glencoe and Central Scotland 148
24 Ben Vrackie 150
25 Leum Uilleim 154
26 Sgorr na Ciche (Pap of Glencoe) 159
27 Beinn a'Chrulaiste 162
28 Beinn Trilleachan 167
29 Sron a'Chlachain 172

Arrochar and the Trossachs 176
30 Meall an t-Seallaidh 178
31 Ben Ledi 184
32 Ben A'an 190
33 Ben Venue 193
34 The Cobbler (Ben Arthur) 199
35 Beinn an Lochain 204

The Islands 208
36 The Storr (Skye) 210
37 Glamaig (Skye) 213
38 An Sgurr (Eigg) 219
39 Dun da Ghaoithe (Mull) 223
40 Goatfell (Arran) 228

APPENDIX A Useful contacts 235
APPENDIX B Bibliography 237
APPENDIX C Glossary of Gaelic words for Common Mountain Features . . 238
APPENDIX D Route Summary Table 239

Route symbols on OS map extracts

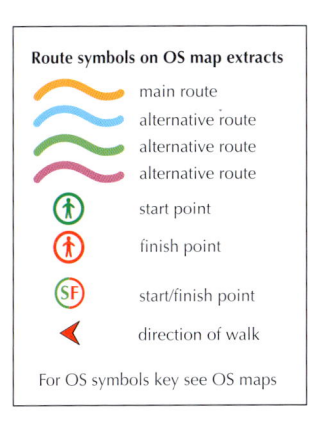

~~~ main route
~~~ alternative route
~~~ alternative route
~~~ alternative route

(🚶) start point
(🚶) finish point
(SF) start/finish point
◄ direction of walk

For OS symbols key see OS maps

Warning

Mountain walking can be a dangerous activity carrying a risk of personal injury or death. It should be undertaken only by those with a full understanding of the risks and with the training and experience to evaluate them. While every care and effort has been taken in the preparation of this guide, the user should be aware that conditions can be highly variable and can change quickly, materially affecting the seriousness of a mountain walk. Therefore, except for any liability which cannot be excluded by law, neither Cicerone nor the author accept liability for damage of any nature (including damage to property, personal injury or death) arising directly or indirectly from the information in this book.

To call out the Mountain Rescue, ring 999 or the European emergency number 112: this will connect you via any available network. Once connected to the emergency operator, ask for the police.

Map Legend

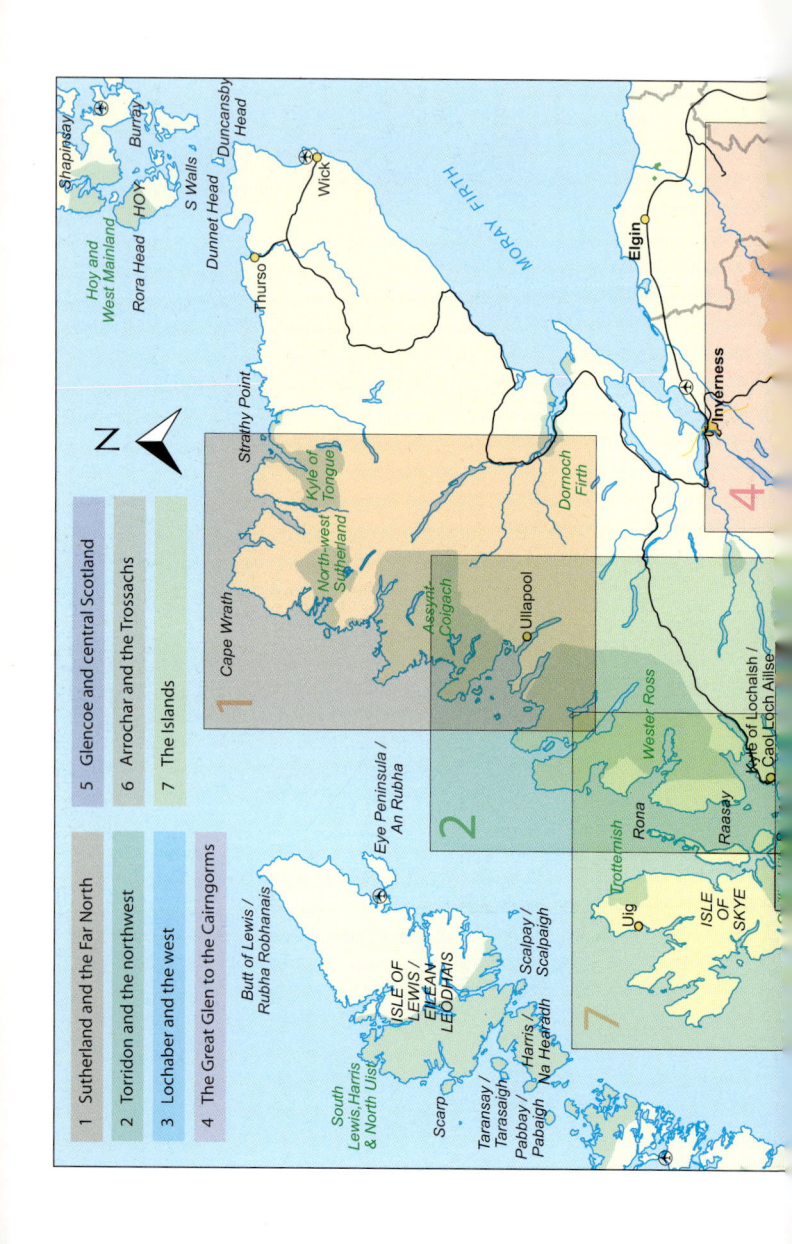

1. Sutherland and the Far North
2. Torridon and the northwest
3. Lochaber and the west
4. The Great Glen to the Cairngorms
5. Glencoe and central Scotland
6. Arrochar and the Trossachs
7. The Islands

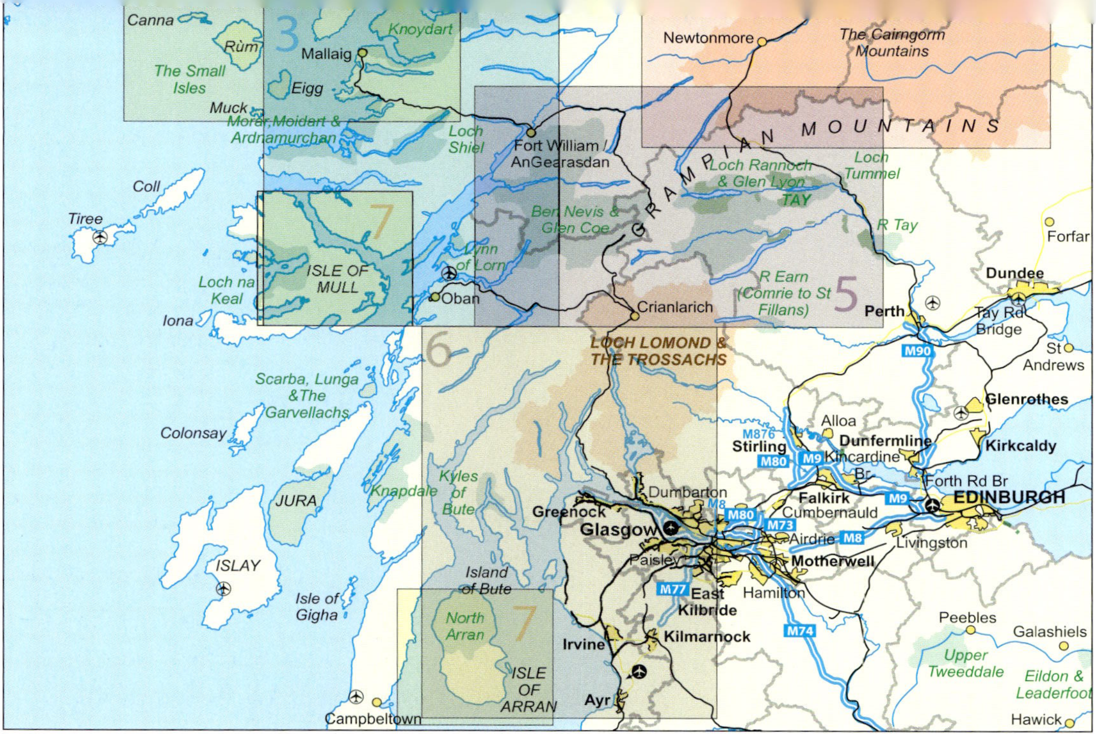

Canna
Rùm
The Small Isles
Muck
3
Mallaig
Eigg
Knoydart
Morar,Moidart & Ardnamurchan
Loch Shiel
Fort William / AnGearasdan
Newtonmore
The Cairngorm Mountains
GRAMPIAN MOUNTAINS
Loch Rannoch & Glen Lyon
Loch Tummel
TAY
R Tay
Forfar
Ben Nevis & Glen Coe
Coll
Tiree
7
ISLE OF MULL
Lynn of Lorn
Loch na Keal
Iona
Oban
Crianlarich
R Earn (Comrie to St Fillans)
5
Perth
Dundee
Tay Rd Bridge
St Andrews
6
LOCH LOMOND & THE TROSSACHS
Scarba, Lunga &The Garvellachs
Colonsay
Glenrothes
Alloa
M876
Stirling
Dunfermline
Kirkcaldy
M80
M9
Kincardine Br
M90
Forth Rd Br
Knapdale
Kyles of Bute
JURA
Dumbarton
M8
Falkirk
Cumbernauld
EDINBURGH
Greenock
Glasgow
M73
Airdrie
M8
Livingston
Paisley
Motherwell
ISLAY
Island of Bute
M77
East Kilbride
Hamilton
Isle of Gigha
North Arran
7
Irvine
Kilmarnock
M74
Peebles
Galashiels
Upper Tweeddale
Eildon & Leaderfoot
ISLE OF ARRAN
Ayr
Campbeltown
Hawick

Scotland's Best Small Mountains

The Cobbler and Allt a'Bhalachain

INTRODUCTION

Bourblaige with Ben More on Mull behind

When Sir Hugo Munro compiled a list of mountains in Scotland over 3000ft (914m), back in 1891, it's unlikely that he would have predicted the enthusiasm that arose for climbing them all. 'Munro-bagging', as it's become known, has fed that part of human nature that loves to collect, to tick off lists and to reach for an ultimate goal. In this case, climbing all 283 of the 3000ft-plus mountains, or Munros, in Scotland.

While this offers a challenge and an opportunity to climb some of the best mountains in the world, the downside is that many of Scotland's finest mountains are overlooked by walkers, purely because they lack a few metres in height. Yet what they lack in stature, they often more than make up for in other ways. This book champions just some of Scotland's best smaller mountains, each of which has been selected for its character, location, views, historical significance, technical difficulty or simply its beauty. From the surreal and striking landscape of the Storr in Skye, the pagan festivals of Ben Ledi in the Trossachs, to the imposing and rugged ridges of Quinag in Sutherland, this guide is, in its own way, 'an antidote to Munro-bagging'.

But neither is this another guide to the Corbetts (2500ft-plus peaks) or the Grahams (2000ft-plus) in Scotland – it is a guide that shuns height altogether as a factor for climbing a mountain. People who climb mountains to tick them off a list, and then do not return, never find out more about the mountain than how to reach its summit. This guide sets out to convey some of the character of the mountain, its history, who lived there and why they left, the wildlife, the flora and the geology. It encourages you to climb a mountain many times, in different seasons, until you know it as you would an old friend.

There is, obviously, a question mark over what a mountain actually is. In England and Wales, a mountain is defined as a landmass over 600m. This fits with other definitions that use 2000ft (610m) as their benchmark. In Scotland, however, there is no such definition and, in keeping with the spirit in which this book is written, no attempt is made to offer one, or to exclude peaks that fall below 2000ft. Few who have gone up the 528m of Ben Hiant from sea level could say it was any less of a climb than the 1245m of the mighty Cairn Gorm, which most climb from a starting point of 625m.

Above all, this guide aims to increase the enjoyment of Scotland's mountains. Whether you are an avid Munro-bagger (please don't take offence), an experienced walker, or new to Scotland's mountains, this book offers something for everyone. While it can't do anything about Scotland's weather or midges, it does describe opportunities to get away from it all on mountains that are far less climbed, with the potential for discovering new peaks and new places, and finding out more about the landscape you're walking in.

There are so many wonderful 'smaller' mountains in Scotland that one guide could not possibly attempt to cover them all. This is a selection of some of the best, but by no means exhaustive.

This book divides Scotland into seven areas (see overview map), with routes in each, so that wherever you are, there will be some of Scotland's best small mountains to explore. The routes range in length and difficulty, so you can easily choose what best suits your experience and plans. Where possible, circular routes are described, and different options are highlighted to increase your choices and make the routes even more interesting.

WALKING IN SCOTLAND

While Scotland is a relatively small country, the combination of stunning mountains and spectacular coastlines make it one of the best walking destinations in the world. Few other locations offer dramatic rocky ridges that rise up from stunning sandy beaches, and fewer still offer this and the opportunity to get away from it all completely.

As one of the least populated areas in Europe, the Scottish Highlands are one of the last great areas of wilderness. Characterised by remote peaks reached, in some cases, only by single-track roads, or occasionally only on foot, walking in Scotland can be a splendidly secluded experience. Rough footpaths and few waymarks are more than made up for by breathtaking sea views, an eagle soaring overhead, or nothing but the sound of the wind in the trees.

Scotland is home to two national parks – the Cairngorms National Park and the Loch Lomond and the Trossachs National Park – but much of northern and western Scotland is mountainous, offering many more beautiful destinations to choose from.

Wherever you go, water is likely to be a major feature. From the coast and the sea to the many beautiful lochs, lochans, rivers and burns that make up a large part of the Scottish landscape, you are never likely to be far from water. And with many great walks on Scotland's islands, you even have to cross the sea to reach some of these routes.

WILDLIFE

Wildlife flourishes in the large areas of mountainous wilderness in Scotland. A walk in the hills could well bring you face to face with a majestic stag and other red deer or a herd of wild goats. High on a mountain plateau you could spot a mountain hare, while you're more likely to come across red squirrels and pine martens in the more wooded slopes of the glens. Most elusive is the Scottish wildcat.

Scotland being home to over 400 breeding pairs of golden eagles, you may also find one of them soaring above your head. Then there is the

Wild goats

The summit of Beinn Ghoblach with Scoraig peninsula beyond

white-tailed, or sea, eagle, the UK's biggest bird of prey, with a wingspan of eight feet (two and a half metres!). Following recent reintroduction of these magnificent creatures, there are now around 40 breeding pairs, with the best chance of seeing them being on Mull, on the Small Isles and in the adjacent west coast hills.

On the coast there are otters and grey and common seals to spot. Porpoise and bottlenose dolphins are often found in coastal waters too and if you are really lucky you may be able to spot minke whale, basking shark, or even the distinctive black and white form of an orca. Ferry journeys from the mainland to the islands or specialised boat trips offer the best opportunities to spot marine wildlife.

THE HISTORY OF SCOTLAND

Scotland is also rich in both natural and human history. From some of the world's oldest rocks to some of the most famous battles, the landscape and culture of Scotland has been shaped over the years by both climate and human activities.

The geographical entity that is now Scotland came into being 40 million years ago, when the continents of North America, of which Scotland was a part, and Europe collided. Many of the rocks and landforms that shape Scotland were formed much earlier, however, through the collision of tectonic plates, glaciation and weather. The Lewisian Gneiss rock of the Northwest Highlands that Scotland shares with North America is 3000 million years old.

The human history of Scotland is clearly much more recent but no less turbulent. From the Picts of Caledonia and the formation of the original Alba, then the wars of independence and Viking marauders, to the Jacobite uprisings and the Highland Clearances, people have long fought and died over the hills and glens of Scotland. The Pict, Gaelic, Norse, Scots and English names that pepper the landscape are evidence of the many waves of settlers.

This guide will tell you all about Scotland's natural and human history as you walk through the landscapes they have formed. Each route reveals something of the people and places, features and events, both past and present, of each of Scotland's best small mountains. From Rob Roy and Jacobite hideouts to battlefields and abandoned villages, Scotland's history is out there to discover.

GETTING THERE

Train travel from Europe and the rest of the UK is straightforward via the east- and west-coast mainlines, travelling to Edinburgh and Glasgow respectively. Both lines originate in London, making it easy to connect to and from Eurostar services. For train information within the UK, visit www.thetrainline.com; for Eurostar see www.eurostar.com.

There are ferry services to Scotland from Northern Ireland and Belgium. Stena Line runs a ferry service between Stranraer in Scotland and Belfast in Northern Ireland (www.stenaline.co.uk), P&O run services from Cairryan and Troon to and from Larne in Northern Ireland (www.poirishsea.com) and Norfolkline runs a service between Rosyth (near Edinburgh) to Zeebrugge in Belgium (www.norfolkline.com).

There are also many international and national flights to Scotland's major airports – Glasgow, Edinburgh, Glasgow–Prestwick and Aberdeen. In addition there are a number of national flights to the smaller airports of Inverness and Dundee.

More details of how to reach Scotland from overseas can be found at www.visitscotland.com/guide/travel/travel-from-overseas.

GETTING AROUND

Within Scotland, most places can be reached by public transport, via trains, buses and ferries. Scotland's train services are operated by Scotrail (www.scotrail.co.uk) with the West Highland line from Glasgow to Mallaig proving particularly useful for accessing the mountains. Most of the ferries to the Scottish islands are operated by Caledonian MacBrayne (www.calmac.co.uk). There are also many bus operators with good services linking Scotland's major towns and cities and, usually, less frequent services in rural areas. Details of public transport to access the mountains in this guide are given in each route description.

For details of public transport options across Scotland see www.travelinescotland.com or call them on 0871 200 22 33.

Given the remoteness of much of the Scottish Highlands, there are some mountains that can only be reached by car. There are car rental agencies at all the major airports, as well as in most large towns and cities.

ACCOMMODATION

A wide range of accommodation to suit differing budgets is available in most of the areas covered in this guide, although sometimes it may be a drive or bus journey from an individual route. With tourism such an important part of Scotland's rural economy, most towns and villages have hotels or guest houses, and there are large numbers of B&Bs and self-catering cottages spread throughout the Highlands. There are also many formal campsites, and responsible wild camping well away from roads is often permitted (if in doubt check with the landowner).

For details of accommodation in Scotland contact the Scottish Tourist Board www.visitscotland.com/guide/where-to-stay.

WEATHER

It is fair to say that the Scottish weather does not always enjoy a good reputation! With prevailing westerly winds bringing rain off the Atlantic, the Scottish hills can certainly be wet and blustery places. Low cloud can even lead to some visitors wondering where the hills actually are. That said, on a sunny, clear day, of which there are many, there is no finer place to be and you will appreciate it all the more.

Check the weather forecast before you go and be prepared for the right conditions. Always carry waterproofs and spare warm clothing – even in mid-summer the weather in the mountains can change rapidly and the higher you go the colder it gets. The Mountain Weather Information Service provides good daily mountain forecasts for the different upland regions of Scotland www.mwis.org.uk.

WHEN TO GO

The routes given in this guide have been described with spring, summer and autumn conditions in mind. While some would provide a pleasant winter excursion, the longer and steeper routes could be very challenging in winter.

The summer school holidays in Scotland are earlier than in England, running from the beginning of July to mid-August. During this period places are busier and accommodation is often more expensive. May, June and September are quieter and often have good spells of weather.

The summer months are also the time of midges, Scotland's infamous small biting insects. While they are unlikely to bother you on a very sunny

When to Go

Sgurr an Fhidhleir and Stac Pollaidh from Ben More Coigach

Taking in the view on Sgurr Dhomhnuill

or on a very windy day, in damp, still conditions they can become pretty unbearable – thankfully it is often windy on Scotland's hills! They can also be avoided by visiting in the spring or autumn.

WINTER WALKING

The mountains in winter can be very different places from during the summer. Check route details and conditions carefully in advance, and only venture out if you are confident of your winter walking abilities and have the appropriate equipment including an ice axe and crampons. Make sure you know how to use them.

Plan winter routes taking into account that winter conditions will make routes longer and that the days are much shorter. Always carry a head torch for use in emergencies.

Avalanches are an additional risk in the winter – it is important to check the avalanche forecast www.sais.gov.uk.

MOUNTAIN SAFETY

The Scottish mountains can be dangerous places and it is important to be properly equipped and prepared. While this guide covers 'small' mountains, they are often in remote and rugged places, and lesser height does not negate the impact of the Scottish weather.

- Wear good walking boots and appropriate clothing, with extra warm and waterproof layers to put on if the weather changes.
- Always ensure you carry a map and compass and know how to use them. Many of the routes in this guide have sections without

paths, and even on those that do it is easy to get lost, particularly in bad weather.
- Be sure to leave word with someone of where you are going and when you expect to return, and let them know when you do.
- Carry a first aid kit and a whistle to alert people to your location in an emergency. The internationally recognised distress call is six blasts on a whistle within a minute.

ACCESS

The Land Reform (Scotland) Act 2003 establishes a clear public right to access land in Scotland, meaning that so long as you act responsibly and do not interfere with the rights of the landowner, you are able to walk where you wish in the Scottish mountains.

The main potential access issue for most of the routes in this guide is deer stalking. The red-stag stalking season is from 1 July to 20 October, although the dates on which estates start stalking vary. The season for shooting hinds is from 21 October to 15 February. Roe-deer stalking is less common, but the roe-buck stalking season is from 1 April to 20 October and the doe-stalking season is from 21 October to 31 March.

Even when an estate is stalking, it is unlikely to prevent you walking many of the routes. The best advice is to contact the estate and find out where they will be. Many will post details at main car parks and popular

Near Cunside on the walk in to Ben Loyal

Scotland's Best Small Mountains

The rocky summit of Beinn Resipol

Looking south across the rocky shoulder of Meallan Diomhain on Cul Mor

route access points. In general, walkers are advised to stay on paths and ridges during the stalking season. It is worth noting that deer stalking does not take place on Sundays. The Hillphones network provides phone numbers for walkers to call a number of estates. The relevant hillphone and other estates' phone numbers are given where available in the information box for each route. However, these can change and it is important to check local information where possible.

Another potential access issue is forestry work, and again the relevant contact numbers are given where available.

Wherever you are walking it is important to follow the Scottish Outdoor Access Code (www.outdooraccess-scotland.com) and to be responsible for yourself and your activities. As they say, leave only footprints and take only memories and photographs.

USING THIS GUIDE

For each mountain in this guide, one main route is described in detail. Where possible this is a circular route, providing an interesting and enjoyable ascent and descent of the peak, taking in any notable features and landmarks. This is often, but not always, the most popular route up a hill. It is not always the shortest or quickest.

Alternative routes, where they exist, are described in less detail, to give walkers a choice of routes or allow them to construct their own. The distance and ascent of each

Little Loch Broom

alternative route is given in brackets at the end of the description. The route descriptions are not designed to be followed without a map, except for armchair planning.

Each route is accompanied by a description of the mountain and the area in which it is located, and a factual information box detailing distance, timing, ascent, difficulty, access, how to get there, grid reference and other nearby attractions and facilities.

Mountain names

The spelling of mountain names and features in this guide is taken from the Ordnance Survey 1:50,000 maps.

Maps

Each route is highlighted on the relevant section of Ordnance Survey's 1:50,000 maps.

The main route described is shown in orange, then any alternatives are first blue, then green, then pink, where applicable.

The small section of map provided is not a replacement for carrying the relevant OS map. For those who prefer to use the more detailed 1:25,000 maps, the map numbers for these as well as for the 1:50,000 maps are given in the route information box. HARVEY Maps also cover many of the mountain areas in this book – www.harveymaps.co.uk.

Grid references

Grid references (expressed as two groups of three digits) are given for the start and end points, and summits of all the mountains included, as well as for some useful points along the way, particularly where routes lack paths or key landmarks to aid navigation. These are six-figure references based on GPS readings taken by the author while on the routes.

Distance and ascent
Figures given for distance and ascent both refer to the whole route from start to end. This means the level of ascent is often greater than the height of the peak being climbed.

Difficulty
Rather than give any kind of grading of difficulty, the guide provides an overview of the type of terrain, gradient, exposure, length and need for navigation on each route, to allow you to judge for yourself how easy or difficult you will find a route. A very long walk without any exposure may be difficult for some, while a short walk down steep scree is easy, and vice versa. This allows you to match routes to your own skills and confidence.

Times
Timings given for each route are the walking time to complete the whole route. They are based loosely on 4km an hour plus 30 minutes for every 300m of ascent (Naismith's Rule) and the author's own timings. They do not include time for breaks, which should be added to give a clearer idea of the length of time needed. A 4hr30 route may appear short, but can easily become a full day out by the time you've stopped for lunch and had a couple of breaks.

Getting to routes
Details of the starting point for each route are given in the information box. In the majority of cases these refer to a car park, but where there is none, details of where you can park are given. Information on how to reach a route by public transport, where possible, is also included and while it is hard to reach many of Scotland's mountains without the use of car, in an age of climate change we should all be encouraged to do so where we can.

Something else
Also in the information box are details of one or two of the best attractions or things to do near the route, with relevant contact details. These attractions range from ruined castles to real ale pubs, and are intended to enhance your enjoyment of your visit to an area, or fill some time while waiting for a train, bus or lift, and are by no means exhaustive. Visiting attractions and facilities in rural areas, rather than just turning up to do a walk and leaving again, also helps the local economy, so you can feel good about yourself while drinking that pint!

Scotland's Best Small Mountains

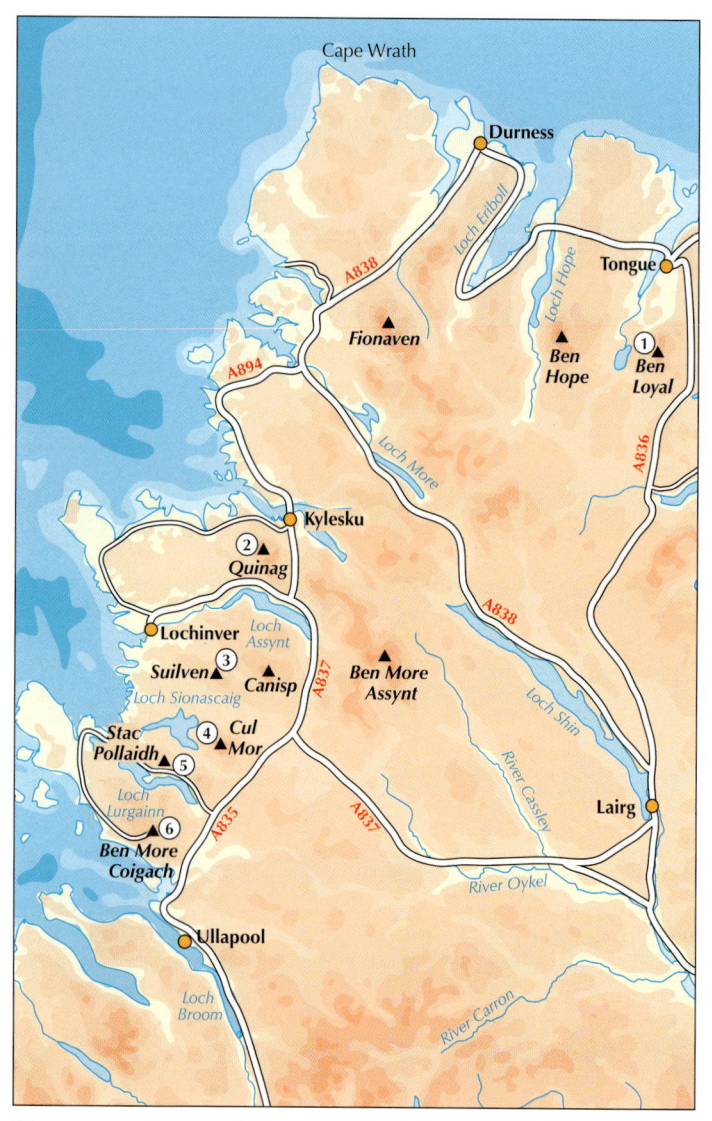

Suilven and Loch Druim Suardalain

SUTHERLAND AND THE FAR NORTH

1 BEN LOYAL (765m)

in Gaelic Beinn Laghail, probably 'the law mountain', from the Norse 'laga fiall'

Distance	14km
Time	5hr30
Ascent	820m
Difficulty	A good walk in on tracks gives way to grassy slopes that are less challenging or steep than the rocky peaks of Ben Loyal might suggest.
Maps	OS Landranger 10, OS Explorer 447
Access	Ben Loyal forms part of the Ben Loyal Estate (01847 611291)
Getting there	Start at the turning to Ribigill Farm off the minor road around the Kyle of Tongue (584 546). There is parking for a couple of cars. You could walk to here from Tongue. There is a daily bus from Thurso to Tongue (Traveline Scotland 0871 200 22 33 www.travelinescotland.com).
Something else	Take a walk on the stunning sands of the Kyle of Tongue, or visit the ruins of Varrich Castle, once home to the MacKay clan chiefs.

A royal hill in Scotland's far north, Ben Loyal is renowned for its queens, castles and treasure. Climbing far above the Kyle of Tongue, this route gives you an opportunity to conquer your own castle, and gaze out to where the North Sea meets the Atlantic Ocean.

Ben Loyal is known to many as 'the queen of Scottish mountains', although it's not clear why, as the name doesn't seem to have royal connotations. But 'queen' or not, Ben Loyal does have an impressive castle.

The granite tower of An Caisteal, 'the castle', is Ben Loyal's highest top, at 765m. It is just one of the five rocky tops that crown the ridge, causing it to be described as

Ben Loyal across the Kyle of Tongue

castellated. From each of these tops you gain fantastic panoramic views over the surrounding countryside, composed as it is of vast swathes of wild land and water. The shifting white sands of the Kyle of Tongue in particular are a sight to be seen.

In the middle of the Kyle you can see the Rabbit Islands, so named because rabbits were introduced to them in the 1700s to provide meat for the local laird. You also look down to small Lochan Harkel. Not that notable in its appearance, it does hold an extraordinary story and, perhaps, treasure!

In 1746, the *Hazard*, a Jacobite ship carrying over £13,000 in gold coins to fund Bonnie Prince Charlie's rebellion, hid in the Kyle of Tongue, hoping to evade capture by HMS *Sheerness*, a navy frigate. The *Hazard*'s crew took the coins ashore with a plan to deliver them by land, but the crew were attacked and threw the coins into Lochan Hakel. Bonnie Prince Charlie sent 1500 men to retrieve the money, but they were defeated en route, and it is thought that the government recovered most of the coins. If the 1500 men had fought at the Battle of Culloden instead, they might have prevented the Jacobites' defeat.

Route

From the start, follow the road to **Ribigill** farm, going left where it divides to pass between the farm buildings.

Continue along the track from here, which runs between the fields heading towards Ben Loyal. Ignore a fork off to the right to head left and across a small ford. This track takes you across level boggy ground towards the ruined farm of **Cunside**.

Cross the **Allt Lon Malmsgaig** (580 515) to the same side as Cunside, but then leave the track to take a small path heading south-southeast towards the **Bealach Clais nan Ceap**. This climbs up the right-hand side of a small burn.

Leave the path before you reach the bealach to climb steeply southwest up the side of **Sgor Chaonasaid** at the end of the Ben Loyal ridge, gaining the summit of Sgor Chaonasaid (712m) from the south. From here there are fantastic views of the ever-changing sand banks in the Kyle of Tongue.

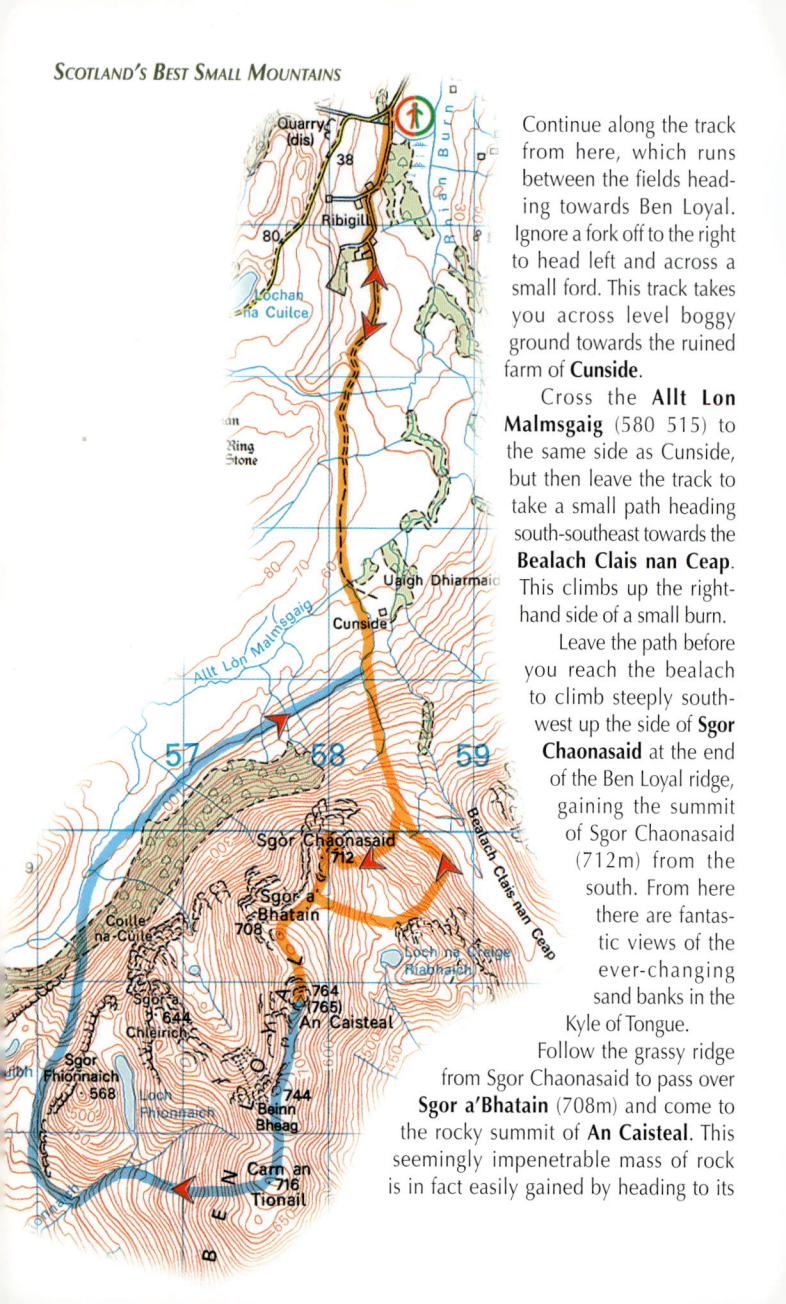

Follow the grassy ridge from Sgor Chaonasaid to pass over **Sgor a'Bhatain** (708m) and come to the rocky summit of **An Caisteal**. This seemingly impenetrable mass of rock is in fact easily gained by heading to its

1 BEN LOYAL

Looking down on the Kyle of Tongue

west side from where a small path takes you to the summit (765m) (578 488, 7.5km, 3hr). All other routes would involve a serious rock climb. From its elevated position, this rocky castle offers brilliant 360° views.

To return, retrace your steps to the shoulder between An Caisteal and Sgor a'Bhatain, then head east down gentle slopes towards **Loch na Creige Riabhaich**. Just north of the loch you can pick up a path that runs north-northeast across the broad plateau, then zigzags down more steeply to rejoin the original path into the Bealach Clais nan Ceap. Follow this to return to the start via the outward route (14km, 5hr30).

Alternatives
A Full Traverse of the Ridge
For a full traverse, return to the west side of the summit of An Caisteal, then go south along the ridge to Beinn Bheag (744m). Carry on south taking you down then back up to the top of Carn an Tionail (716m), the last top of the ridge. From here, head west down grass and heather slopes to come to the top of a gully. Follow the gully down to meet the Allt Fhionnaich and head down its left bank, crossing it before it enters a steeper gorge (564 476). Head north then northwest around Sgor Fhionnaich before following a second burn steeply down through the birch forest to level ground below. Continue northwest across rough grassland to rejoin the path just before Cunside (20km, 960m, shown in blue).

2 QUINAG (808M)

from the Gaelic cuinneag, meaning 'milking pail'

Distance	13km
Time	5hr30
Ascent	1200m
Difficulty	This is a long, challenging route across rocky, narrow ridges, with some exposure and a lot of ups and downs.
Maps	OS Landranger 15, OS Explorer 442
Access	Quinag is owned by the John Muir Trust and there are no access restrictions. Contact the JMT on 0131 554 0114 or visit www.jmt.org.
Getting there	Start at the car park on the A837 (232 273). There are buses during the summer from Inverness to Skiag Bridge at the junction of the A837 and the A894 (Traveline Scotland 0871 200 22 33, www.travelinescotland.com).
Something else	Take a walk around the ruins of Ardvreck Castle or visit the Bone Caves at nearby Inchnadamph, where human remains dating back 4500 years were found.

> Five tops, stunning scenery, several ridge walks and sea views make this an absolute epic, one of the best mountains in one of the wildest parts of Scotland.

More of a massif than a single mountain, Quinag has five tops, three of them Corbetts (if you are counting). Its huge Y-shaped form dominates north Assynt, stretching from Loch Assynt at the foot of its southern slopes, to the village of Kylesku to the north.

Loch Assynt is home to the ruins of Ardvreck Castle, standing on a peninsula jutting out into the loch. Built by the Clan MacLeod, who had owned much of Assynt since the 13th century, Ardvreck Castle is the scene of betrayal, conflict and ghosts.

2 QUINAG

Heading towards to Quinag

The Marquis of Montrose, a famous Royalist fighting against the Covenanters, sought sanctuary in the castle following his defeat at the Battle of Carbisdale in 1650. But instead of finding sanctuary, he was tricked into capture and transported to his execution in Edinburgh. The ghost of Montrose is said to still haunt the ruins.

Less than three decades later, the castle and much of Assynt were captured by the Mackenzie clan, who went on to build neighbouring Calda House, now also in ruins. Their stay was short lived too, as the Crown seized the castle and land following the Mackenzies' participation in the failed Jacobite Rebellion of 1745.

From Kylesku, to Quinag's north, you can travel by boat along Loch Glencoul to the site of Britain's highest waterfall – Eas a'Chual Aluinn. At 200m, it is more than three times as high as Niagara Falls, though perhaps not quite as wide!

Now owned and protected by the John Muir Trust, Quinag is part of both the North West Highlands Geopark and the Assynt National Scenic Area. Its long ridges and fine peaks give rise to views over one of the wildest landscapes in Scotland. The surrounding land is studded with a myriad of lochs and lochans with white sandy beaches, stretched along the west coast beyond.

Scotland's Best Small Mountains

Route

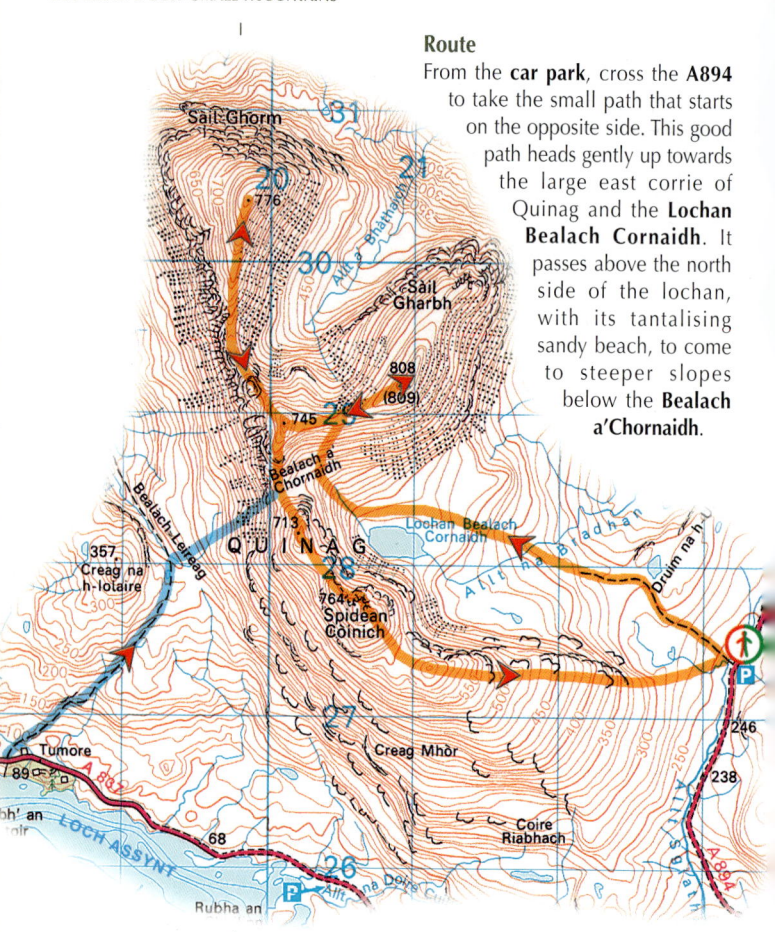

From the **car park**, cross the **A894** to take the small path that starts on the opposite side. This good path heads gently up towards the large east corrie of Quinag and the **Lochan Bealach Cornaidh**. It passes above the north side of the lochan, with its tantalising sandy beach, to come to steeper slopes below the **Bealach a'Chornaidh**.

Instead of climbing directly to the bealach, take the path off to the right (202 285) to double-back on yourself and traverse steeply northeast up onto the shoulder of **Sail Gharbh** by a large cairn (203 289). From here, head right along the broad rocky shoulder to reach the summit of Sail Gharbh (808m) (209 291, 5km, 2hr). Looking

2 QUINAG

Spidean Coinich and Lochan Bealach Cornaidh

south you see the rocky buttresses of your last top of the day, Spidean Coinich.

Retrace your steps along the shoulder, but once at the cairn continue straight on, dropping slightly before making the steep ascent up the grassy slope of an unnamed peak at **745m**. From here, on a clear day, the views out to sea and the Summer Isles are magical.

A steep path leads you north-northwest down off the top and along a narrow section of ridge. Once past an impressive square-topped knoll, a long but gradual ridge, with great views west, takes you all the way to the summit of **Sail Gorm** (776m) (198 303, 7km, 3hr).

Again retrace your steps, this time back to the unnamed top, from which the path zigzags steeply south on loose rock down to the Bealach a'Chornaidh. You could choose to return to the start from this point for a shorter day, but it is well worth continuing.

Climb very steeply south on an increasingly narrow ridge and along its interesting and airy rocky crest to reach a second unnamed top (713m). A gentler descent brings you to a small lochan and the final climb of the day. Pass the lochan on its left to gain the steep, rocky path to the summit of **Spidean Coinich** (764m) (206 277,

10km, 4hr30). Here the best views are over Loch Assynt and the peaks of Canisp and Suilven to the south.

To descend, head steeply southeast, balancing your way down across the large boulders of Spidean Coinich's summit. The gradient soon lessens and the large boulders shrink, giving way to smaller stones and large slabs of rock. Use these slabs to pick a way east down the stony slopes, keeping near the edge of the shoulder. The route then crosses a short section of boggy ground to rejoin the path back to the car park (13km, 5hr30).

Alternatives
The route up Quinag can be easily reversed or shortened by only climbing the peaks to the north or to the south of the Bealach a'Chornaidh, or by omitting Sail Gorm.

From Loch Assynt
The only other route onto Quinag is from the road alongside Loch Assynt, the A837. A track leaves the road to the west of Tumore (182 267). Follow this to the Bealach Leireag, from where a very steep, rocky ascent can be made to the Bealach a'Chornaidh and then the main route above followed (3km, 500m to the Bealach a'Chornaidh, shown in blue).

3 SUILVEN (731M)

the 'suil' part meaning 'pillar', from the Norse sular, the 'ven' part meaning 'mountain', from the Gaelic bheinn

Distance	23km (+ 6km road walk if no transport)
Time	7hr
Ascent	1170m
Difficulty	This is a long and demanding route. A good approach path gives way to boggier ground and a very steep, rocky ascent. The descent is equally steep, with a long walk out on boggy paths until the good path down the River Kirkaig.
Maps	OS Landranger 15, OS Explorer 442

3 Suilven

Access	www.assyntfoundation.org 01571 844100
Getting there	The route starts on the road to Glencanisp Lodge from Lochinver. There is parking just before the public road ends (107 219). If walking from Inverkirkaig back to Lochinver, it would be worth parking in the village itself to avoid a climb at the very end of the day. There are buses to Lochinver from Inverness and Ullapool (www.rapsons.com or contact Traveline Scotland 0871 200 22 33, www.travelinescotland.com).
Something else	Visit the Achins bookshop and cafe at Inverkirkaig (01571 844262) or get one of the best pies in the world at the Lochinver Larder (01571 844356, www.piesbypost.co.uk).

Scottish mountains don't come any more iconic than Suilven. Instantly recognisable, this small but mighty peak rises up as if from nowhere to dramatic effect. A long, classic route with rewards aplenty.

When the Vikings came to their 'south land' – Sutherland – they saw Suilven from the sea and named it 'pillar

Meall Meadhonach from the summit

mountain', so much did it dominate the landscape. Today geologists refer to it as an inselberg, or island mountain.

An isolated peak rising dramatically out of moorland, Suilven is formed of Torridonian Sandstone capped with Cambrian Quartzite. This tougher quartzite cap protected the sandstone beneath during the ice ages, creating the inselberg shape, as the rocks all around were eroded away. The surrounding landscape, worn down to the ancient Lewisian Gneiss that forms the base here, was scoured out to leave hundreds of little lochans and hummocks.

The human history of the area is pretty groundbreaking too. Sitting above the fishing village of Lochinver, Suilven forms part of the Glen Canisp Estate. In an area of Scotland hardest hit by the Highland Clearances, this estate was long held in private hands.

In 1886, the Lochinver branch of the Highland Land League agreed to demand the restoration to the people of the deer forest of Glencanisp 'where there is plenty of provision for ourselves and our families. It extends twenty-one miles...and the land of our fathers lying waste.' In 2005, their demand was met.

Suilven – the classic view

3 SUILVEN

The Assynt Foundation, formed by a group of local residents, managed to secure a community buy-out of the Glencanisp Estate and neighbouring Drumrunie Estate, under the 2003 Land Reform Act. The foundation now owns and manages the 44,000 acres, including Suilven, for the benefit of the community and the public, and the sustainable development of the natural environment.

This route on Suilven takes in both Glen Canisp itself and a descent down the beautiful River Kirkaig, passing the stunning 20m cascade of the Falls of Kirkaig.

Route

Starting from the parking area on the road to **Glencanisp Lodge**, continue along the road and take a left fork to pass behind the lodge. From here head right, the road becoming a gravel track with great views of Suilven and Canisp ahead.

The track divides after 4.5km (147 209) at **Suileag**. You take the right fork to pass in front of the lovely old wall of a sheiling. This brings you alongside the **Abhainn na Clach Airigh**, aptly meaning 'river of the stone sheiling'. The track crosses the river via a bridge just beyond **Lochan Buidhe**.

From here you climb gently until you reach a cairn, where you turn off the track onto a path to the right (167 196). This is before the second bridge marked on the map. This small path is boggy at first and climbs up a series of shelves in the landscape to come to **Loch a' Coire Dhuibh**.

The path takes you round the west side of the loch, between it and some smaller lochans, to reach the base of the climb up to the bealach. The route up is steep and eroding in places, but the zigzags in the path make it reasonably straightforward, and the narrow, airy bealach (at 600m) is soon reached. From here the views south over to Stac Pollaidh and the Inverpolly Estate are breathtaking.

To gain the highest top, Caisteal Liath ('the grey castle'), follow the path right over a couple of lumps and some exposed sections of ridge before the final climb up some step-like rocks to the summit of **Caisteal Liath**

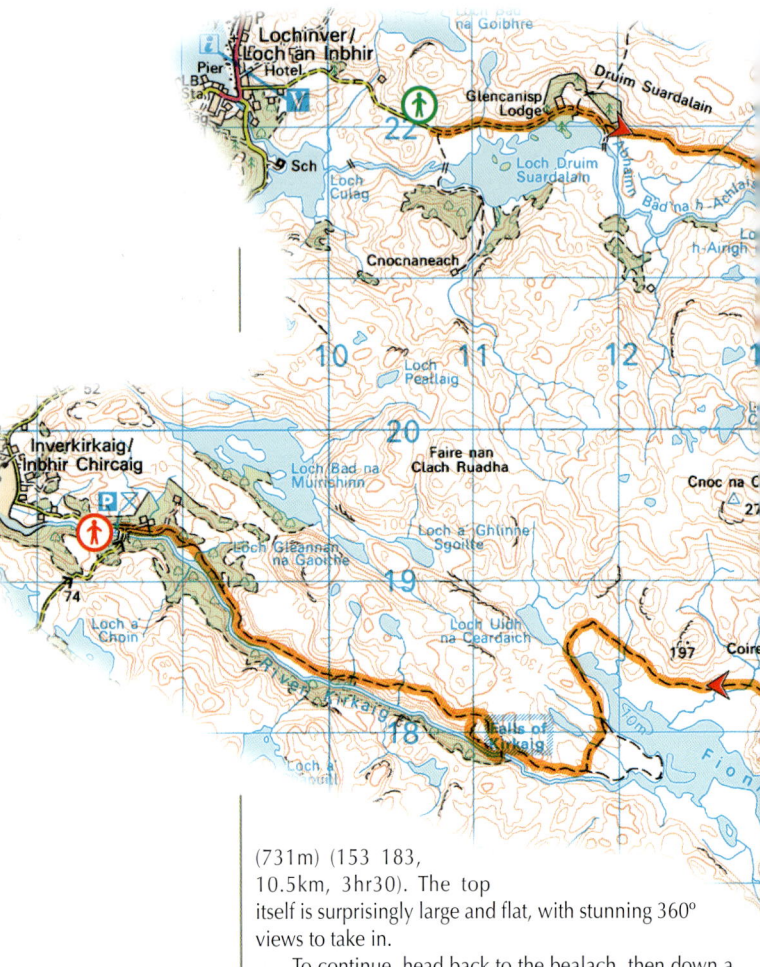

(731m) (153 183, 10.5km, 3hr30). The top itself is surprisingly large and flat, with stunning 360° views to take in.

To continue, head back to the bealach, then down a path on the other side. This takes you first down a steep scree gully before giving way to a slightly less steep path cutting diagonally down the hillside below crags. A final steep descent down the side of a small gully brings you

3 SUILVEN

onto the level by a small **burn**. Follow the burn to meet a path at the side of **Fionn Loch**, along which you go right. The path, very boggy in places, runs the length of Fionn Loch, bending round the northwest end to pass between it and **Loch Uidh na Ceardaich**. You then double-back on yourself to walk down the other side of the loch. There is a great view back to Suilven here, with Fionn Loch in the foreground. When the path divides, take the right fork, happily cutting a corner to come to the **River Kirkaig**.

Follow the path down the River Kirkaig, detouring, if you have the energy, to see the beautiful **Falls of Kirkaig**.

39

The path ends at a small road. Head left along it to reach the main single-track road by the **parking area** (086 193) (23km, 7hr).

Alternatives
Avoiding the road
Either the Glencanisp or River Kirkaig routes could be used for either approach or return, eliminating the road walk at the end.

4 CUL MOR (849M)

'big back'

Distance	12km
Time	4hr30min
Ascent	760m
Difficulty	With a good path to start and end, this is a relatively straightforward route, but does involve navigating across some rough, pathless ground, and a steep, rocky final ascent up the ridge to the summit.
Maps	OS Landranger 15, OS Explorer 439
Access	Cul Mor is part of the Drumrunie Estate owned by the Assynt Foundation (01571 844100).
Getting there	Start at a lay-by on the left of the A835 just past the Knockan Crag car park (188 093). The Ullapool to Lochinver bus passes by Knockan Crag, (Traveline Scotland, 0871 200 22 33, www.travelinescotland.com).
Something else	Visit the Knockan Crag visitor centre to find out more about the fascinating geology of the area (01854 613418, www.knockan-crag.co.uk).

One of the highest peaks in Assynt, Cul Mor's rocky summit is a window to both beautiful views, and the history of the formation of the surrounding landscape.

4 Cul Mor

The twin peaks of Cul Mor

The 'big back' that is Cul Mor rises up from Knockan Crag to the east to overlook Loch Sionascaig and the peak of Stac Pollaidh to the west. Located in the Drumunie Estate, it is now part of the land owned by the Assynt community, who formed the Assynt Foundation to buy the estate and neighbouring Glencanisp in 2005. Together with the smaller peak of Cul Beag, Cul Mor's rocky flanks dominate the view as you drive north from Ullapool.

While just one of the famous Assynt peaks, and less well known than Suilven and Stac Pollaidh, Cul Mor does sit at the heart of a major geological debate.

The so-called 'Highland controversy', over the way the landscape and rocks of Scotland were formed, began here in the 1850s, and has gone on to shape our understanding of the geology of the world. Prominent Victorian geologists Murchison and Geikie argued that the layers of rock in the Northwest Highlands must have formed vertically, younger rocks forming on top of older ones. They dismissed claims from less well-established figures, such as Nicol and

Lapworth, that there were in fact younger rocks beneath older ones, demonstrating that there must be horizontal forces at work in the formation of the landscape.

It was not until the 1880s that this latter theory was accepted as correct, and with it the identification of the Moine Thrust. We now know that the Moine Thrust was formed 430 million years ago when Scotland, then part of America, collided with England and Wales, causing huge sheets of rock to be thrust up to the west to form many of the Northwest Highlands' most recognisable mountains.

Knockan Crag, at the foot of Cul Mor, was one of the most important sites in identifying the Moine Thrust and the horizontal movement of rocks. Today it forms the Knockan Crag National Nature Reserve, and is home to a visitor centre explaining more about the geology and global processes at work on the rocks and landscapes all around us.

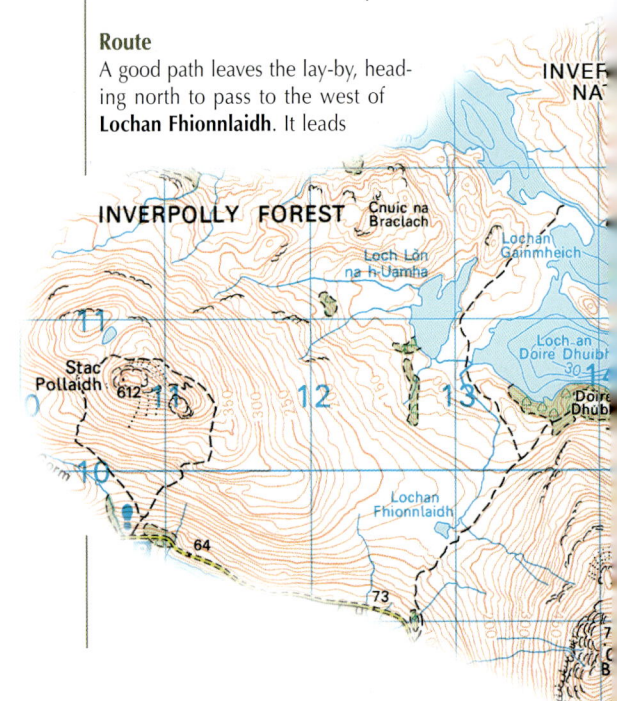

Route
A good path leaves the lay-by, heading north to pass to the west of **Lochan Fhionnlaidh**. It leads

4 Cul Mor

you gently up and round the hummocky landscape, with good views back to Knockan Crag.

This good path ends at a large cairn (185 111) at the foot of the wide shoulder of **Meallan Diomhain**, just over 2km from the start. From here, head west-northwest on a rough, peaty path up the shoulder. It becomes rockier, with the gradient easing at about 500m. The path is hard to spot in places, but continue west with a line of cairns guiding you towards the summit.

Once at the cairn marking the high point of Meallan Diomhain at 600m (170 116), the severe rock crags on the face of Cul Mor make it apparent why a direct ascent from here is not possible. Instead, after taking in the good views southwest to Cul Beag, go north-northwest, descending briefly to head towards the northeast ridge of **Cul Mor**. The ridge is easily gained by way of rough but not too steep ground.

Knockan Crag

Ascend the ridge, climbing southwest as it becomes increasingly steep and narrow. On the lower section of the ridge you can avoid most of the rocky outcrops, but as you climb, the ridge becomes almost entirely rock, with the final section requiring you to clamber over large boulders to reach the summit trig point (849m) (162 119, 6km, 2hr30). There are great views over the lochs and peaks of Inverpolly, particularly that of Coigach.

To continue, descend gently west then south to the col between the summit and Creag nan Calman. It is then worth the short steep climb to the top of **Creag nan Calman** (828m) for the views of Cul Beag and Stac Pollaidh.

The easiest descent is to return to the col from here, then head east down the heather and grassy slopes, keeping to the north of the burn. At about 550m, head north and then round to the east to climb briefly back to the high point of Meallan Diomhain. The outward route can then be followed back to the start (12km, 4hr30).

Alternatives
Omitting Creag nan Calman
Rather than continuing to climb Creag nan Calman, return from the summit by the same route (12km, 630m).

5 STAC POLLAIDH (613M)

'the stack', or 'steep rock', 'by the pool'

Distance	5km
Time	2hr–2hr30
Ascent	520m
Difficulty	This short circuit round the hill presents no difficulties, and, although steep, nor does the ascent to the ridge. A traverse along the ridge, however, requires exposed scrambling, to grade 3 for the final summit, and anyone attempting it needs to remember they will have to return the way they came.
Maps	OS Landranger 15, OS Explorer 439
Access	Polly Estates 01854 622 452
Getting there	Start at the Stac Pollaidh car park off the Achiltibuie road next to Loch Lurgainn (107 095). A local bus runs from Ullapool to Achiltibuie (Traveline Scotland 0871 200 22 33, www.travelinescotland.com).
Something else	Take a drive around the beautiful Inverpolly landscape.

Something of a national treasure, Stac Pollaidh is beloved by many. A circular route up to, and possibly along, its rocky pinnacles, offers a mini adventure at the heart of the beautiful Inverpolly Estate.

Based on 3000-million-year-old rock that was once a part of North America and Greenland, Stac Pollaidh is now very much a Scottish institution. This small mountain has

The dramatic rocky pinnacles of Stac Pollaidh's ridge

long held a place close to the heart of many walkers and it is easy to see why.

Its dramatic rocky towers and pinnacles rise up from the banks of Loch Lurgainn, presumably the pool that gives Stac Pollaidh its name. Right in the centre of what was for many years the Inverpolly National Nature Reserve, Stac Pollaidh rubs shoulders with the likes of Cul Mor, Cul Beag and Coigach, some of the giants of the Sutherland landscape, though they too fall into the 'small' category. With sea views and a backdrop to die for, it really is the epitome of picturesque.

But perhaps the reason Stac Pollaidh is so loved is that it is slowly shrinking. Worn down over the years by walkers and weather alike, the Torridonian sandstone that makes up Stac Pollaidh's ridge appears to be eroding far quicker than its neighbours. Scientists at the British Geological Survey believe that weathering has taken place for so long as to suggest that the ridge was not covered by ice during the last ice age, when other hills were. But don't worry – it's unlikely Stac Pollaidh will disappear any time soon, especially with its new path.

Route

From the **car park** cross the road to take the well-built path on the other side. This starts off steep, but the gradient soon eases. When the path divides, take the left fork to pass through a gate in a deer fence and climb steadily northwest.

The path then heads north to bring you over the west shoulder of **Stac Pollaidh** and round the back of the hill. As you come round the back, ignore an older, eroded path off to the right that leads to the pinnacles. Instead, continue round until the path divides again, the left fork heading down to the east. You take the right fork, climbing steeply southeast up some rock steps and then along the top of a fence line to gain the ridge and a large cairn at 543m (110 104, 2km, 1hr15).

This point, with its great views south to Coigach and north to Suilven, is where many walkers stop. The ridge from here involves some reasonably serious exposed

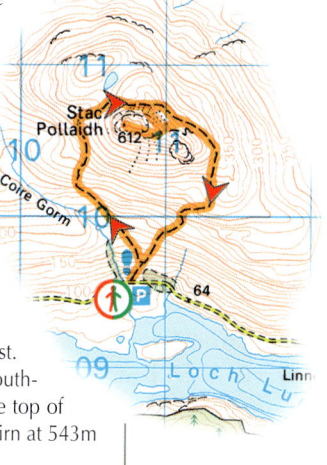

Stac Pollaidh from Ben More Coigach

Scotland's Best Small Mountains

scrambling, particularly on the final top, which is classed as a grade 3 scramble.

To continue, head west, making use of the small path that runs along the north side of the ridge to avoid the first rocky towers. This brings you to the unavoidable final tower for which you will need a good head for heights and scrambling skills to gain the summit (613m) (107 106, 2.5km, 1hr45). You are rewarded with great views west to the Summer Isles and across to neighbouring peaks.

Retrace your steps to the cairn, then head northeast down a path on the far side of the previously mentioned fence line. This brings you down to the main path around the hill, which this time takes you round the east of the peak.

A few large zigzags bring you to the front of Stac Pollaidh again, then back to car park (5km, 2hr–2hr30).

Alternatives
Avoiding the Ridge
An easy circular route of Stac Pollaidh can be made without gaining the ridge at all. To do this, take the left turn when the path divides to the north of the peak and continue round (3.5km, 400m).

6 BEN MORE COIGACH (743m) AND SGURR AN FHIDHLEIR (705m)

'big hill of Coigach', Coigach coming from the Gaelic coigeach, meaning 'a fifth share of land', in this case thought to mean a fifth of the then Cromarties; Sgurr an Fhidhleir translates literally as 'peak of the fiddler'

Distance	10km
Time	4hr
Ascent	900m
Difficulty	A short route with some steep slopes and exposed sections of ridge. Stretches without paths make for some

6 BEN MORE COIGACH AND SGURR AN FHIDHLEIR

	rough walking and the need for good navigation in poor visibility.
Maps	OS Landranger 15, OS Explorer 439
Access	Ben More Coigach is located in its entirety within the Scottish Wildlife Trust's reserve. For up-to-date access information, contact 0131 312 7765.
Getting there	Park in a lay-by at Culnacraig, near the very end of the road that passes through Achiltibuie (061 041). There are some buses from Ullapool to Achiltibuie (Traveline Scotland 0871 200 22 33, www.travelinescotland.com).
Something else	Take a boat trip on the *Hectoria* from Achilitibuie to the seal colonies of the Summer Isles (01571 622200).

Rising dramatically out of the sea, the Ben More Coigach range dominates the Coigach peninsula while remaining fairly unknown to walkers. The great ridge walk combined with some of the best views in the world make for a brilliant day out.

Ben More Coigach is the highest peak on the peninsula that gives it its name. Together with its neighbour and

The long ridge to Ben More Coigach

subsidiary peak, Sgurr an Fhidhleir, it forms part of a stunning mountain massif.

Carved out of sandstone by glaciers, the peaks form part of the North West Highland Geopark. The first of its kind in Scotland, the geopark celebrates the unique geology, landscape and communities of the far northwest of Scotland. With the Ben More Coigach ridge dominating the view north from Ullapool, it is easy to see why it is geology to be celebrated.

The ridge ends abruptly, dropping dramatically to the sea, with the spectacular views out to the Summer Isles more famous than the peaks themselves. The Summer Isles, a collection of picturesque islands out to the west, when caught at sunset on a descent from Ben More Coigach and Sgurr an Fhidhleir, offer one of the best vistas there is.

While once widely inhabited by farmers, herring fishermen and even illicit whisky distillers, it is now only Tanera Mor, the largest of the Summer Isles, that still has a few occupants, though it is a very popular destination for day-trippers in the summer months.

History has played its part in shaping the landscape of the Coigach peninsula too. Visited or occupied at various times by Vikings, Bronze Age farmers and Picts, some evidence of these prehistoric settlers remains. Perched on a promontory not far from Ben More's crags are the remains of the Pictish fort of Dun Canna.

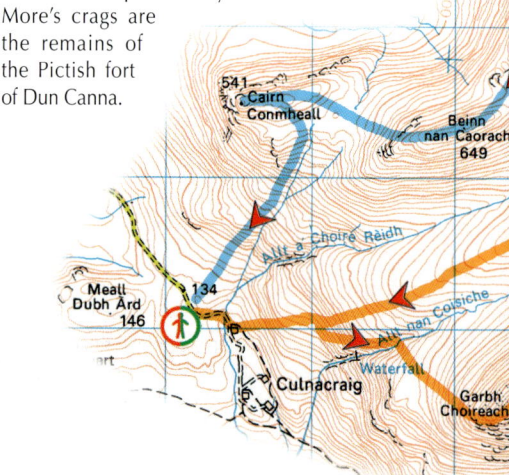

6 BEN MORE COIGACH AND SGURR AN FHIDHLEIR

More recently, the settlements of Achiltbuie, Culnacraig and others came into being as people crofted the land and fished off its shores. Perhaps surprisingly, the post office has played a role too. The current 10km path from Blughasary, and a potential route to Ben More Coigach, was formed by a hardy postman delivering the mail to Achiltibuie from Ullapool.

Route

From the car parking area walk left down the road to cross the bridge. Take a small path off to the left just after the bridge to climb steeply northeast (this path looks as if it is used by sheep more than people). At about 280m the path levels out and heads southeast towards Garbh Choireachan and the start of the ridge.

The path divides soon afterwards – go right to continue towards the ridge, contouring southeast still. The path disappears just before the gorge of the **Allt nan Coisiche**, or 'walker's burn', but bear east along the burn to find a crossing place. Once across, head southeast again towards the end of the ridge. This is ascended on the west side by bearing east all the way to the top and making use of bits of sheep paths. While steep, and on some well-eroded rock, it is never too difficult.

Once on **Garbh Choireachan** (738m), follow the path along the hugely enjoyable ridge. It sticks to the west side to avoid some rockier sections, though there is the option of scrambling along the very top. This brings you to the summit of **Ben More Coigach** (743m) (094 042, 4km, 2hr). The view from here over to better-known neighbour Stac Pollaidh is spectacular and unique.

From the summit head northeast briefly until the gradient down to the left lessens, then head north diagonally down across short grass to the bealach (544m).

From the bealach the prominent peak of **Sgurr an Fhidhleir** (705m) (094 054, 6km, 2hr45) lies ahead. Climb northwest to gain the summit, and stunning views over its precipitous northern edge.

To return, head southeast, picking up a path that runs the length of the shoulder from the summit back to the junction where you originally turned right. This gentle descent allows you to take in the great view out over the sea to the Summer Isles. Once back on the original path, follow it back to the start (4hr, 10km).

Alternatives
One Peak Only
The route could be shortened by climbing either Sgurr an Fhidhleir by the same ascent as the descent, or Ben More Coigach by joining the path from the bealach, missing out the ascent of Sgurr an Fhidhleir (7.5km, 630m former; 8.5km, 710m latter).

Taking in Beinn nan Caorach and Cairn Conmheall
The route could be extended by continuing along the ridge from Sgurr an Fhidhleir to take in the tops of Beinn

6 BEN MORE COIGACH AND SGURR AN FHIDHLEIR

Looking out to the Summer Isles from Sgurr an Fhidhleir

nan Caorach (649m) and Cairn Conmheall (541m). Rather than heading down the southeast shoulder from Sgurr an Fhidhleir, go southeast briefly then drop northwest to the bealach with the unnamed peak (648m). Ascend this (no paths) then follow the shoulder southwest to Beinn nan Caorach. From there, cross the broad plateau with little further climbing to Cairn Conmheall. Retrace your steps briefly to avoid crags and follow the burn down to the road (12km, 1100m, shown in blue).

From the Northeast, following the Allt Claoniadh

Approach the peaks from the northeast following the Allt Claoniadh on a small path from the end of Loch Lurgainn, past Lochan Tuath, then up steeply to the bealach between Sgurr an Fhidhleir and Ben More Coigach (10km, 400m to/from bealach, shown in green).

Scotland's Best Small Mountains

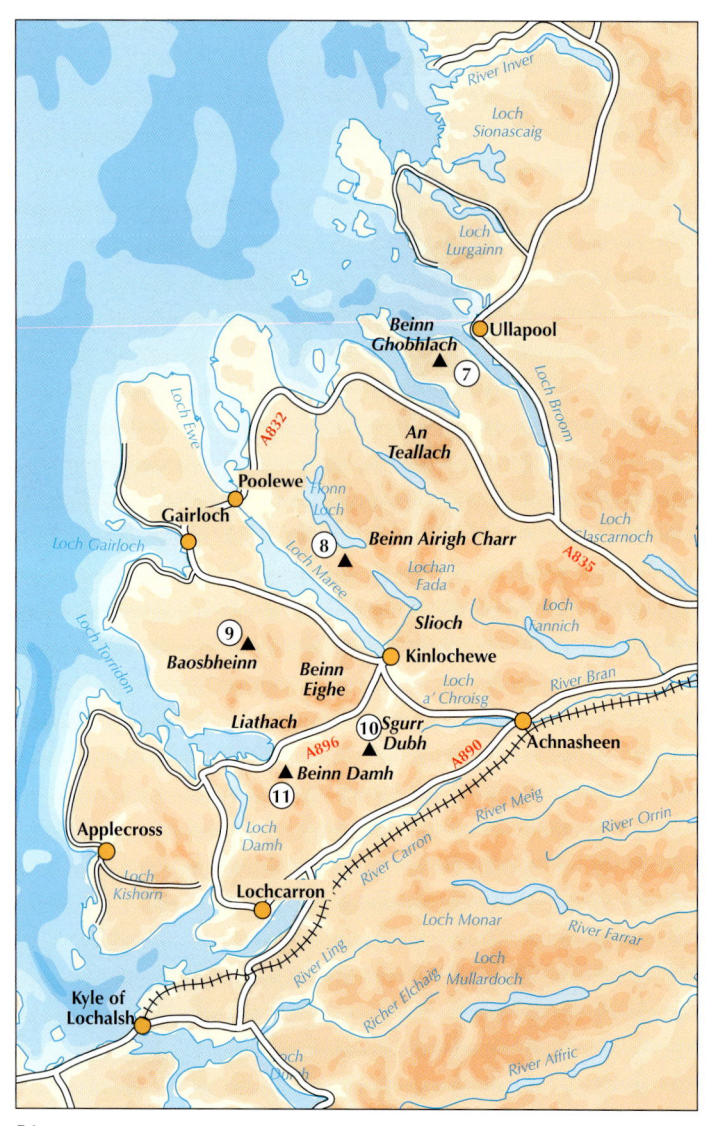

TORRIDON AND THE NORTHWEST

Ling Hut and the Coire of the Hundred Hills

7 BEINN GHOBHLACH (635m)

'forked hill'

Distance	12km
Time	4hr30
Ascent	760m
Difficulty	A remote rugged route that soon leaves all paths behind to climb rough heather then rocky slopes. Good navigation required.
Maps	OS Landranger 19, OS Explorer 435
Getting there	Start at the parking area at the end of the road to Badrallach (055 918). The nearest public transport is to the other end of the road, about 11km away (Traveline Scotland 0871 200 22 33, www.travelinescotland.com).
Something else	Visit the remote village of Scoraig and consider staying a few days to get away from it all, accommodation details at www.scoraig.com.

Occupying a unique location on a remote peninsula, Beinn Ghobhlach offers the opportunity to really get away from it all. This wild and rugged walk with sea views also holds the possibility of eagles soaring overhead.

Beinn Ghobhlach easily qualifies as one of Scotland's best small mountains because of its unique location. With Loch Broom to the north and Little Loch Broom to the south, Beinn Ghobhlach's slopes descend to meet the sea on both sides of the remote Scoraig peninsula. In its isolated position, without any paths, it is a great place to escape to. Rich in wildlife and with great views over the Summer Isles and the pinnacles of the mighty peak of An Teallach, it is well worth visiting.

The village of Scoraig itself can only be reached by boat from Badlurach on the south shore of Little

7 Beinn Ghobhlach

Start of the route at Badrallach

Loch Broom, or by way of an 8km walk along the north shore. With no road and no mains electricity, the 90 or so full- and part-time villagers of Scoraig have had to be inventive. It is home to both a self-taught wind-turbine designer/builder, and organic-vegetable growers –producing both electricity and fresh food for the inhabitants. Everything else comes in by boat or on someone's back.

While many of the settlements that scatter the Scottish countryside have been left as ruins due to the clearances or lack of work, Scoraig has bucked the trend. From the 1960s onwards, new inhabitants moved into the abandoned village, resettling the crofts there and building their own homes. It now has a school, a postal service and a museum.

Route

Take the path that continues from the end of the road at **Badrallach**. This good level route is the only access, apart from by boat, to the village of **Scoraig**, which is located near the end of the peninsula. Follow the path around the coast for almost 2km to reach its high point and a small cairn (039 924).

Head right from the cairn to climb northeast quite steeply up a grass and heather slope. This levels out at about 270m when Beinn Ghobhlach comes into view straight ahead, with Loch na h-Uidhe in the foreground. Descend slightly to go round to the right of **Loch na h-Uidhe** across boggy ground.

At the far side of the loch pass by a tempting sandy beach to start the climb onto Beinn Ghobhlach's ridge. Head north-northeast for what appears to be a small saddle to the left of the top. The climb is steep in places, up heather slopes, but if anything it is shorter and less steep than it looks. Once you gain the boulder-clad ridge (around 053 942), head east up it the short distance to **Beinn Ghobhlach**'s summit (635m) (055 943, 5km, 2hr30).

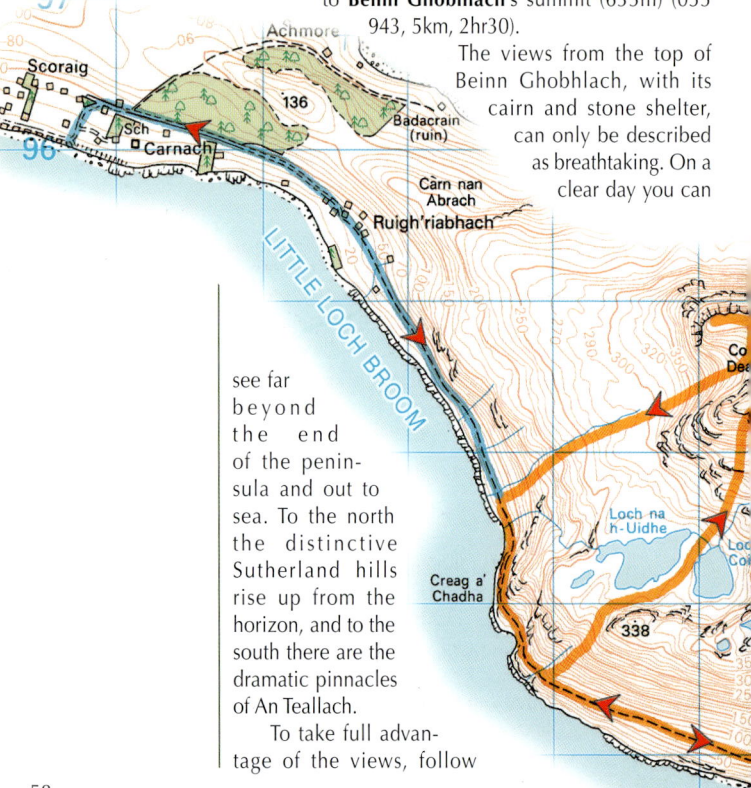

The views from the top of Beinn Ghobhlach, with its cairn and stone shelter, can only be described as breathtaking. On a clear day you can see far beyond the end of the peninsula and out to sea. To the north the distinctive Sutherland hills rise up from the horizon, and to the south there are the dramatic pinnacles of An Teallach.

To take full advantage of the views, follow

7 BEINN GHOBHLACH

Looking down on Loch na h-Uidhe and Loch na Coireig

the ridge round from the summit and out to the end top. From there double-back briefly to reach less steep terrain, then head down south into **Coire Dearg**.

From Coire Dearg head southwest down rough ground all the way back to the Scoraig path. The last section down to the path is the hardest, due to its steepness and long grass. Once on the path, head left to return to the start along a spectacular cliff-hugging route (12km, 4hr30).

Alternatives
Straight There and Back
Return via the outward route to make a slightly shorter day (10km, 600m).

From Scoraig
If you are staying in Scoraig or have travelled there by boat, by walking the opposite way along the path to the start, the same route as above could be followed (17km, 850m, shown in blue).

8 BEINN AIRIGH CHARR (791M)

'hill of the mossy' or 'rough sheiling'

Distance	25km
Time	8hr
Ascent	1100m
Difficulty	This is a long route, but on good, straightforward tracks and paths for the walks in and out, with a small but clear path to the col. No path on the tops and some steep slopes. It is possible to use a bike to shorten this route.
Maps	OS Landranger 19, OS Explorer 433 & 434
Getting there	Start at the car park beside the bridge over the River Ewe in the centre of Poolewe (858808). There are some buses to Poolewe from Inverness, Dingwall and Achnasheen station (see www.rapsons.com or contact Traveline Scotland 0871 200 22 33, www.travelinescotland.com).
Something else	Visit the National Trust for Scotland's beautiful Inverewe Gardens (0844 4932225, www.nts.org.uk/Property/36/) or celebrate the end of the walk in the Poolewe Hotel (01445 781 241, www.poolewehotel.co.uk).

A long but simple walk into the heart of some of Scotland's most beautiful countryside. With stories of legendary shepherdesses, Arctic convoys and exotic plants, this is a real gem of a mountain, which very much deserves to be explored.

Rising up out of the watery landscape of Letterewe, Beinn Airigh Charr stands proud behind Poolewe, flanked by Loch Maree on one side and Fionn Loch to the other. The Torridon hills spread out to the south and An Teallach peeks up to the north. This countryside is truly beautiful and unique in many ways.

Poolewe is home to Inverewe Gardens, famous for growing exotic plants in the Highlands of Scotland, at a

8 BEINN AIRIGH CHARR

On the shoulder with the summit behind

latitude further north than Moscow. Established in the late 1800s by Osgood Mackenzie, it is home to an amazing array of rhododendrons and a beautiful walled garden.

Loch Ewe, at whose end Poolewe sits, is the only north-facing sea-loch on the west coast of Scotland. This makes it particularly sheltered, and for that reason it was of great importance during the Second World War. Navy convoys bound for Russia with vital supplies sheltered in the loch before making the hazardous Arctic trip. Pool House, now one of Poolewe's hotels, was used as a command centre for the convoys, and the ruins of the navy's coastal defences can still be seen at Rubha nan Sasan, at the end of the Cove road from Poolewe.

The start of the walk to Beinn Airigh Charr is along the length of the River Ewe. This is actually not very far, though, as at less than a mile long, the River Ewe is the shortest river in Scotland. The route then climbs above the banks of beautiful, islanded Loch Maree, passing ruins of the former sheilings that give the hill its name. The shepherds who used these summer dwellings when grazing their animals have left their mark on the hillside. Not only are there the ruins, but also lazy beds (patches where potatoes were grown by laying them on the surface and covering them with soil from a trench on either side of the patch in rows), giving evidence of where they'd cultivated the land, and one unfortunate shepherdess has given her name to one of Beinn Airigh Charr's peaks.

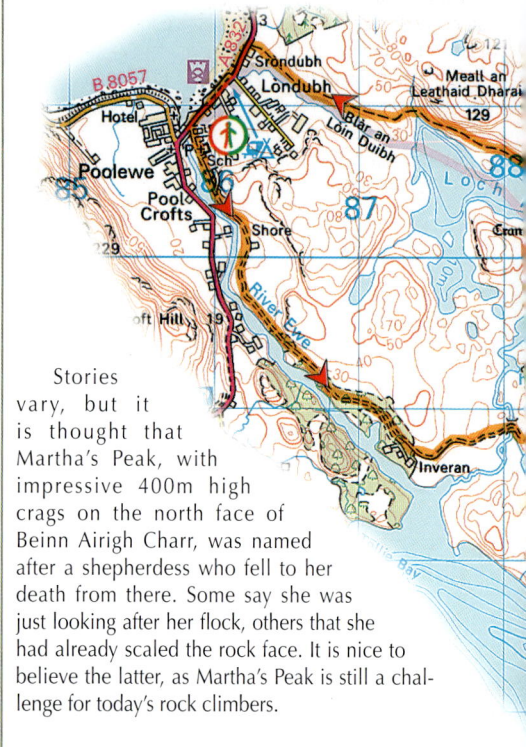

Stories vary, but it is thought that Martha's Peak, with impressive 400m high crags on the north face of Beinn Airigh Charr, was named after a shepherdess who fell to her death from there. Some say she was just looking after her flock, others that she had already scaled the rock face. It is nice to believe the latter, as Martha's Peak is still a challenge for today's rock climbers.

Route

From the **car park**, follow the small road that runs alongside the **River Ewe** as it heads upstream. This turns into a private road at a cattle-grid. Continue, and 2km from the start you come to a deer fence with gate and stile. Just after this the road divides – head left up the now gravel track, signed to Loch Maree and Kernsary.

8 Beinn Airigh Charr

The track leaves the river and trees behind to head out into open countryside. It crosses a burn then passes **Loch an Doire Ghairbh** on its left. Once past the lochan the track bends to the north; at this point (883 788) take a small path off to the right, starting in a lay-by and marked by a small cairn. This path, boggy in places, is a shortcut, heading southeast to cut out a large loop in the track before returning to it (if you are cycling, stay on the track).

On regaining the track, follow it to the right for about 1km as it heads towards the banks of **Loch Maree**. Here (893 768) a small cairn marks the path off to the left; take it to start climbing the hill (leave bikes here – see the alternative, below). The small path passes the ruins of a sheiling and goes round an old pasture to come down and across a small pretty ford. The path then heads east, contouring around the hillside, with the **burn** on your left. When the path divides, take the right fork to continue round the hillside, still following the burn.

Keeping the burn on its left, the path begins to climb more steeply, zigzagging up into the corrie between the rocky peak of **Spidean nan Clach** to the left and **Meall Chnaimhean** on the right. It finally crosses the burn at this point, just before a final short steep climb south up to the col between these two peaks.

From the col, double back to head north up the shoulder of Spidean nan Clach. From the summit of Spidean at 703m, drop down southeast (no path) to the col (670m) between it and **Beinn Airigh Charr**.

From this col, head east up the steep rocky and grassy slope to gain the summit (791m) (930 761, 12.5km, 4hr). This vantage point gives spectacular views over Fionn Loch, the length of Loch Maree, surrounding peaks and out to sea.

To return, head southeast then southwest down to about 600m on gentler slopes, the islands of Loch Maree directly ahead. At this point (926 756) cut northwest to contour around the hillside back to the col between Spidean nan Clach and Meall Chnaimhean. Follow the ascent route back down to the track.

The wilderness of Fionn Loch

For a different walk out, stay on the track (don't take the previous short-cut) to come to **Kernsary**. The track divides here. Take the right fork across the bridge to pass in front of Kernsary Cottage and past some sheds to go through a gate. Just after the gate take a track to the left down to and across a metal footbridge. Head up a grassy field towards a ruined building from where a path takes you round the east side of **Loch Kernsary**.

This is a lovely lochside path that improves as it crosses a stile into National Trust for Scotland land. It takes you all the way back to **Poolewe** via a small hill at the end of the loch and through the Cnoc na lise community woodland, before reaching the main road. Follow the road to the left for 1km to return to the start (25km, 8hr).

Alternatives
Avoiding Loch Kernsary
The return round Loch Kernsary could be omitted, allowing a bike to be used to and from where the hill path leaves the track. To do this, you should keep on the track rather than taking the short cut at Loch an Doire Ghairbh (25km, 1140m, shown in blue).

9 BAOSBHEINN (875m)

'hill of the forehead' or perhaps, more interestingly, ' wizard's peak', from baobh, meaning 'wicked person'

Distance	23km
Time	8hr
Ascent	1200m
Difficulty	A good track for the long walk in, but then rough ground over open hillside with no paths to gain the summit. Rocky, steep slopes with some small paths on main ridges.
Maps	OS Landranger 19 & 24 OS Explorer 433
Access	Information is posted in the car park during the stalking season; more information from Gairloch Estate (01445 712378).

Getting there	Start at the car park on the A832 by a green barn (known locally as the red barn, due to its previous colour) (856720). Limited buses to Gairloch from Inverness and Achnasheen station (www.rapsons.com or contact Traveline Scotland 0871 200 22 33 www.travelinescotland.com).
Something else	Drive north to stunning Red Point beach, to watch the sun set over the Torridon hills, then camp in the dunes at Gairloch's Sands campsite (01445 712152, www.sandscaravanandcamping.co.uk).

> A magical journey into the wilderness of a remote Torridon hill. This long and rugged route takes you back in time to the end of the last ice age, to see, in all their glory, the mountains that the ice age created.

With a name that roughly translates to mean 'wizard', perhaps it shouldn't be a surprise to start the day at a 'red barn' that's actually green. The rational explanation – that the barn used to be red, and the name stuck – doesn't detract from the magic of this route.

Leaving behind the red/green barn, you climb gently, passing through contrasting landscapes and gaining a glimpse into other eras. Regenerating native woodland with evidence of past settlements gives way to wild, barren terrain that could have you believing the glaciers have just melted.

Baosbheinn sits in what was the Flowerdale Deer Forest. Established in 1847, it would have seen most of the remaining trees in the area chopped down to make way for deer stalking. Attitudes to deer and forestry are beginning to change though.

The Bad na Sgalag native pine wood was established in 1997 as part of the shifting approach towards forestry in Scotland. After many years of favouring large

9 Baosbheinn

Baosbheinn and Loch Bad an Sgalig

plantations of foreign species, the emphasis is now on promoting habitats and biodiversity through the sensitive planting of native species. The seeds used to start the woodland came from the Beinn Eighe Nature Reserve and the islands of Loch Maree.

Leaving the pine woods behind, you pass by the Grouse Stone, a large sandstone boulder deposited by a glacier during the last ice age. Its name comes from the early 20th century, when grouse shoots were common and shooting parties often stayed out on the hill for several days. The grouse shot each day were left by a ghillie on the stone to be collected and taken to Gairloch.

By the time you reach Loch na-h-Oidhche, it really feels as though you've left all civilisation behind. While the ruins of the bridge you hoped to cross may make you briefly wish this not the case, the unspoilt climb and views ahead will soon change your mind.

Lying across the landscape like some sleeping monster, the long ridge of Baosbheinn not only offers some of the best and most unusual views of its more well-known Torridon neighbours, but also a great day out in itself. Climbing up from the loch to the summit brings first

Slioch, then the north faces of Beinn Eighe, Liathach and Beinn Alligin into view. A fantastic, well-earned reward – but it doesn't end there.

From the summit the route follows the rocky ridge as it takes in two more tops, with yet more jaw-dropping views, before heading down to the Poca Buidhe bothy and along the loch back to the start.

Route

From the **car park** at the red/green barn, cross the road to follow the Bad an Sgalaig native pine wood trail (marked as a red trail). This track takes you gently up through beautiful regenerating Scots pine, with information panels along the way acting as convenient rest stops. Ignore both the blue and yellow trails, when they cut off to the right, to stay on the main track along the east side of the **Abhainn a' Gharbh Choire**.

The track leaves the woodland behind, passing through a gate in the deer fence, to head out onto open, exposed hillside, with **Beinn an Eoin** directly ahead. A branch of the river is crossed via some stepping-stones.

After 7km, just as **Loch na-h-Oidhche** comes into view, take a less distinct track off to the right (885 667) to cross along the north shore of the loch to the outflow of the river. Even though there is no longer a bridge, the river is easily crossed here in dry conditions, but could become impassable when in spate. (If so, an alternative route is to leave the track earlier, just before the stepping-stones, and cross via a bridge just north of where the river divides.)

Head west-southwest from the river across rough ground into the corrie, **An Reidh-choire**, then south to gain the shoulder at about 700m. Follow the edge of the shoulder southwest to the col at 845m, gaining stunning views west over Shieldaig Forest and out to sea. A small path heads left from here the short distance up to the summit of **Baosbheinn** (875m) (870 654, 10km, 3hr45).

From the broad grassy summit, head southeast down a steep grassy slope, then east on more rocky terrain to a col. Climb back up east-southeast to gain an **unnamed**

9 Baosbheinn

top. From there head south to the end of the top, then southeast down the narrow ridge to and over the small peak of **Ceann Beag**, with the end of the loch coming into view.

Map continued on page 70

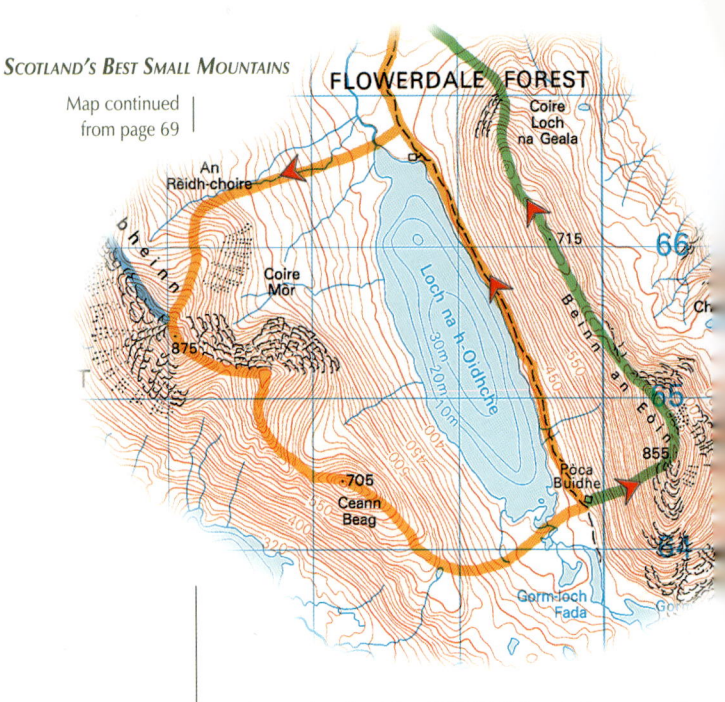

Leave the shoulder (887 639) just before a small **lochan** to head east then northeast over rough but not steep ground. Pick your way between the lochans at the south end of the loch to head directly for the **Poca Buidhe bothy**.

Once at the bothy (open at one end, providing shelter for two) you regain the main track. Follow this down the side of the loch, the full length of Baosbheinn laid out to your left, for the 10km walk back to the start (23km, 8hr).

Alternatives
Full Traverse of the Ridge
Traversing the entire ridge is possible, but it involves crossing very rough ground and an extremely steep ascent. To do this, follow the route as above, but after 3km take a turning to the right with yellow waymarking (872 700). This track takes you down to the Abhainn a'Gharbh

Looking back at the summit

Choire. Find your way across the river and head southwest across rough ground towards the end of Baosbheinn. Ascend very steeply on the east side to gain the shoulder just to the south of Creag an Fhithich. Follow the shoulder southeast, making use of small paths to skirt round the two rock towers, just before meeting the route described above at the col (23km, 1300m, shown in blue).

Ascent of Beinn an Eoin
An ascent of Baosbheinn could be combined with an ascent of neighbouring Beinn an Eoin (855m). From the Poca Buidhe bothy climb very steeply, avoiding crags, to the summit, then follow the full length of the ridge to drop back down to the main route just before the stepping-stones over the Abhainn Loch na h-Oidhiche (25km, 2000m, shown in green).

10 SGURR DUBH (782M)

'dark' or 'black peak'

Distance	16.5km
Time	6hr
Ascent	830m
Difficulty	While there are sections with good stalking paths, much of this route is characterised by rough ground and confusing terrain. Good navigation is essential. The final section involves several stiles over deer fence and a two-rope river crossing.
Maps	OS Landranger 25, OS Explorer 433
Access	Coulin Estate 01445 760383
Getting there	Start at the Beinn Eighe car park in Glen Torridon (957 568). Buses go to Torridon from Strathcarron train station, (contact DMK motors 01520 722682 or Traveline Scotland 0871 200 22 33, www.travelinescotland.com).
Something else	Take a walk around the Beinn Eighe nature trails, part of the first National Nature Reserve (visitor centre 01445 760254).

A wild excursion with an opportunity to take a trip into Scotland's geological past. Sgurr Dubh may be one of Torridon's least climbed peaks, but it offers some of the best views.

Sgurr Dubh sits on the south side of Glen Torridon, looking up to its bigger and more famous neighbours, Beinn Eighe and Liathach. An unassuming and more rounded hill, it is often overlooked by walkers. But what it lacks in ridges, it more than makes up for in wild ruggedness, not to mention being one of the best viewpoints in the glen.

By virtue of being relatively un-walked, any ascent soon leaves paths behind to enter a jumbled world of hummocks, lochans and rock. And it is Sgurr Dubh's very

10 Sgurr Dubh

Sgurr Dubh from Beinn Damh

form that makes it so interesting, telling, as it does, so much about Scotland's geological past.

It could be argued that Sgurr Dubh is misnamed as a 'dark peak', as it is wears a cap of brilliant white quartzite , though this is relatively young compared to the Torridonian sandstone on which it sits.

Eight thousand million years ago, vast river systems left behind the sediment that became an enormous plain of Torridonian sandstone as much as 1000 million years ago. The Torridon mountains, with their newer quartzite caps, are the remnants of that eroded plain.

Much erosion was caused by glaciation, and nowhere is this more evident than at the Corrie of the Hundred Hills, which sits at Sgurr Dubh's foot. This is a myriad of little pyramidal hills and hummocks formed 10,000 years ago from material deposited as the glaciers of the last ice age receded and melted. Thought to be the best example of its kind in Scotland, it is a fantastic sight, and a quite a maze to walk through. And it is at the Corrie of the Hundred Hills that the Sgurr Dubh route begins, though thankfully on a path.

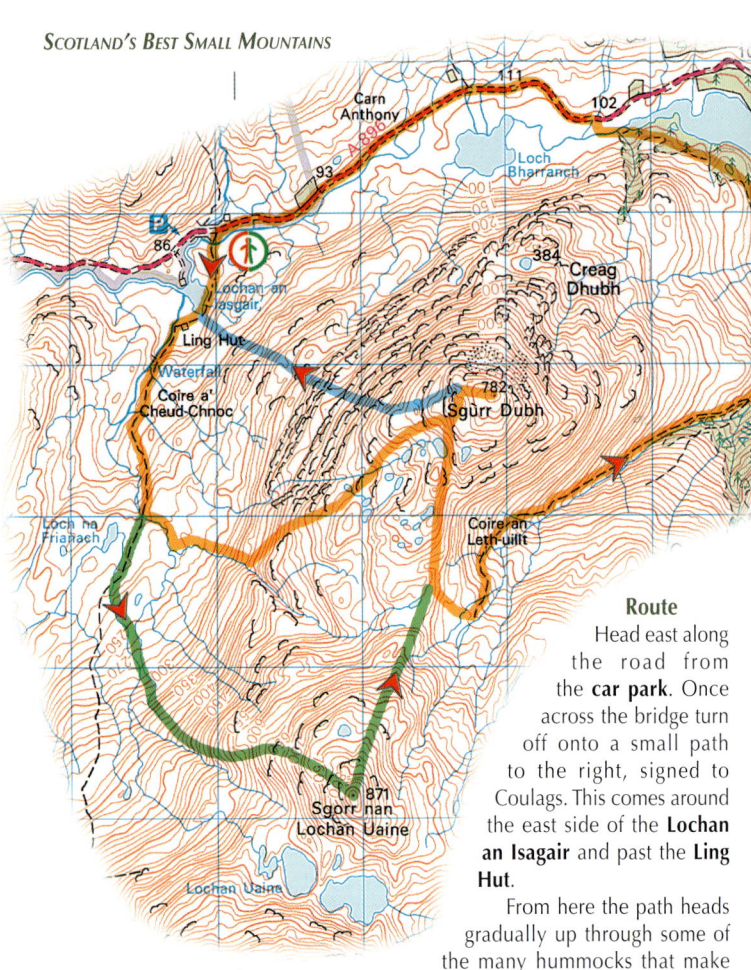

Scotland's Best Small Mountains

Route

Head east along the road from the **car park**. Once across the bridge turn off onto a small path to the right, signed to Coulags. This comes around the east side of the **Lochan an Isagair** and past the **Ling Hut**.

From here the path heads gradually up through some of the many hummocks that make up the Corrie of a Hundred Hills, with the **river** to its right. Cross one ford, then at a second, larger ford 2.5km from the start (954 549) leave the path. Go left, southeast, keeping the small **burn** to your right.

A faint path used more by deer than people sticks to the bank of the burn as it heads across flatter ground. While being a bit circuitous, it does make the going easier.

10 SGURR DUBH

As the gradient steepens, stay on this little path to the left of the burn. Just as the burn enters a gorge, by a small cairn, head left away from it to traverse northeast. The path soon stops, and at this point you climb east-northeast up increasingly steep and rocky terrain until it levels out by a cairn (964 547).

From the cairn, continue climbing northeast to gain the vast, hummocky plateau between **Sgorr nan Lochan Uaine** and **Sgurr Dubh**. This lumpy, rocky terrain can be confusing enough in good weather – in poor visibility it is a nightmare. There are some cairns, but these are hard to spot amongst the rocks and should not be relied on.

Avoid climbing too much to the east at this point – however tempting, this is not the top. Rather, continue on your northeast route to pass by the first of many **lochans**, where the real summit comes into view. Keep most of the lochans to your right to ascend the northeast shoulder. A flat plateau is reached – from here head southeast to gain the brilliant white rocky summit (782m) (979 557, 6.5km, 2hr30). The views from here down the entire length of Glen Torridon are fantastic.

The most obvious route down seems to be south from the summit on a scree path, but this leads you down perilously steep scree and heather to reach the path in Coire an Leith-uillt. It is easier to retrace your steps down to the lochans then head south to the east side of the col. From here (973 544) the slopes into **Coire an Leth-uillt** are gentler and you can pick up the path higher up.

Once on the path, follow it down alongside the **Allt na Luib** and into a lovely Scots pine woodland. It widens and arrives at a gate. Pass through and head left down a track to pass between buildings to reach the Coulin estate road (**Coulin Lodge** is to your right).

Follow the road briefly, then just before a white house and bridge take a track off to the left. This takes you behind the house and down to the shore of **Loch Clair** via another deer gate. Beinn Eighe, with Loch Clair in the foreground, looks great from here. The track fords the

Interesting bridge with Beinn Eighe behind

river and then divides before it reaches a boathouse. Go left, briefly away from the shore.

The track then narrows to a path and contours round above the loch. Ignore a rough track off to the left to stay on the path as it passes through two gates before dividing just after a small **lochan**. The right fork takes you to a bench and viewpoint; the left, which is overgrown and hard to spot, is the continuation of the route. It takes you over three quite rickety stiles across deer fences, then north down to the river by a final rickety stile and an 'interesting' river crossing. This two-rope affair is not for the faint-hearted, although thankfully the drop is not great.

Once over it is simply a matter of walking up to the road and following it left back to the start (16.5km, 6hr).

Alternatives
Via the Ling Hut
A shorter, much steeper and craggier descent can be made by heading southwest from the summit then northwest towards the Ling Hut, picking your way between rock outcrops (9.5km, 715m, shown in blue).

Including Sgorr nan Lochan Uaine

To combine an ascent of Sgurr Dubh with an ascent of Sgorr nan Lochan Uaine, the same outward route is followed, but instead of leaving the path at the second ford, stay on it until you reach the next ford (952 545). Follow the burn up towards Lochan Uaine before gaining the summit by way of the northwest ridge. Head north from the summit of Sgorr nan Lochan Uaine to join the original route (20km, 1150m, shown in green).

11 BEINN DAMH (903M)

'mountain of the stag'

Distance	14km
Time	5hr30
Ascent	1180m
Difficulty	Most of this route is on very good paths, though the ridge itself is very rocky and becomes steep and narrow as it nears the summit.
Maps	OS Landranger 24 & 25, OS Explorer 428
Access	Beinn Damh estate (01445 791252, 01241 830258)
Getting there	Park at the Torridon Hotel (889 541), which is signed off the road as 'parking for the Beinn Damh hill path'. Buses go to Torridon from Strathcarron train station (DMK motors 01520 722682 or Traveline Scotland 0871 200 22 33 www.travelinescotland.com).
Something else	Enjoy some great food and real ale right at the foot of the mountain in the Torridon Inn, winner of the pub of the year 2008–2009 (01445 791242, http://thetorridon.com).

One of Glen Torridon's most distinctive peaks, this is a hill of two halves. Pleasant pony paths take you up past waterfalls and through lush forest, in contrast to a striking, rocky ridge that reveals the full drama of the spectacular mountain scenery.

Heading up through Scots pine

Glen Torridon is acclaimed as one of the most spectacular mountain areas in Scotland. Characterised by buttresses, pinnacles, crags and jagged ridges, the mountains of the glen have been sculpted over time by glaciers and weather. Now they offer a challenge to hill-walkers from around the world.

Geologists too are drawn to Glen Torridon. The mountains are formed of Torridonian sandstone, which dates back 1000 million years, and, in many instances, are capped with quartzite. This combination is striking, with the red of the Torridonian sandstone contrasting against the light hues of quartzite, never more so than at sunset. On Beinn Damh the contrast is so great that it has been given a name – the Stirrup Mark. This is a semicircular area of white quartzite, topping the highest peak of Spidean Coir an Laoigh, which stands out from the grey rocks that surround it.

Ben Damh sits proudly at the far west of Glen Torridon, rising up from the sandy shores of Upper Loch Torridon. Named the 'mountain of the stag', deer have played a major role in the history of the landscape here, Beinn Damh forming part of the 14,500 acre Beinn Damh hunting estate.

11 Beinn Damh

The paths you follow to ascend Ben Damh were built in the late 1800s by the then estate owner, the Earl of Lovelace, for use by deer ponies. He too was responsible for building the fairytale-like turreted building that is now the Torridon Hotel, from where you begin to climb Beinn Damh.

The Earl of Lovelace was a far more benign owner of the estate than at least one of his predecessors. Colonel McBarnet, who owned the estate for many years from the 1830s, was notorious for his treatment of plantation workers in the West Indies and his tenant farmers in Torridon alike. He oversaw a massive clearance of farmers and their families from the glen, resettling them on little and poor land in Annat, at the foot of Ben Damh, making way for sheep.

Thankfully the fortunes of the farmers improved when the estate was sold to Duncan Darroch, a man who became loved by the people of Torridon after he cleared the sheep to make way for his own deer forest, and allowed the farmers to graze in the glen once more. There is still a memorial stone in Torridon that reads, 'In memory of the devotion and affection shown by one hundred men on the estate of Torridon, who, at their request, carried his body from the house here on its way to interment in the family burial place at Gourock.'

Route

From the car park, walk to the rear of the **Torridon Hotel** to cross the bridge over the **Allt Coire Roill**. This brings you to a sign to the Beinn Damh hill path, directing you off up to the left. Walk up through rhododendrons and over a stile to cross the main road. The path continues on the other side of the road, with stunning views down to the river on the left.

This very good path climbs steeply up through Scots pine, passing a waterfall before it emerges from the trees. The path divides here, with great views down to the beach at Torridon. Take the right fork to leave the river behind.

The path levels out, crossing a broad plateau before climbing more steeply again up to the col between Beinn

Scotland's Best Small Mountains

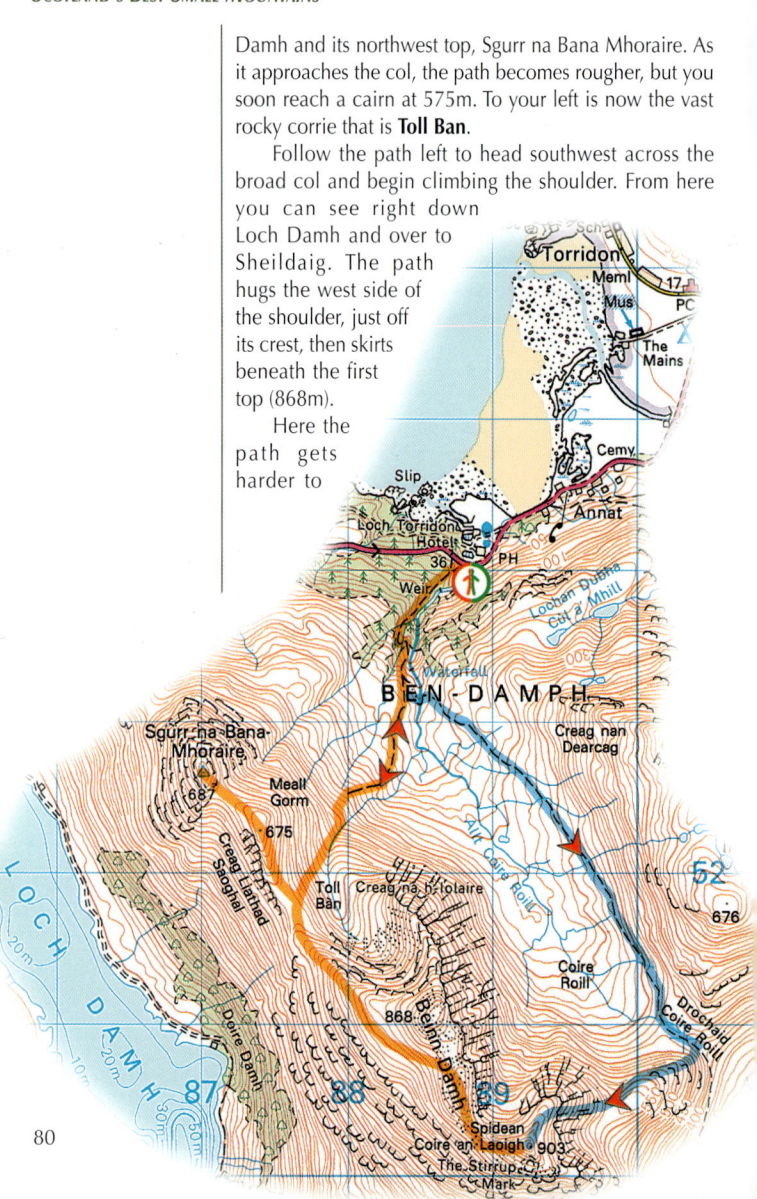

Damh and its northwest top, Sgurr na Bana Mhoraire. As it approaches the col, the path becomes rougher, but you soon reach a cairn at 575m. To your left is now the vast rocky corrie that is **Toll Ban**.

Follow the path left to head southwest across the broad col and begin climbing the shoulder. From here you can see right down Loch Damh and over to Sheildaig. The path hugs the west side of the shoulder, just off its crest, then skirts beneath the first top (868m).

Here the path gets harder to

follow, with the terrain becoming rockier all the time. Head southeast, making use of some small and hard-to-spot cairns. This brings you back, across a boulder field, onto the shoulder. Follow it along to reach a very narrow col and the final dramatic rocky ridge to the summit of **Beinn Damh** (903m) (892 502, 6km, 2hr40).

Return by same route, but if time permits, follow the path up the broad ridge over **Meall Gorm** to the summit of **Sgurr na Bana Mhoraire**, before descending from the col. This peak at the northwest end of the ridge has the best views out to sea (14km, 5hr30).

Alternatives
A Circular Route
A more challenging ascent, and one which makes it possible to complete a circular route of the peak, is from the pass Drochaid Coire Roill. When the path divides just as you leave the woods, take the left fork to come down to and across the river. Follow this good path, now on the left-hand side of the river, right up to the pass. From here leave the path to climb very steeply southwest up the ridge, avoiding most crags by keeping to the north side. It levels out before coming to the base of Beinn Damh's northeast ridge. This is very steep and buttressed, and should be climbed with care, levelling out just before it reaches the summit. This is not recommended as a descent route. Descend by the route above (15.5km, 1200m, shown in blue).

The shifting sands of the beach at Torridon

Scotland's Best Small Mountains

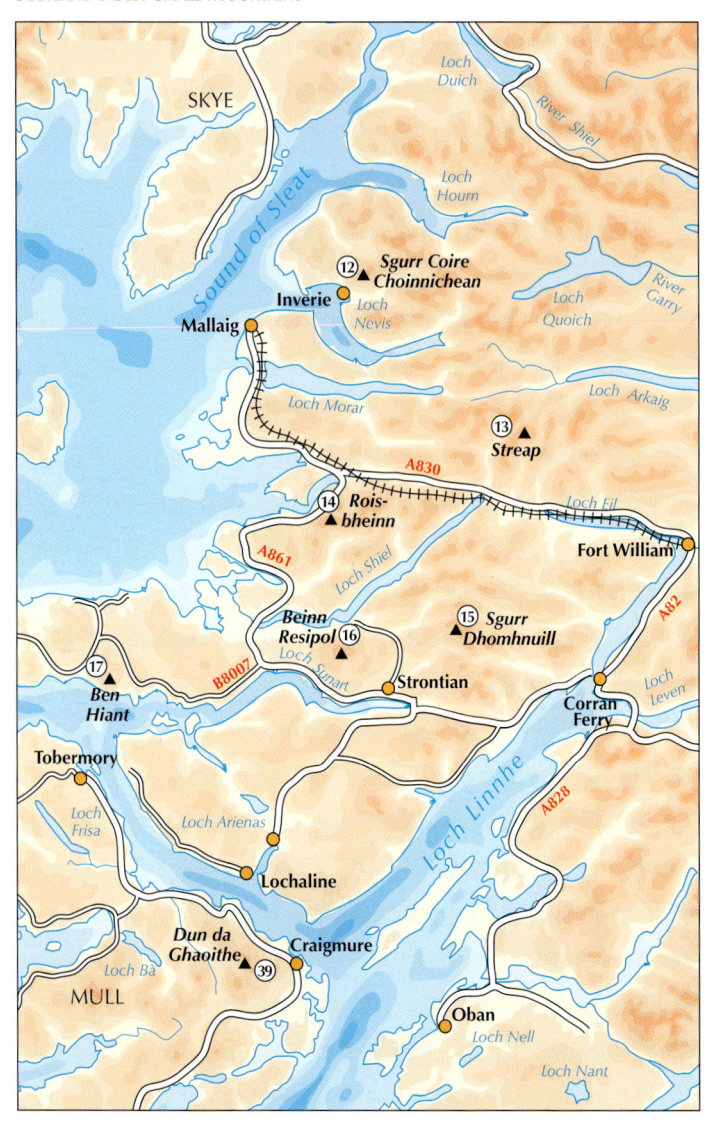

Looking down the gorge to Inverie beach

LOCHABER AND THE WEST

12 SGURR COIRE CHOINNICHEAN (796M)

'peak of the mossy corrie'

Distance	13km
Time	4hr30
Ascent	900m
Difficulty	A shorter route but one that takes in steep, pathless heather slopes and a narrow rocky ridge.
Maps	OS Landranger 33, OS Explorer 413
Access	For stalking information contact the Knoydart Foundation (01687 462242).
Getting there	Ferry from Mallaig to Inverie, Mon, Wed & Fri all year plus Tue and Thu mid-May to mid-Sept, Bruce Watt Cruises (01687 462320, www.knoydart-ferry.co.uk). Mallaig can be reached by train or bus (Traveline Scotland 0871 200 22 33, www.travelinescotland.com). Start the route outside the Old Forge pub (766 001).
Something else	Hang out in the Old Forge. Arguably Scotland's remotest pub, it's famous for its live music and fresh seafood (01687 462267, www.theoldforge.co.uk).

A remote ridge walk located in the wonderful wilds of Knoydart, a peninsula sitting 'between heaven and hell'. This route is only accessible by boat from Mallaig or by a long walk, and ends at the mainland's remotest pub.

Sgurr Coire Choinnichean easily qualifies as one of Scotland's best small mountains, and not least because of its stunning location. Situated on the Knoydart peninsula, Sgurr Coire Choinnichean, and the village of Inverie at its foot, are only accessible by boat from Mallaig or by way of a two-day walk. This makes Knoydart, known as the Rough Bounds, one of the remotest areas of wilderness left in Scotland and the UK.

12 Sgurr Coire Choinnichean

The ridge rising about Inverie

The peninsula sticks out into the Sound of Sleat, with Loch Hourn to the north and Loch Nevis to the south. It has been described as being 'between heaven and hell', not necessarily a reflection on the character of these two sea lochs, but rather, interestingly, because of their meanings. Loch Hourn most likely comes from the Gaelic 'Loch Iuthairne', meaning 'loch of hell', while Loch Nevis could be from the Gaelic *nimheis*, meaning 'heaven'.

Today the 17,200 acre Knoydart Estate, which makes up part of the peninusla, is owned by the Knoydart Foundation, after a community buy-out of the land in 1999. Inverie is the only village and is home to half of the estate's 100 residents, as well as mainland Britain's most remote pub, the Old Forge.

The Old Forge, famous for its live music and fresh seafood, is happily located at the end of the ascent of Sgurr Coire Choinnichean.

The hill itself is also well worthy of the ferry trip. It lives up to the translation of *sgurr* as a 'jagged, rocky peak', with its long narrow ridge rising up and dominating the

Scotland's Best Small Mountains

view above Inverie. While it is a short route, its pathless slopes give a real taste of the wild character of Knoydart.

Route

Start outside the Old Forge **pub**. Facing the pub, take the track to the left of it up past some A-frame buildings. Turn right when this joins a forestry track and continue, ignoring small paths off to the right, until you reach a path off to left (769 000).

This path heads uphill steeply, zigzagging its way through conifer trees. Ignore smaller paths off, to stay on the main path marked by rocks painted with red feet symbols. The path levels out and leaves the woods. Just after this, cut off the path to head right to a deer stile (771 003). Cross the stile and continue right to pass through a gap in a fence and wall. The path ends here.

Go northeast uphill on heather slopes heading for a rocky knoll. This takes you towards the impressive gully of the **Allt Slochd a'Mhogha**. There is no way across the gully here, so continue northeast beyond the knoll to reach a broad grassy plateau, known locally as 'the flats'. A faint path brings you around the top of the gully, with

12 Sgurr Coire Choinnichean

Ascending the narrow crest of the ridge

great views down to the beach at Inverie, and then doubles-back to gain the ridge at around 550m (781 006).

Ascend the increasingly narrow and exciting ridge to the two tops of **Sgurr Coire Choinnichean**, the second being the summit (796m) (790 010, 4km, 2hr). The views over to Skye and to the peaks to the north are fantastic.

To continue, carry on along the ridge. As it starts dropping down to the col between Sgurr Coire Choinnichean and **Stob an Uillt-fhearna** (798 013), head right off the ridge and down the rough grassy slopes to the track below. This track runs the length of **Gleann an Dubh-Lochain** from Barrisdale Bay to Inverie. Head right along the track as it runs alongside the **Inverie river**.

87

Stay on the main track, ignoring two turnings to the left, until it ends at a white gate. Pass through the gate and turn left downhill, then right to reach the shore and the tarmac road. Go right along the road to return to the start (13km, 4hr30).

Alternatives
Straight there and back
The easiest option is to return to Inverie by the ascent route. This is a much shorter route and would potentially allow the very fit to make the afternoon ferry back (8km, 760m).

Continuing to Mam Suidheig
The traverse of the ridge could be extended by continuing over the top of Stob an Uillt-fhearna (661m) and dropping down to the track by Loch an Dubh-Lochain from the col of Mam Suidheig (17km, 970m, shown in blue).

13 STREAP (909m)

'a climb' or 'climbing'

Distance	17.5km
Time	7hr
Ascent	1400m
Difficulty	A long, challenging route across rugged ground with no paths; a lot of climbing, steep slopes and a very narrow rocky ridge to the summit.
Maps	OS Landranger 40, OS Explorer 398
Access	Gleann Dubh Lighe is part of the Fassfern Estate. From Aug to mid-Feb they request walkers to gain the ridge of Beinn an Tuim as quickly as possible. For information on the day during stalking season contact 07767 267443 or 07767 270594.
Getting there	Start at the beginning of the track up Gleann Dubh Lighe off the A830 (931 799) where there is space to park a few cars. Glenfinnan, 4km from the start, can be reached

13 Streap

Something else by train or bus from Mallaig and Fort William (Traveline Scotland 0871 200 22 33, www.travelinescotland.com). Visit Glenfinnan Monument (0844 4932221, www.nts.org.uk/Property/26/), ride a steam train across the Glenfinnan viaduct (www.steamtrain.info), or take tea in a converted train carriage (01397 722300, www.glenfinnanstationmuseum.co.uk).

With a knife-edged ridge and several rugged tops along the way, this long and challenging route up Streap is enough to rival most Munros and offer a great adventure.

The dramatic peak, razor-edged ridges and rugged slopes of Streap make it one of the most challenging of Scotland's small mountains, an ascent of which will take you far from people and paths. Rising up from

Taking a rest on the bridge over the Dubh Lighe with Streap Comhlaidh behind

Glenfinnan, it holds great views north to the remote peninsula of Knoydart and south to the hills of Moidart and Ardnarmuchan.

Glenfinnan, at Streap's foot, is famous for some very different characters. Historically, it is best known as the gathering place for the Jacobite army of Prince Charles Edward Stuart (or Bonnie Prince Charlie) in 1745. The prince raised the Jacobite standard, declaring his rebellion, after rallying around 1200 Highlanders to his cause. Eight months later his rebellion came to an end at the Battle of Culloden.

The Glenfinnan monument, sitting at the head of Loch Shiel, was built 70 years later, in 1815, by Alexander MacDonald of Glenaladale as a tribute to the Highlanders who fought for the Jacobite cause. The monument is now a visitor attraction managed by the National Trust for Scotland.

A modern day, and fictional, character associated with Glenfinnan is Harry Potter, the Hogwarts Express steam train being seen to cross the famous Glenfinnan viaduct in the films.

The picturesque viaduct with its 21 arches forms part of the West Highland line from Fort William to Mallaig. It was designed by Robert McAlpine, and when completed in 1901 was one of the most pioneering and largest feats of engineering of the day. One of the routes up Streap starts by passing beneath an arch of the viaduct.

Route

Pass through the gate that marks the start of the forestry track up **Gleann Dubh Lighe**. This follows the left side of the **Dubh Lighe river**, passing by some lovely waterfalls and pools. Ignore a turning to the left by a small quarry to stay by the river.

When the track divides again, about 2.5km from the start, turn left to leave the river. Ignore a track to the left, not marked on the map, to pass through and then out of the woods at a gate in the deer fence (941 821).

From here, climb northwest up the grassy open hillside. Without any paths, the lumpy terrain can be quite

13 STREAP

hard work, and there are several false tops before you gain the true summit of **Beinn an Tuim** (810m). The hard work is rewarded, though, with great views back down Loch Shiel and ahead to the ridge to come.

From Beinn an Tuim head north back down to the col at about 700m before regaining the height immediately by ascending

Map continued on page 93

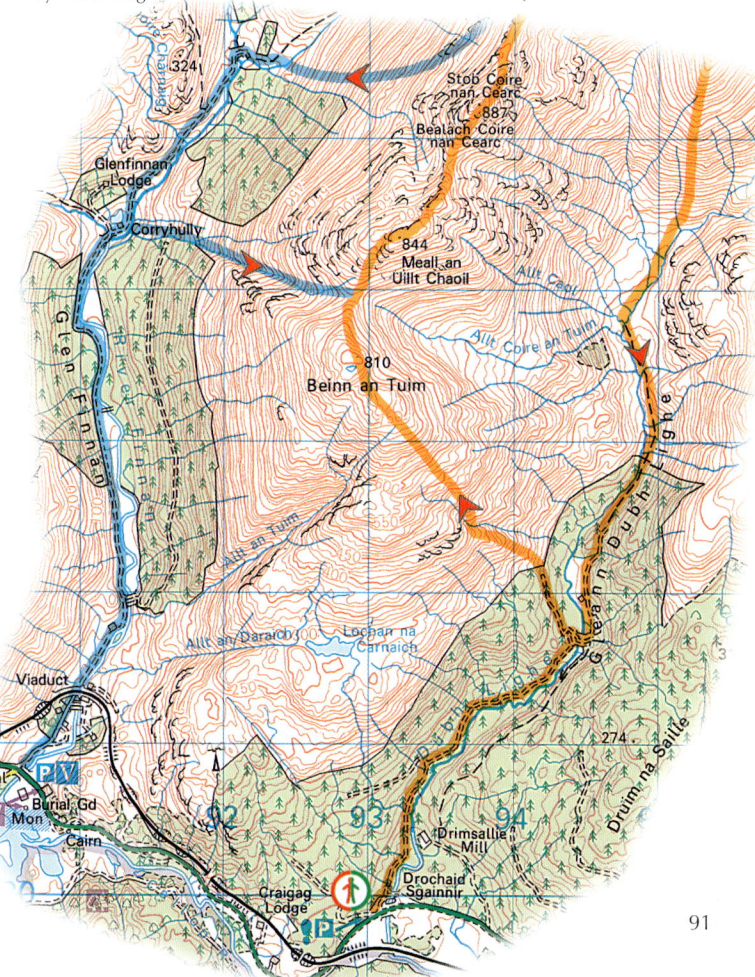

Streap from Strathan

to **Meall an Uillt Chaoil** (844m), the majority of the climbing now done. Continue along the ridge to the rocky top of **Stob Coire nan Cearc** (887m).

The last section of ridge from Stob Coire nan Cearc to the summit of Streap, while gaining little in height, is an impressive and extremely narrow rocky crest, which calls for a good head for heights and sure footing. Follow this to reach the distinctive and prominent summit of **Streap** (909m) (946 863, 9km, 4hr30).

From the summit, go down a short distance to the southeast to follow another narrow ridge to the slightly lower top of **Streap Comhlaidh** (898m). From here a descent can be made to the south down a steep grassy slope to reach the burn below. A rough track follows the burn downstream to come to a bridge (947 837). After crossing the bridge the track improves, making for an easier return route as it takes you all the way down Gleann Dubh Lighe.

After entering woodland you pass by an open bothy before crossing another bridge and coming to the junction where you earlier left the track. From here retrace your steps back to the start (17.5km, 7hr).

Alternatives
From Glen Finnan
Streap can also be climbed from Glen Finnan. To do this, start from the car park at the start of the glen (906 808) and take the private

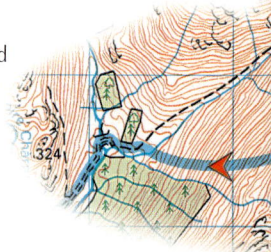

13 STREAP

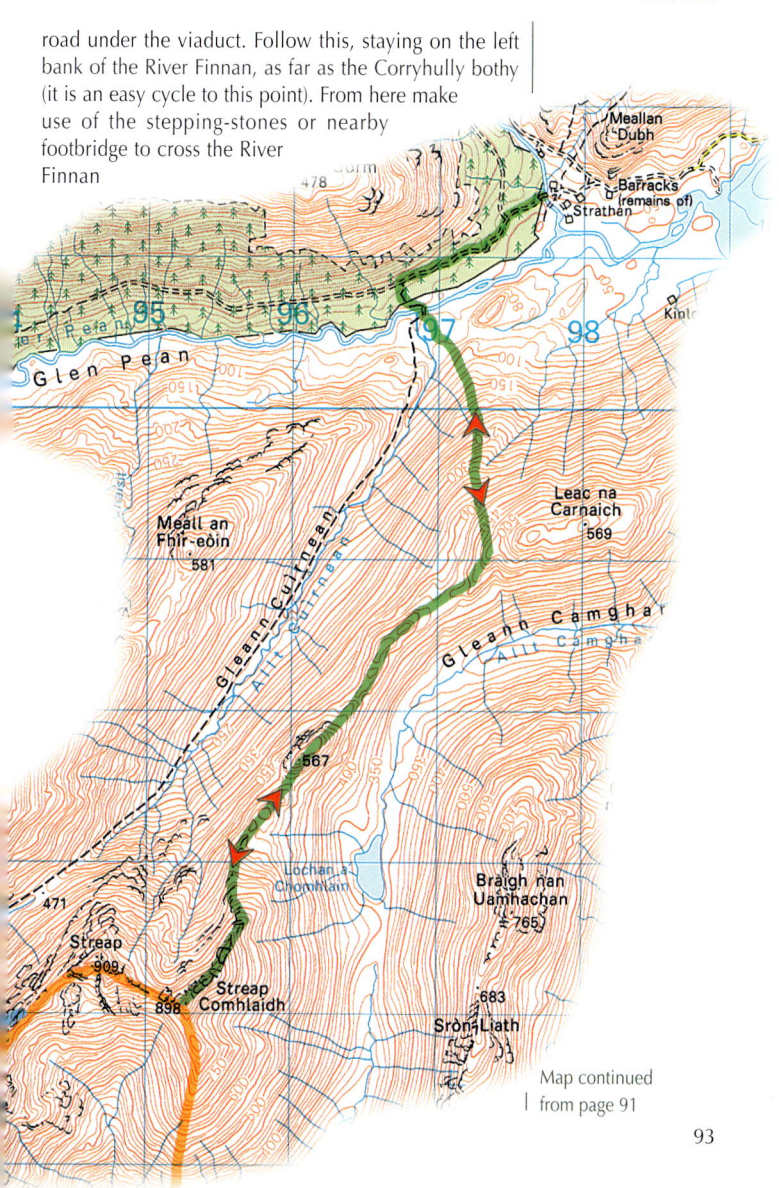

road under the viaduct. Follow this, staying on the left bank of the River Finnan, as far as the Corryhully bothy (it is an easy cycle to this point). From here make use of the stepping-stones or nearby footbridge to cross the River Finnan

Map continued
from page 91

and make a steep ascent up the side of the burn to the col between Beinn an Tuim and Meall an Uillt Chaoil.

From the col follow the route above to the summit of Streap. Retrace your steps from the summit to the lowest point on the ridge between it and Stob Coire nan Cearc. From there, leave the ridge to traverse southwest down the hillside, making use of the visible fault line in the landscape to reach the river below. Find a way across the river to join the path back to Corryhully, then retrace your steps along the private road to the start (18km, 1200m, shown in blue).

From the north via Glen Pean

Streap can also be climbed from the north from the end of the road at Strathan. From there follow the track into Glen Pean, leaving it to cross a bridge over the River Pean. Once across, head south across rough ground to the ridge of Leac na Carnaich. Follow this undulating ridge southwest then south over the top of an unnamed peak at 567m and up onto Streap Comhlaidh. Follow the narrow ridge to the summit of Streap. Return by the same route (18km, 1350m, shown in green).

14 ROIS-BHEINN (882M), AN STAC (814M), SGURR NA BA GLAISE (874M) AND DRUIM FIACLACH (869M)

Rois-Bheinn – from the Norse 'mountain of horses' or from Gaelic 'mountain of showers'; An Stac from the Gaelic 'steep hill'; Sgurr na Ba Glaise could be 'peak of the grey cow'; Druim Fiaclach, from the Gaelic 'toothed ridge'

Distance	18km
Time	8hr
Ascent	1600m
Difficulty	This is a long and demanding route. It starts on a boggy all-terrain-vehicle (ATV) track, but then there are virtually

14 ROIS-BHEINN, AN STAC, SGURR NA BA GLAISE AND DRUIM FIACLACH

	no established paths, making good navigation skills essential. Steep ground and rocky outcrops going up, then following grassy/rocky ridges, with some exposure, and descending across rough ground.
Maps	OS Landranger 40, OS Explorer 390
Access	Stalking takes place between August and February, contact the Inverailort Estate for information (01687 470 206).
Getting there	Ask at the Lochailort Inn if you can park there (767 823) or park off the main road at Inverailort. Alternatively, four trains a day Mon–Sat, three on Sun, to/from Fort William or Mallaig stop on request at Lochailort Station (contact Scotrail 08457 55 00 33, www.scotrail.co.uk or Traveline Scotland 0871 200 22 33, www.travelinescotland.com).
Something else	Enjoy a post-walk drink in the Lochailort Inn (01687 470208, www.lochailortinn.co.uk) or head round to Glenuig to watch the sun set over the Small Isles.

'Four peaks for the price of one' make this a long and challenging circuit to rival any of its higher counterparts. Rugged ridges and superb views are the rewards for the adventurous.

If Ben Nevis has always seemed just a little bit small to you, not to mention somewhat on the busy side, you need to head 30 miles west to its Moidart neighbour, Rois-Bheinn.

OK, so Ordnance Survey haven't made a big mistake, and Rois-Bheinn isn't technically taller, but when you combine an ascent of this with its fellow peaks – An Stac, Sgurr na Ba Glaise and Druim Fiaclach – a nice day out in the hills suddenly becomes a more than 1500m (5000ft) adventure.

With 1600m of ascent, this circular route is a fantastic, full day out. Dramatic drops, rocky, sometimes exposed ridges, and incredible sea views over a demanding distance make it a challenge worth taking.

Scotland's Best Small Mountains

Eigg and Rum from the col on An Stac

Starting almost at sea level in Lochailort, the route climbs first to the triangular point of An Stac. It then heads a disturbingly long way down just to climb back up to the twin peaks of Rois-Bheinn, but once there you are rewarded with stunning views out to sea and the Small Isles of Eigg and Rum. You then follow the ridge as it takes in Sgurr na Ba Glaise and the wonderfully rocky top of Druim Fiaclach.

With pretty much only deer paths to follow and most people off up nearby Munros, this really is an opportunity to get out and explore in the wilds.

The four peaks form part of the 9000 acre Inverailort Estate, which was once the main deer forest for the MacDonalds of Clanranald, a branch of the MacDonald clan closely associated with the Lord of the Isles, who during the 1400s owned much of the West Highlands and Islands.

In more recent history, Inverailort House was requisitioned in 1940 for use by first the army and then the navy

14 Rois-Bheinn, An Stac, Sgurr na Ba Glaise and Druim Fiaclach

during the Second World War. Inverailort House became the Special Training Centre, and then HMS Lochailort, while the estate land was widely used for training Special Services units and Royal Navy commandos before being handed back to its owners in 1945.

Route

From the **Lochailort Inn** head right along the main road to Glenfinnan for 100m and then take the first track down to the right. Head down across a wooden bridge, then left along a track signed to **Glenshian Lodge**. Pass the lodge, and when the track divides go left to pass an old walled cemetery.

Beyond here the track becomes more of an ATV route and can be very wet. Stay on it, heading east alongside the river, then south as it starts to climb. A couple of small paths cut out some of the track's longer loops. The track divides, with the left fork heading down to a bridge across the **Allt a'Bhuiridh** (this is the way you will return). Take the right fork to continue south, with the horseshoe of the day's peaks ahead.

Leave the ATV track to head west at 772 803 for the lowest part of the col between **Seann Chruach** and An Stac. Climb over rough ground following a small burn to reach the col and your first views of the Small Isles of Eigg and Rum. From the col, the imposing rocky ridge of An Stac dominates to the south. Climb quite steeply, picking your way, with the aid of some deer paths, between rocky outcrops to gain the summit of **An Stac** (814m) (763 792, 5km, 2hr45).

The summit of An Stac provides brilliant views over the twin peaks of Rois-Bheinn and the rest of the horseshoe. Descend steeply down An Stac's south shoulder, staying to the east of it to avoid the largest rocky outcrops, to the col below.

After dropping back down to 560m you have to regain the height almost instantly, climbing south to meet an old wall and a line of old fence posts. These provide a useful guide, with the wall ultimately leading you all the way to the top of Rois-Bheinn. Follow them southeast

Scotland's Best Small Mountains

then steeply southwest to reach **Bealach an Fhiona**. From the bealach head right, following the wall as it heads west up the shoulder to the summit of **Rois-Bheinn** (882m) (756 778, 7.5km 4hr15).

The first peak of Rois-Bheinn is the slightly higher of the two, but it's worth the short, gentle walk to the large cairn of the second peak for the stunning views out to sea. Return to Bealach an Fhiona the same way, then climb southeast up the steep grassy slope of **Sgurr na Ba Glaise** (874m) (770 777, 9.5km, 5hr30).

From the peak of Sgurr na Ba Glaise, the ridge narrows with some impressive drops down to the River Moidart to the south. Descend east from the peak to follow the lumpy but fairly gentle shoulder of **An t-Slatbheinn** as it bends

14 Rois-Bheinn, An Stac, Sgurr na Ba Glaise and Druim Fiaclach

northeast then north before dropping down to the **Bealach an Fhalaisg Dhuibh**. A short but very steep climb north from here takes you onto the ridge of **Druim Fiaclach**, the last top of the day. To reach the summit, follow the toothed ridge northeast atop exposed rock blocks (869m) (791 791, 12.5km, 6hr30).

From the summit of Druim Fiaclach, head north down grassier slopes to the lochan on the col between Druim Fiaclach and **Beinn Coire nan Gall**. It is then downhill all the way across grassy, and often wet, but gentle open hillside. Head down west at first to avoid the steeper upper slopes of Beinn Coire nan Gall, then northwest, heading directly for the **bridge** over the Allt a'Bhuiridh (778 813, not marked on map). As long as you head for the river you won't go wrong.

From the bridge you simply need to follow the track up to the original ATV track and follow it back to the start (18km, 8hr).

Alternatives

There are several alternative shorter routes, which only take in one or two of the four peaks. The full circuit could also be done in reverse.

Circuit of An Stac Only

A circuit of just An Stac could be completed by following the same route as above to climb An Stac and drop down the south shoulder to the col, but then head east down into Coire a'Bhuiridh to join the river and follow it back to the ATV track (12km, 860m, shown in blue).

This return route could also be used if climbing Rois-Bheinn and/or Sgurr na Ba Glaise, but not wishing to complete the full horseshoe and Druim Fiaclach. Equally it could be used as an alternative ascent of Rois-Bheinn, Sgurr na Ba Glaise and Druim Fiaclach, omitting An Stac.

Rois-Bheinn from Roshven Farm

A shorter, alternative ascent/descent of Rois-Bheinn can be made from Roshven Farm (720 785). This makes use of a stalker's track through the wood before ascending the west shoulder (8km, 910m). The views out to sea when descending by this route are spectacular. This could also be used as a way of accessing the other peaks (shown in green).

Rois-Bheinn with the Small Isles out to sea

Via the Alisary Burn

A further alternative ascent of Rois-Bheinn or An Stac is by way of the Alisary Burn. The steep side of the burn is followed into Coire na Cnamha and up to the col between An Stac and Bealach an Fhiona, from where the original route can be followed (to An Stac and back 7.5km, 800m, to Rois-Bheinn and back 8km, 870m, shown in pink).

Circular route of Rois-Bheinn

A good circular route of Rois-Bheinn can be completed by following the Alisary Burn route (pink) to the summit, then returning to Roshven Farm (green) (8km, 930m, plus 2.5km road walk).

15 SGURR DHOMHNUILL (888M)

'Donald's peak', likely to be so named after the Donald clan, who ruled much of the West Highlands and Islands.

Distance	20km
Time	6hr30
Ascent	1150m
Difficulty	While this walk starts on a pleasant path, the rest of the route is pathless across rough ground. The ridges of Sgurr Dhomhnuill itself are very steep and rocky.
Maps	OS Landranger 40, OS Explorer 391
Access	SNH reserve manager 01397 704716, Forestry Commission 01397 702184
Getting there	Park at the Ariundle National Nature Reserve car park (825 633). There is a bus to Strontian from Fort William once a day, Monday to Saturday, (contact Shiel Buses 01967 431272, www.shielbuses.co.uk or Traveline Scotland 0871 200 22 33, www.travelinescotland.com).
Something else	Go for tea and cakes at the lovely Ariundle Centre set amongst the woods, or stay for dinner and make use of their bunkhouse (01967 402279, www.ariundle.co.uk).

> The shapely conical peak of Sgurr Dhomhnuill is the highest peak in Ardgour, and with dramatic drops on all sides it has great panoramic views. But that's not all – this is a mountain with many tales to tell, a place where natural and human history meet.

The route starts in the beautiful Ariundle National Nature Reserve, designated for its beautiful oak trees, the remnants of the ancient Atlantic oak woodlands that once blanketed the area. As you walk through the oaks, birch and hazel trees, it is like stepping into a lush rainforest. Hundreds of lichens and liverworts thrive here, giving a green covering to the tree trunks and branches.

These woods have survived where many others have not because of their necessity to human activity in the area. While other forests were decimated for firewood or by grazing, these woods were protected and carefully coppiced to produce charcoal. The charcoal was transported for use in iron smelting.

Sgurr Dhomhnuill

15 SGURR DHOMHNUILL

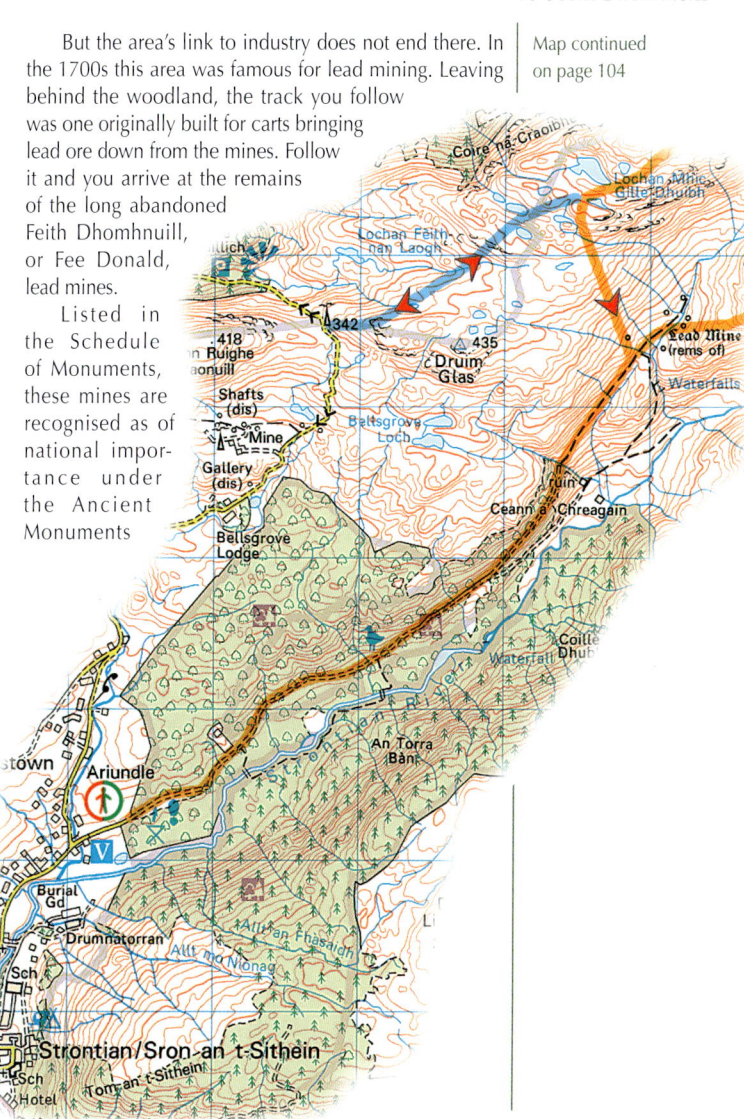

But the area's link to industry does not end there. In the 1700s this area was famous for lead mining. Leaving behind the woodland, the track you follow was one originally built for carts bringing lead ore down from the mines. Follow it and you arrive at the remains of the long abandoned Feith Dhomhnuill, or Fee Donald, lead mines.

Listed in the Schedule of Monuments, these mines are recognised as of national importance under the Ancient Monuments

Map continued on page 104

Scotland's Best Small Mountains

Ben Nevis down Glen Scaddle

and Archaeological Areas Act. In fact lead mined here was a major source for bullets in the Napoleonic Wars. These are also some of the mines where strontianite, from which strontium is extracted (named after the village of Strontian), was discovered.

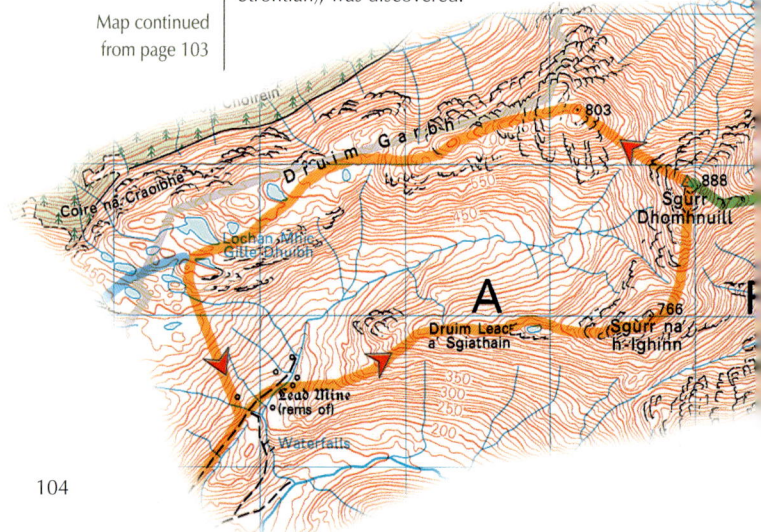

Map continued from page 103

15 SGURR DHOMHNUILL

While the mines have not been active for around 200 years, fascinating evidence of them remains in the form of shafts, ruined buildings, and spoil heaps where you can still find glinting silver-blue crystals of galena.

Route

Leaving the nature reserve car park, a good track (the reserve's main walk) provides an easy route for the long walk in.

Stay on the main track, ignoring some smaller paths off (which loop back to the car park). After 3km you pass through a gate in a deer fence, and immediately after this the track divides, where you take the left fork. From here the track, which gets a little rougher underfoot, brings you to a wooden gate. Pass through it to cross a small bridge. Here you leave the trees behind and the track becomes more of a hill path. Rounding the corner the first views of the top come into sight.

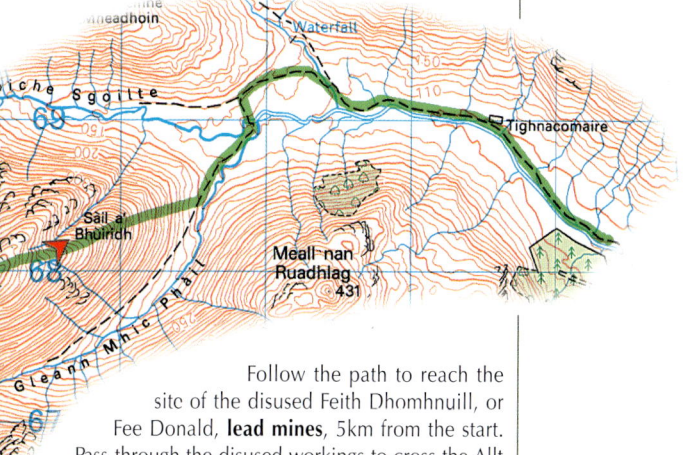

Follow the path to reach the site of the disused Feith Dhomhnuill, or Fee Donald, **lead mines**, 5km from the start. Pass through the disused workings to cross the Allt Feith Dhomhnuill and, leaving the path behind, head northeast onto the shoulder of **Druim Leac a' Sgiathain**. The going here is fairly rough, across heather and peat bog, but straightforward enough in good visibility.

Once on the shoulder, follow it east and up to attain the summit of **Sgurr na h'Ighinn** (765m). From here there are great views down Glen Scaddle to Ben Nevis and beyond. Leaving Sgurr na h'Ighinn, a rough path takes you down to the col at 682m before the very steep and rocky 200m ascent north to the peak of **Sgurr Dhomhnuill** (888m) (889 678, 9km, 3hr30).

Continue by descending the equally rocky northwest ridge of Sgurr Dhomhnuill to the col at 660m. From there head northwest to gain the summit of **Druim Garbh** (803m), which aptly translates as 'rough ridge'. From this high point it is a long, bumpy descent over rough terrain, which can prove very difficult in poor visibility.

Pick your way west southwest down the ridge to reach the lochans, the largest of which is named on the map as **Lochan Mhir Gille Dhuibh**. Pass by this lochan at its southeast end. This should allow you to avoid the steeper crags as you then descend left off the ridge. Head south down another rough slope to meet the track from the lead mines. Follow the outward route back to the start (20km, 6hr30).

Alternatives
From the Strontian to Polloch road
An alternative ascent can be made by climbing the length of Druim Garbh from the highest point (342m) on the small road from Strontian to Polloch, although this is rough walking the whole way and does miss out the interesting top of Sgurr na h-Ighinn (12km, 700m). This could also be used as a different return route (shown in blue).

From Glen Scaddle
Sgurr Dhomhnuill could also be climbed from Glen Scaddle. This is a very long route, making it more desirable as a two-day wild camping trip. It starts from Aryhoulan on the A861 (018 684) and follows first a track then a path the length of Glen Scaddle. The path is left shortly after it divides to make an ascent of Sail a'Bhuiridh, Sgurr Dhomhnuill's northeast ridge (31km, 1100m, green, but not all shown).

16 BEINN RESIPOL (845M)

possibly 'mountain of the horse farmstead', from the Norse 'hross bolstadar'

Distance	16km
Time	5hr30
Ascent	920m
Difficulty	This is a relatively straightforward day out on small, mainly clear, but often muddy hill paths, with a pathless section across open hillside calling for good navigation, and a single-track road walk to finish.
Maps	OS Landranger 40, OS Explorer 390 & 391
Getting there	There is parking at Resipole Studios (721 641) off the single-track road that runs from Strontian to Salen. There is also a bus from Fort William once a day, Monday to Saturday (contact Shiel Buses 01967 431272, www.shielbuses.co.uk or Traveline Scotland 0871 200 22 33, www.travelinescotland.com).
Something else	Enjoy some culture at Resipole Studios (01967 431 506, www.resipolestudios.co.uk before a great dinner at the Salen Hotel (01967 431661, www.salenhotel.co.uk) and a night under canvas at the Resipole campsite (01967 431 235, www.resipole.co.uk).

A traverse across the Ardnamurchan peninsula's highest peak, with some of the best views to be had of the west coast. Not only that, but Beinn Resipol is flanked by unique oak woodlands and steeped in local history too.

It's the highest peak for miles, yet it's not a Munro. You can take a ferry to it, yet it's not on an island. You can see Skye, the Small Isles, Mull and Ben Nevis from the top, yet it's on one of Scotland's remotest peninsulas. Beinn

Resipol might seem like a mass of contradictions, but it is those very contradictions that make it the classic mountain that it is.

As the highest peak on the Ardnamurchan peninsula, Beinn Resipol commands one of the finest views on the whole west coast. For starters, it is almost surrounded by water – Loch Shiel to the north, the sea loch of Loch Sunart to the south, the Atlantic out west and Loch Linnhe to the east. It is by ferry across Loch Linnhe that Beinn Resipol is most easily accessed.

Then add the stunning array of islands and peaks you can see when you reach the top – Skye, Eigg, Rum, Coll, Tiree, Ben Nevis, Glencoe…on a clear day the list seems almost endless. Not to mention the views of white sandy beaches or the potential of an eagle flying by.

And then there is the walk itself. Traversing from west to east you pass through some of the beautiful native oak and birch woodland that this area is famous for. The Sunart Oak Woods are one of the last UK remnants of ancient temperate oak woodland that once stretched the whole length of Europe's Atlantic coast.

Leaving behind the trees, you climb alongside a mountain stream to gain the prominent summit. A rocky ridge leads you down grassy slopes to an old miners' path, notable because much of the area's history was dominated by mining. The village of Strontian, where the route ends, was established in 1724 to provide accommodation for miners working in several lead mines nearby. Strontian went on to lend its name to the element strontium, which was discovered in one of these mines in 1790. The mines were at their peak in the 1730s, but now all that remains are some interesting ruins of the disused workings.

Route

Leave **Resipole Studios** car park via the bridge at the far end. Turn left to pass some static caravans, then through a gate, heading towards a large metal shed. Before reaching the shed go off to the right through a wooden gate and onto a new track. This climbs gently to reach a gate in a deer fence that you pass through, the **Allt Mhic Chiarain**

16 BEINN RESIPOL

Beinn Resipol above Loch Sunart

burn on your left. Carry on until you see a wooden shed. Just before reaching the shed take a small path uphill into the woods on your right. This very quickly reaches a wider path that you head left along.

This path takes you uphill through lovely oak and birch glades. It becomes smaller and rougher underfoot through this section, but is always clear.

You emerge from the trees onto open moorland with the summit of Beinn Resipol straight ahead. Aim directly for the summit, passing through a wooden gate, then continue along the path as it keeps the Allt Mhic Chiarain to its left virtually all the way to its source. The higher you go, the less distinct the path becomes, but the burn provides a good guide all the way to the shoulder.

From the shoulder, head east along level ground for a short distance, then south to pick your way between rocky outcrops up a gentle slope to the summit of **Beinn Resipol** (845m) (766 655, 6.5km, 3hr).

From the summit, follow the path east along the rocky bumps of Beinn Resipol's ridge. As the ridge ends, the path disappears and the rock gives way to grass.

SCOTLAND'S BEST SMALL MOUNTAINS

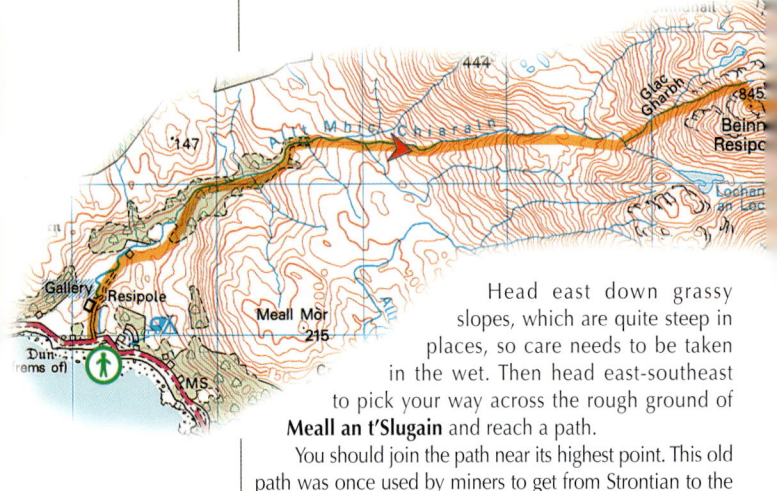

Head east down grassy slopes, which are quite steep in places, so care needs to be taken in the wet. Then head east-southeast to pick your way across the rough ground of **Meall an t'Slugain** and reach a path.

You should join the path near its highest point. This old path was once used by miners to get from Strontian to the long abandoned mines in Coire an t'Suidhe. The cairns you pass mark the resting point for funeral parties carrying coffins. Head right and follow the path down as it runs along

On Resipol's rocky ridge

16 BEINN RESIPOL

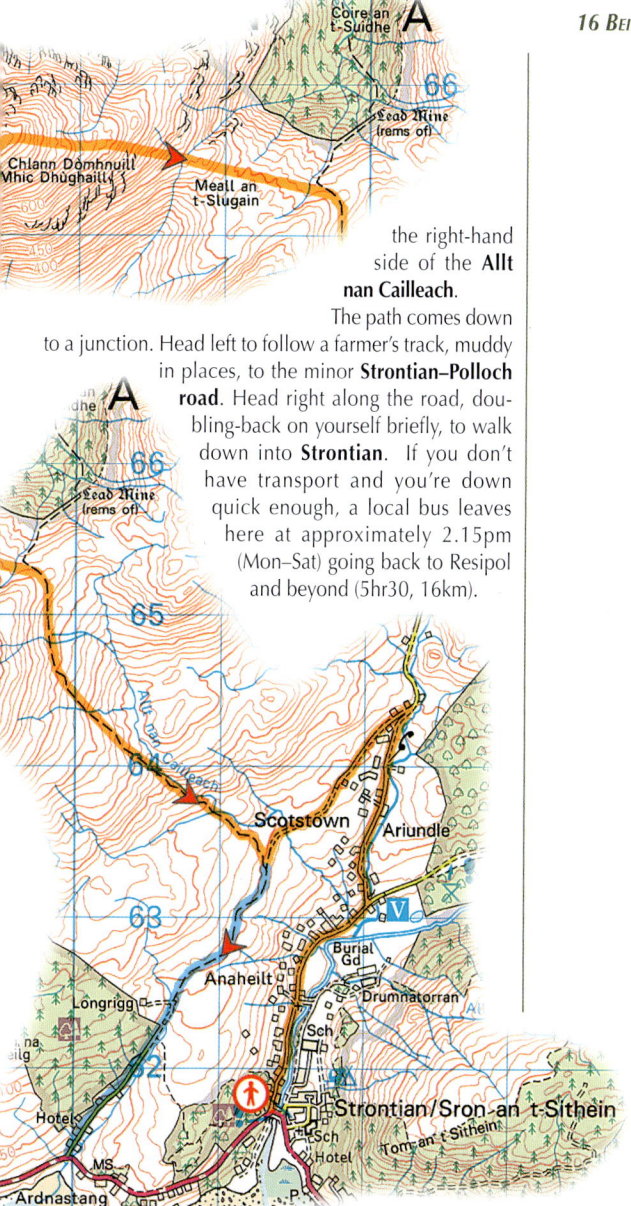

the right-hand side of the **Allt nan Cailleach**.

The path comes down to a junction. Head left to follow a farmer's track, muddy in places, to the minor **Strontian–Polloch road**. Head right along the road, doubling-back on yourself briefly, to walk down into **Strontian**. If you don't have transport and you're down quick enough, a local bus leaves here at approximately 2.15pm (Mon–Sat) going back to Resipol and beyond (5hr30, 16km).

111

Alternatives

Reversing the Traverse
The traverse could be reversed without encountering any difficulties and, equally, walkers could ascend and descend by the same route to avoid the need for transport.

Avoiding Strontian
If you don't want to go into Strontian, when the miners' path comes to the junction you could follow the path to the right to come out on the main road (14km, 880m, shown in blue).

17 BEN HIANT (528M)

'holy peak'

Distance	10.5km
Time	4hr
Ascent	620m
Difficulty	A compact route on small but mainly clear paths on hill and coast, but the pathless middle section needs good navigation. The walk starts and finishes on a single-track road.
Maps	OS Landranger 47, OS Explorer 390
Access	Ben Hiant is part of the Ardnamurchan Estate. Contact the estate office for details of stalking – 01972 510208, www.west-highlands.co.uk.
Getting there	Park just off the single-track road from Salen to Kilchoan in an old borrow (or quarry) pit (556 626). There is also a bus from Fort William once a day, Monday to Saturday (Shiel Buses 01967 431272, www.shielbuses.co.uk, or Traveline Scotland 0871 200 22 33, www.travelinescotland.com).
Something else	Head out to the lighthouse that marks mainland Britain's most westerly point (01972 510210, www.ardnamurchanlighthouse.com) and stop off at the Sonachan Hotel for a drink on the way back (01972 510 211, www.sonachan.com).

17 Ben Hiant

> Hills, history, beaches and breathtaking views out over Britain's most westerly point, Ben Hiant is a compact route that has it all.

The phrase 'size isn't everything' could have been made for Ben Hiant. While only reaching 528m, it dominates the end of the Ardnamurchan Peninsula, mainland Britain's most westerly point. Combining stunning 360° views over the Small Isles, Mull and Skye, with sea eagles, abandoned villages and rugged coastline, the only thing this peak lacks is people. It truly is an opportunity to get away from it all and, amazingly, in a short day out.

This compact but varied circuit starts with an ascent of Ben Hiant's rugged and lumpy shoulder. The small but clear path wends its way up, steeply in places, with the views becoming more tantalising as you climb. From the peak's panoramic vantage point on a clear day, with the Cuillin Ridge one way and Ben Nevis the other, you'd be forgiven for imagining you could see America out to the far west!

Ben Hiant rising up from the sands of Camus nan Geall

If you can tear yourself away from the top, it is to abandon the path and head into the wilds proper, heading down and off the west shoulder only to arrive at the busy village of Bourblaige – or at least it would have been in the 1800s. The 30 or so ruins here, which were cleared in 1828 to make way for sheep, prove to be eerily atmospheric, allowing you a sense of what life would have been like for the villagers.

Then, just when you couldn't believe it could get better, you follow the villagers' path down to follow the beautiful rocky coastline around to the stunning white sands, chambered cairn and Neolithic standing stone of Camus nan Geall. The standing stone, with an early Christian cross, is situated within the small fenced Clan Campbell cemetery.

Route

From the car parking, turn right and walk up the road for 1.5km to the brow of the hill. From there a small path leaves the road to the left. Follow this as it climbs west, and after 200m take a left where the path divides (the faint right turn is an old droving road to Kilchoan) to gain the east shoulder of Ben Hiant.

The path stays on top of the shoulder as it climbs southwest in stages. The shoulder then bends round to the west bringing you to a narrow col, with views to Eigg, Rum and Skye to the north and Ben More on Mull to the south.

From the col, carry on along the top of the shoulder for 100m until you reach the last rise. Here the path skirts

17 BEN HIANT

round to the left, avoiding a steep rocky slope, to traverse the hillside to the south and arrive at the summit of **Ben Hiant** from the rear (528m) (537 632, 4km, 1hr45).

Leaving behind the top and the path, continue following the line of the grassy shoulder as it heads southwest. Follow it down and west, being careful on some steep grassy slopes, to reach a broad, flat area of the shoulder. Leave the shoulder here (533 627), heading southeast at first steeply downhill then on more level, open moorland. The rocky tops of **Stallachan Dubha** are to the south. If you keep heading in this direction, towards a distinctive pyramid-shaped knoll, you should have no problems, but navigation could become very difficult in low cloud.

By the foot of the pyramid-shaped knoll you will come across an old line of metal fence posts. Follow this line left for 50m to reach the top of a distinct gully (540 624). Staying on the west of the gully, follow it downhill (but avoid its steep edge) to arrive at a gate in a new fence and the edge of the old village of **Bourblaige**.

You can head through the gate to explore the village, but return to it to take the small path that heads southeast following a fence line down to the shore at **Port a'Chamais**.

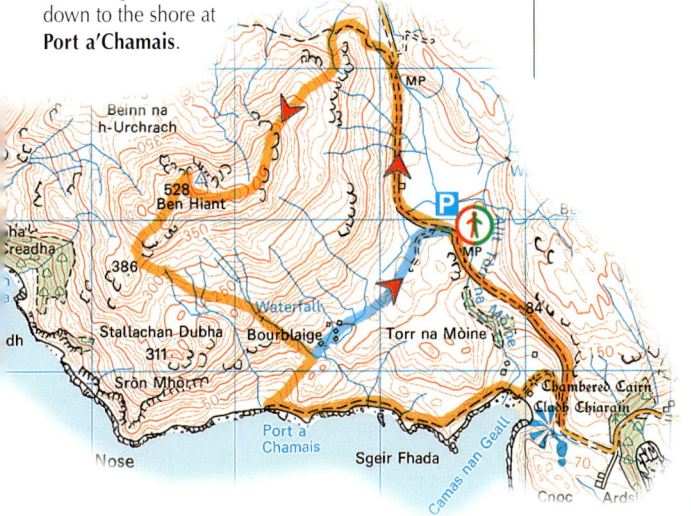

Once there you simply need to head left, keeping to the shoreline until you reach the large sandy beach at **Camus nan Geall**, though there is a small, occasionally faint path to follow. Along the way you pass the site of an Iron Age fort on the point of **Sgeir Fhada**.

Once on the beach, head through a kissing-gate onto a track passing the Neolithic standing stone on the right and the remains of a **chambered cairn** on the left. Go through a second kissing-gate to follow the track back up to the road and a great **viewpoint** over Ben Hiant. Complete the walk by going left along the road to return to the start (10.5km, 4hr).

Alternatives
Straight there and back
Descend the hill by the same path as you ascended it. If this is the preferred option, parking is available at the start of the hill path on the opposite side of the road (551 641) (5km, 350m).

Eigg and Rum from the summit

17 Ben Hiant

From the shoulder with Eigg and Rum beyond

Avoiding the Coast
An alternative circuit avoiding the coast can be made by heading northwest from Bourblaige around the left of a mound to come to a gate. Passing through the gate takes you onto a track, which returns to the road near to the parking (7km, 500m, shown in blue).

Scotland's Best Small Mountains

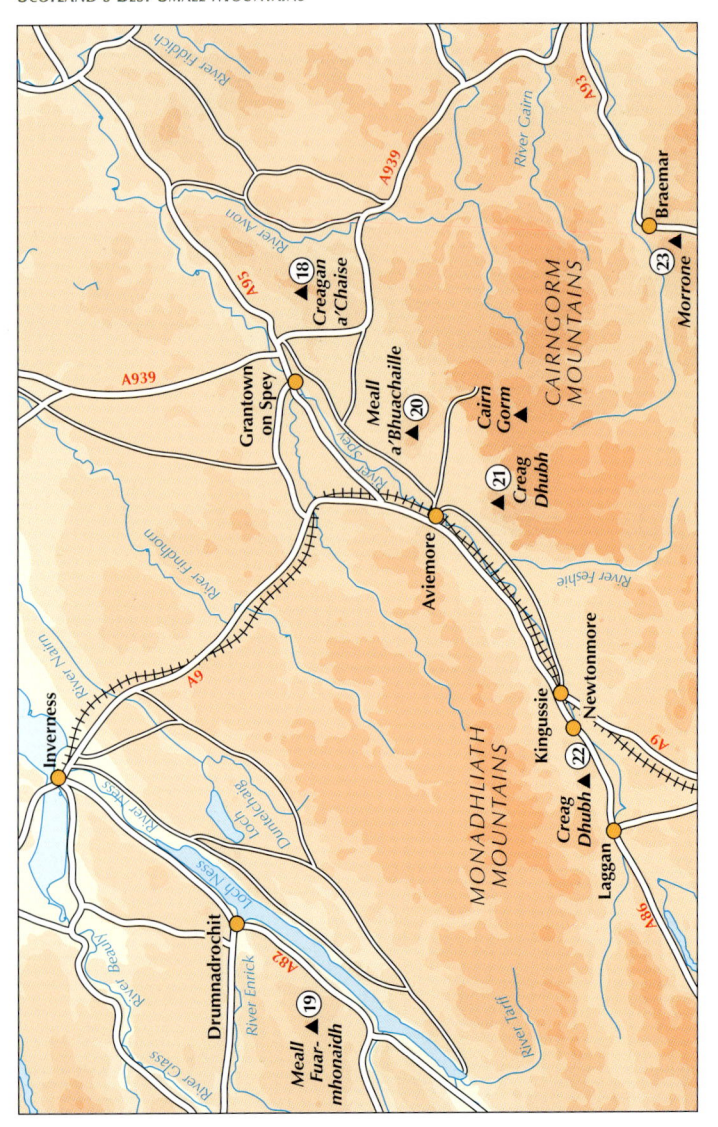

THE GREAT GLEN TO THE CAIRNGORMS

The dark rock face that gives Creag Dhubh its name

18 CREAGAN A'CHAISE (722M) AND THE HILLS OF CROMDALE

'steep rock'

Distance	13.5km
Time	4hr
Ascent	580m
Difficulty	This is a gentle route up grass and heather slopes, but with few paths and broad shoulders, navigation can be very difficult in poor visibility.
Maps	OS Landranger 36, OS Explorer 419
Access	The land to the east of the Cromdale ridge and the summit of Creagan a'Chaise itself is part of the Glenlivet Estate (01479 870070 or info@glenlivetestate.co.uk)
Getting there	Start at Wester Rynaballoch in a small parking area off the road (106 287). There are some local buses from Aviemore to Cromdale (Traveline Scotland 0871 200 22 33, www.travelinescotland.com).
Something else	Go on the Malt Whisky Trail to visit some of the many Strathspey distilleries (www.maltwhiskytrail.com).

> Famous for a bloody battle, the rounded, heather-clad Hills of Cromdale offer great gentle but wild walking with wonderful views.

Creagan a'Chaise is the highest top of the long broad shoulder that forms the Hills of Cromdale. A natural barrier between Strath Avon and Strathspey, their heather slopes were the site of a battle between the Jacobites and government soldiers in 1690.

The battle took place on the Haughs of Cromdale beneath the summit of Creagan a'Chaise. Government troops led by Sir Thomas Livingston surprised and killed

18 Creagan a'Chaise and the Hills of Cromdale

At the Jubilee Cairn on the summit

or captured 400 Jacobites under the command of Colonel Cannon. The Highlanders had been making raids in Strathspey from their bases in Lochaber and the west. Livingston, with the help of the local Grant clansmen, attacked the unsuspecting Jacobite camp on horse and foot. This defeat at the Battle of Cromdale had a major effect on the strength of the Jacobites, with their next uprising not taking place until 1715.

The landscape gives little evidence of the bloody scenes that took place upon it. A stone reputed to be where one piper stood, continuing to play while injured to encourage the Jacobite forces, still remains though. The Clach nam Piobair, or Piper's Stone, is near the return route from Creagan a'Chaise.

It is now mainly monuments to royal personages that are to be found on the Hills of Cromdale. The Jubilee Cairn crowns Creagan a'Chaise, commemorating the

Scotland's Best Small Mountains

jubilee of Queen Victoria in 1897, and en route you pass the Coronation Cairn, dedicated to King Edward and Queen Alexandra, to mark King Edward VII's coronation.

Route

From **Wester Rynaballoch** walk along the road towards Cromdale, taking the first turning off to the left to pass through a gate just beyond the plantation. Follow the track until it bends, then leave it to walk straight on across rough ground towards another gate. Pass through this gate to join a track, which you go left along.

This track zigzags uphill then peters out, to be replaced by a less distinct quadbike track. It continues uphill, passing several grouse butts to reach the shoulder. From here on there is little in the way of paths, and the broad grassy shoulders can prove very hard to navigate in poor visibility.

Follow the line of the shoulder southwest, passing by the top of a fence line and over one distinct top. This brings you to a second top, with the large **Coronation Cairn**. From this top the grass is shorter and there are more sections of path, making the walking easier as you head round and up onto the rocky summit

Map continued on page 124

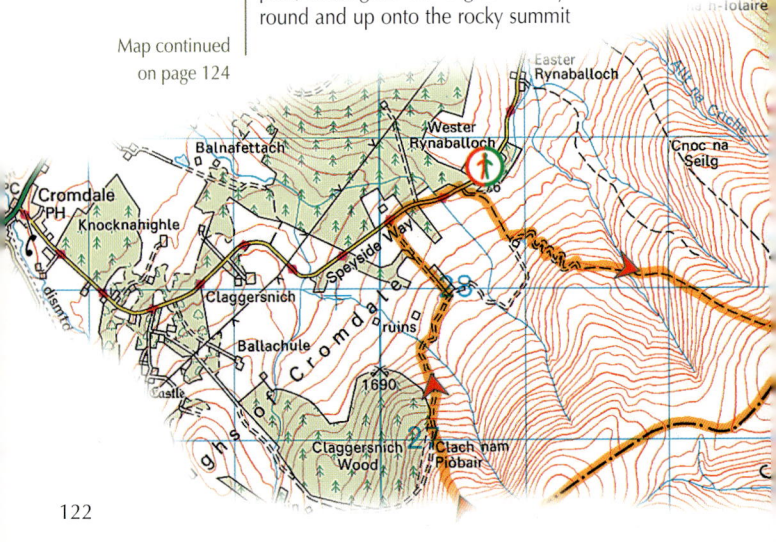

18 Creagan a'Chaise and the Hills of Cromdale

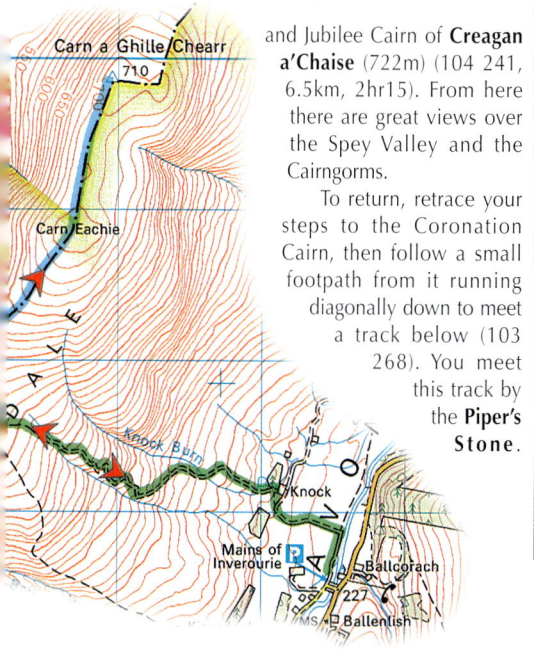

and Jubilee Cairn of **Creagan a'Chaise** (722m) (104 241, 6.5km, 2hr15). From here there are great views over the Spey Valley and the Cairngorms.

To return, retrace your steps to the Coronation Cairn, then follow a small footpath from it running diagonally down to meet a track below (103 268). You meet this track by the **Piper's Stone**.

On the return down from the Coronation Cairn

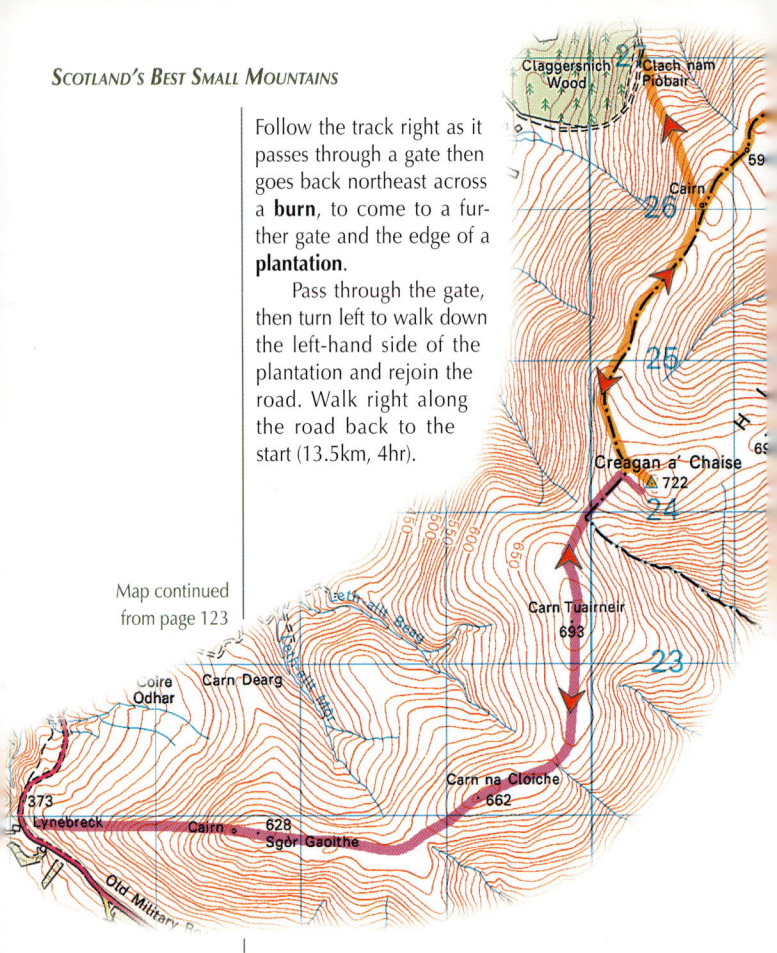

Follow the track right as it passes through a gate then goes back northeast across a **burn**, to come to a further gate and the edge of a **plantation**.

Pass through the gate, then turn left to walk down the left-hand side of the plantation and rejoin the road. Walk right along the road back to the start (13.5km, 4hr).

Map continued from page 123

Alternatives
Including Carn a Ghille Chear
Combine an ascent of Creagan a'Chaise with fellow Cromdale top Carn a Ghille Chear. To do this head left, northeast, once on the shoulder passing over the top of Carn Eachie to reach the summit (710m). Retrace your steps to where you joined the shoulder, then follow the main route as described above (19km, 720m, shown in blue).

From Ballcorach

Creagan a'Chaise can be climbed from Ballcorach on the east side of the Cromdales. From the Ballcorach car park (155 265) follow the track along the River Avon then up the hill to Knock Farm. From there take the left fork to continue uphill. When the track ends, continue uphill to gain the shoulder near where the main route (above) also does so, then follow it to the summit. Return the same way (17km, 650m, shown in green).

Including Sgor Gaoithe, Carn na Cloiche and Carn Tuairneir

An ascent of the Creagan a'Chaise can also be combined with the southern tops of the Hills of Cromdale by starting near Lynebreck on the A939. Following the shoulder, you ascend first to Sgor Gaoithe (628m) then Carn na Cloiche (662m) and Carn Tuairneir (693m) in turn, before gaining the summit of Creagan a'Chaise. Return by the same route (12km, 540m, shown in pink).

19 MEALL FUAR-MHONAIDH (699m)

*'cold hill-mass' or 'hill of the cold slopes',
from Gaelic fuar, meaning 'cold'*

Distance	10km
Time	3hr
Ascent	525m
Difficulty	This is a short route on clear paths. The section along the shoulder can be boggy in places.
Maps	OS Landranger 26 & 34, OS Explorer 416
Getting there	Start at the car park near the end of the small public road from Drumnadrochit to Balbeg and Grotaig (490 238). Buses between Fort William and Inverness stop at Drumnadrochit, though this is 6km from the start of the route (Traveline Scotland 0871 200 22 33, www.travelinescotland.com).

| Something else | Take a boat trip down Loch Ness to try and catch a closer glimpse of Nessie (01463 233999, www.jacobite.co.uk) or visit the Loch Ness Exhibition (www.lochness.com). |

> Monster-spotting above the banks of Loch Ness. Whether or not you believe in Nessie, Meall Fuar-mhonaidh commands a great vantage point over Scotland's longest glen and largest loch. A short walk with a big character.

While only 699m tall, Meall Fuar-mhonaidh is the most prominent of the peaks that flank Loch Ness. Rising up from the loch's north bank, it occupies a spot halfway along the Great Glen, with fabulous views down its entire length.

The Great Glen is more accurately called Glen Mor, or Glen Albyn – Glen Albyn from the Gaelic Gleann Albainn, literally meaning 'glen of Scotland'. It can lay

Meall Fuar-mhonaidh

claim to such a grand name by being Scotland's longest glen. At 100km it runs from Fort William all the way to Inverness, dissecting Scotland along a fault line. Much of the Great Glen is filled with water, in the form of rivers, canals and lochs, the most famous of which is obviously Loch Ness.

Loch Ness is Scotland's largest loch by volume and its second deepest, reaching a depth of 230m in places. But this is not its biggest claim to fame. In 1933, when the *Inverness Courier* reported several sightings of an unknown 'monster', tales of the Loch Ness Monster, later to become known as Nessie, spread across the world.

While some argue that the first recorded sighting was by St Columba in the 6th century, there will always be those who need at least a little scientific proof before they believe an ancient dinosaur or monster exists in the depths of Loch Ness. Over the years, 'sightings' of Nessie have been put down as hoaxes, waves, submarines and fish.

Some credibility was given to the sightings, though, when in 1912 Nessie was included in the Protection of Animals (Scotland) Act. Nessie is still protected under this legislation today.

Route

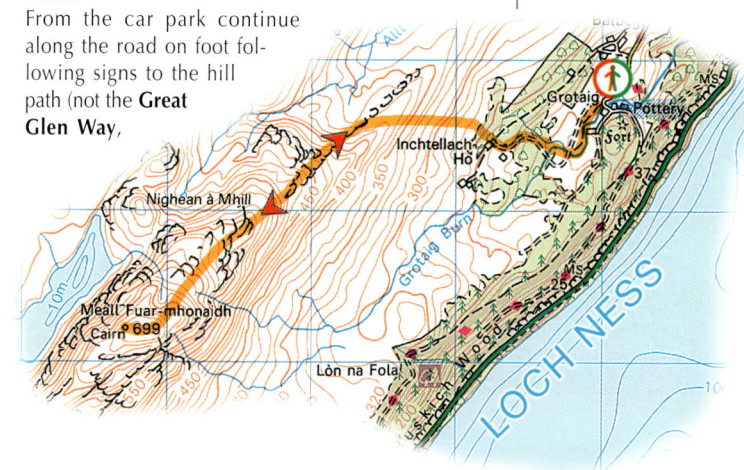

From the car park continue along the road on foot following signs to the hill path (not the **Great Glen Way**,

Scotland's Best Small Mountains

Loch Ness and the first top

which is down to the left). Just before the road crosses a bridge (signed to a pottery), take the well-marked hill path off to the right, passing through a gate.

The pleasant path runs alongside the **Grotaig Burn**, passing through a second gate from where you get a great view of your destination. Two further gates take you across a track to head northwest uphill through some very pretty woodland, with the Grotaig Burn still on your left.

A final gate brings you out of the trees and onto the open hillside, the shoulder of Meall Fuar-mhonaidh straight ahead. As you leave the gate, ignore a path off to the left by an old ruin. Head northwest still on a clear path up towards the shoulder. As you climb you gain your first glimpse of Loch Ness below. The path bends to climb southwest, gaining the shoulder at 400m by a stile over a deer fence (477 238).

From here the path follows the long shoulder southwest all the way to the top. This is fairly gentle in the most part, with occasional boggy patches. A prominent cairn on the first top gives a good indicator of where to head for. The last section up to this cairn is steeper with some rocky sections.

From this first top it is a short, easy walk to the summit of **Meall Fuar-mhonaidh** (699m) (457 222, 5km, 1hr45) and great views down the whole length of Loch Ness and over the Great Glen.

Return by the same route (10km, 3hr).

20 MEALL A'BHUACHAILLE (810M)

'hill of the herdsman' or 'shepherd'

Distance	16km
Time	5hr30
Ascent	750m
Difficulty	Good paths and broad shoulders make this a relatively easy route, though care should be taken on the tops in poor visibility.
Maps	OS Landranger 36, OS Explorer 403
Access	The route is in the Glenmore Forest Park. For more information contact the Forestry Commission on 01463 791575.
Getting there	The start is from the Glenmore Visitor Centre (978 098), which can be reached by car by taking the Glenmore road from Aviemore (parking charge) or by the Cairngorm bus from the centre of Aviemore (contact Rapsons 01463 222244, www.rapsons.com or Traveline Scotland 0871 200 22 33, www.travelinescotland.com).
Something else	Have a picnic on the sandy shores of Loch Morlich before trying your hand at windsurfing (01479 861221, www.lochmorlich.com) and stay at the Glenmore campsite, populated with red squirrels (01479 861271, www.forestholidays.co.uk/glenmore).

A great circular walk atop broad shoulders and over four tops, accompanied along the way by fairies, rogues and great views of the Cairngorms.

Meall a'Bhuachaille

Meall a'Bhuachaille forms part of the Glenmore Forest Park. Rising up from the banks of beautiful Loch Morlich, its good paths and great views offer the walker a wonderful day out. Its wooded slopes are home to red squirrels and pine martens, but once out on the hill it's fairies and the ghosts of local rogues long dead you need to watch out for.

Just as you begin to leave the beautiful remnants of Caledonian pine forest, you come to An Lochan Uaine, 'the green lochan'. Legend has it that the striking green colour came about when Dòmhnall Mòr, King of the Fairies, and his kin washed their clothes in the water.

There appears to be some link between tales of fairy folk, *sith* in Gaelic, and green lochs in Scotland. The Fairy Loch in Arrochar is also known as Lochan Uaine.

Leaving the lochan and fairies behind, you come to Ryvoan Bothy. Ryvoan comes from the Gaelic *ruighe a'bhothain*, meaning 'slope of the bothy', and the building is said to have stood there since the 18th century. One of its occupants was Grigor Ruighe Bhothain, presumably

20 Meall a'Bhuachaille

Grigor of Ryvoan, who was known for his strength and his ability to drink the local liquor. Abandoned as a croft in 1877, Ryvoan Bothy is now managed by the Mountain Bothy Association.

Ryvoan Pass was once a notorious place, being part of the Rathad an Merileach, or 'the cateran's road'. Caterans were rogues and thieves, and this cateran road ran from as far west as Lochaber through Ryvoan to Moray. Keeping away from the main roads and settlements, it allowed the Cameron and MacIntosh clans in the west to steal cattle from the more fertile land in Morayshire. In 1645, Allan Cameron of Locheil was said to have written that 'Morrayland' was the place where 'all men taks their prey'.

Climbing up the slope of the bothy brings you to the broad shoulder and tops of Meall a'Bhuachaille, with their great views over the Rothiemurchus forest to the Cairngorm plateau beyond.

Route

From the **Glenmore Forest Park visitor centre** take the road signed to **Glenmore Lodge**. After 100m take the wide path off to the left that follows the route of the road until its end. From here a wide, well-maintained track continues northeast into Scots pine forest, passing beautiful **An Lochan Uaine**, *uaine* meaning 'green', which it is. When the track divides, take the left fork, signposted to Nethybridge, to arrive at **Ryvoan Bothy**.

From Ryvoan, take a small path that heads up northwest from behind the bothy. The path climbs steeply on stone steps to gain the shoulder of **Meall a'Bhuachaille**. From here views back to Braemar and across the Cairngorm plateau emerge. Follow the shoulder to the summit (810m) (990115, 6km, 500m).

From the top, stay on the path as it descends down the west shoulder, with lovely views over Loch Morlich, to reach the col at 650m (985 115). From here you can choose to either go down to return to the visitor centre, or continue along the shoulder to complete the circuit taking in the peaks of Creagan Gorm and Craiggowrie.

To complete the circuit, continue along the shoulder, climbing to 732m to reach the summit of **Creagan Gorm**. From here the path becomes less distinct and boggier. Keep heading in the same direction to pass over another minor **unnamed top** (711m), with views over Boat of Garten and Aviemore.

To reach the last top, Craiggowrie (687m), continue along the shoulder for a 1km, heading northwest then north to reach the stone shelter that marks the summit of **Craiggowrie**.

From Craiggowrie the path continues briefly in the same direction before taking a sharp left downhill, to enter the woods by a wooden post marked orange (950 131). Shortly after entering the woods you meet another path. Turn left along this, still following orange-marked posts. This in turn brings you to a wide forestry track, which you turn left along, following it as it heads straight, southeast, to arrive at the **Badaguish Outdoor Centre**.

20 MEALL A'BHUACHAILLE

Head left through the outdoor centre complex on a small road, then left again to head back onto a forestry track (957113), where the orange posts reappear. Follow this track, ignoring one turning to the left, to arrive back at the Glenmore Forest Park visitor centre (16km, 5hr30).

A bracing wind at the top

Alternatives
A shorter circuit

A shorter circuit can be completed by returning to the visitor centre from the col at 650m (985 115). Take the path downhill from the col to enter the pine trees. Ignore a path to the right and continue down through the trees. Take the next turn to the right to arrive back at the visitor centre (9km, 500m, shown in blue).

21 CREAG DHUBH AND THE ARGYLL STONE (848M)

'black cliff' or 'crag'

Distance	16km
Time	5hr30
Ascent	650m
Difficulty	This reasonably long route follows good paths in the forest, but involves a long stretch on open hillside without paths that calls for good navigation.
Maps	OS Landranger 36, OS Explorer 403
Access	Rothiemurchus Estate information centre 01479 812345
Getting there	Start at the car park for Loch an Eilein (897 085), where there is a parking charge of £1.50 per person. It is 5km from Aviemore train station to the start of the walk, so it would be possible to walk or cycle from there, where there are trains to/from Inverness and Glasgow/Edinburgh (Scotrail 08457 55 00 33, www.scotrail.co.uk or Traveline Scotland 0871 200 22 33, www.travelinescotland.com).
Something else	Go for some amazing cake at the Inshriach plant nursery (01540 651 287, www.drakesalpines.com).

A ruined castle on an island in a picturesque loch, beautiful native Scots pine forest and a wild and windswept rocky summit, Creag Dhubh has it all. This is a good circular route through a real mixture of landscapes.

Creag Dhubh is technically a lower top of nearby Sgor Gaoith, which is a Munro, and as a result, sadly, Creag Dhubh is rarely climbed. Known more often as the Argyll Stone, for the granite boulder of that name on its shoulder, Creag Dhubh's wooded slopes, rocky summit and stunning views make it well worth a walk in its own right.

21 CREAG DHUBH AND THE ARGYLL STONE

Taking a rest at the stone

The Clach Mhic Cailein, or Argyll Stone, is an enormous granite tor, a remnant of the last ice age. Mhic Cailein translates as 'son of Colin', and refers to the chiefs of Clan Campbell, who were descended from the Great Colin Campbell, the first Earl of Argyll. The stone is said to be named after the seventh Earl of Argyll, who travelled by it after his defeat at the Battle of Glenlivet in 1594. The battle saw the Catholic forces of the earls of Huntly and Errol, numbering around 2000, defeating 10,000 men under the command of the Protestant Earl of Argyll.

At the foot of Creag Dhubh is beautiful Loch an Eilein, meaning 'the loch of the island'. The island for which it is named is home to an ancient castle, thought to have been built in the 13th century. The castle was besieged by Jacobite soldiers in 1690, following their defeat at the Battle of Cromdale, then in 1745 it was used to shelter fugitives from the Battle of Culloden.

Both loch and mountain are part of the Rothiemurchus Estate. The estate at the heart of the Cairngorms National

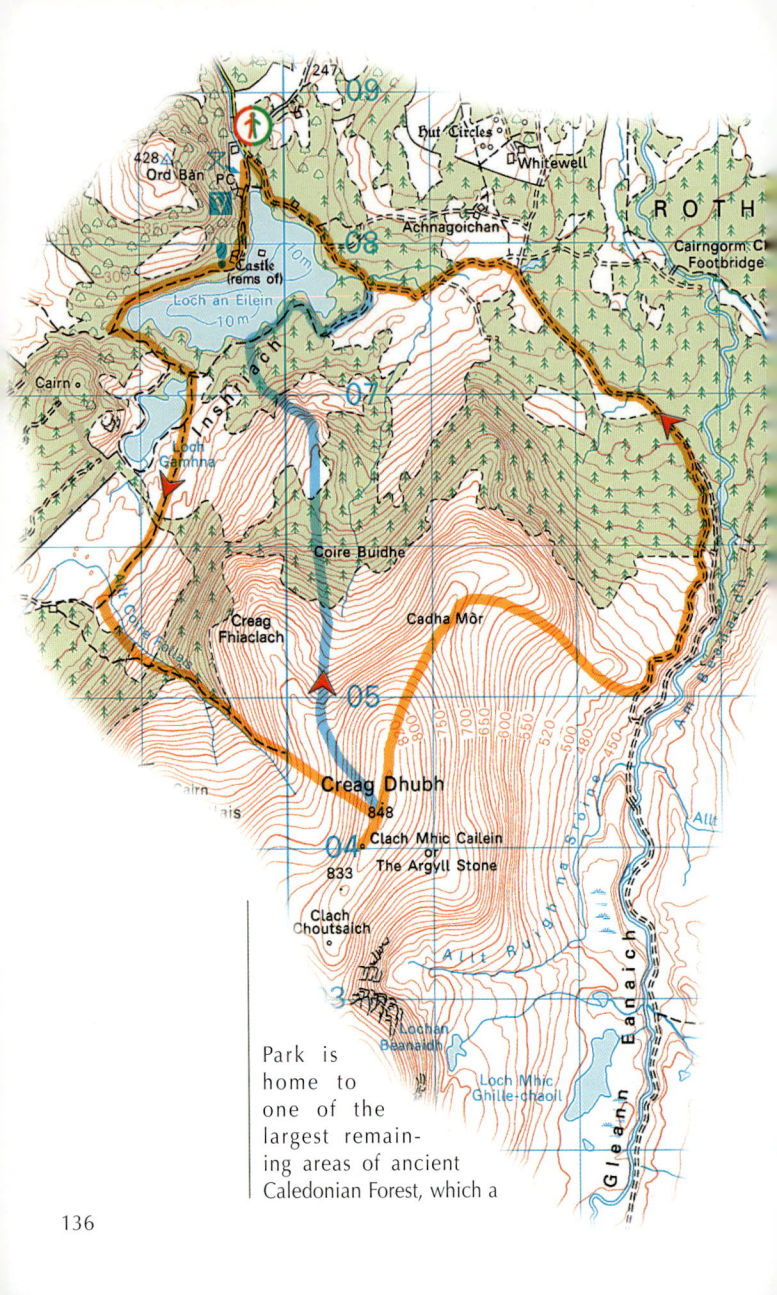

Park is home to one of the largest remaining areas of ancient Caledonian Forest, which a

21 CREAG DHUBH AND THE ARGYLL STONE

walk up Creag Dhubh allows you to pass through.

Route

From the car park follow the path signed to Loch an Eilein, taking the path down the **loch's** west side. Stay on the main path until it divides at the end of the loch, then turn left (following a footpath sign). This takes you briefly along the south side of the loch, then down to a bridge at the outflow of **Loch Gamha**. Cross the bridge and go up the hill on the far side before taking a small path off to the right by some fire beaters (893 071).

This path takes you around Loch Gamha across level heather terrain to the **Allt Coire Follais**. Shortly after crossing the burn and just as you enter the trees (886 055), take a small overgrown path to the left. This heads uphill, quite steeply in places, on the right-hand side of the burn, passing between beautiful Scots pines.

As you leave the tree line, cross to the left bank of the Allt Coire Follais, with the Clach Mhic Cailein, or Argyll Stone, coming into view ahead. The path peters out, but continue southwest up the heather slope, heading for the shoulder just to the left of the **Argyll Stone** to avoid the steepest section. Go right along the shoulder to reach the Argyll Stone from which there are great views down into Gleann Einich and over to the peaks of the Cairngorm plateau.

The actual summit of **Creag Dhubh** (848m), at about 5m higher, is a short gentle walk to the north of the Argyll Stone (906 042, 7.5km, 2hr45).

From the summit of Creag Dhubh continue north then northeast down the shoulder of **Cadha Mor**. As you near the end of the shoulder, bear southeast to come down the short grass and heather slopes to meet the track in **Gleann Einich** below. It is pathless to here, but never too difficult.

There are two tracks at this point in Gleann Einich, but they soon merge. Walk left along either of them to

Looking into Gleann Einich from the top

enter the **Rothiemurchus** forest. Take the left fork at an intersection of paths, then ignore a turning off to the left to come back to Loch an Eilein. This time turn right to walk round the east side of the picturesque loch and return to the start (16km, 5hr30).

Alternatives
The Mule Track
An interesting, shorter descent can be made by heading from the summit north-northwest into Coire Buidhe. Continuing north through attractive woodland, but which is also hard going, you come to the end of a spur (902 067) from where you descend more steeply northwest to pick up what is known as 'the mule track'. This appears on the 1:25 000 map but not the 1:50 000, and could be the mule track that was reputed to have been built during the Second World War by Sikh horse and mule handlers stationed in the area. This overgrown track zigzags downhill to bring you onto the main path around Loch an Eilein. Go right to follow the path back to the start (13km, 650m, shown in blue).

22 CREAG DHUBH (NEWTONMORE) (756m)

'black cliff' or 'crag'

Distance	6km
Time	2hr30
Ascent	500m
Difficulty	This is a short but challenging route. The lower slopes require good route finding, with the path disappearing for short sections in the woods. The upper slopes are steep and rocky with some sharp drops.
Maps	OS Landranger 35, OS Explorer 402
Getting there	Start at a small parking area off the A86 on the opposite side of the road from Lochain Uvie (673 957). Buses run to Newtonmore from Aviemore and Inverness (Traveline Scotland 0871 200 22 33, www.travelinescotland.com).
Something else	Find out all there is to know about the Clan Macpherson by visiting the museum (01540 673332, www.clan-macpherson.org).

A battle cry, a mountain hideout and a rock climbers' paradise, the route up this Creag Dhubh also offers a great short walk with fantastic views of Badenoch.

Shout 'Creag Dhubh!' and it may well mean you're a member of the Clan Macpherson on your way to do battle. The black crags and cliffs of this shapely peak have long played a part in Macpherson history.

Located in the heart of their territory, the clan gathering still meets at the foot of Creag Dhubh once a year, with those tough enough competing in a hill race up its northeast ridge. But it is probably best known and loved for providing a hiding place to the clan chief following the failed Jacobite Rebellion in 1746.

A local inhabitant

Ewan, or 'Cluny', Macpherson, as he was known, hid out in the hills of Badenoch, amazingly, for nine years following the Battle of Culloden. While he and his men were not part of the battle, he was an important Jacobite leader and as such wanted by the government. With his house destroyed and his men scattered, he sought refuge in the hills, making use of several hiding places.

Uamh Chluanaidh, or Cluny's Cave, on the side of Creag Dhubh, was one such, though it is now almost impossible to find and only really accessible to rock climbers. Another was Cluny's Cage, on Ben Alder, and it is this hideout that has become better known, due to it and Cluny himself appearing in Robert Louis Stevenson's novel *Kidnapped*. In the book, Cluny plays host to on-the-run Balfour and Alan, providing them with food and shelter in his 'cage'. The book also tells of how he hosted Bonnie Prince Charlie.

After nine years in hiding Cluny made it to France, only to die there shortly afterwards, but the legend and stories live on.

22 Creag Dhubh (Newtonmore)

Creag Dhubh, rising up from the village of Newtonmore, is also one of the most prominent hills in the area, resulting in great views of the surrounding countryside, including Glen Banchor, the River Spey and the Monadhliath mountains, from its summit.

Route

From the parking area walk right along the road to the **Creagdhubh Lodge**, obvious because of the sentry box at its entrance. Go through a gate across the road from the lodge and follow the track until you come to another gate (668 954).

Pass through the gate then cross the burn to head west up through birch trees. The way here is hard to find, as it crosses boggy ground, but becomes clearer as you continue up through the trees. Here there are impressive cliffs to your right, which are home to **Cluny's Cave**.

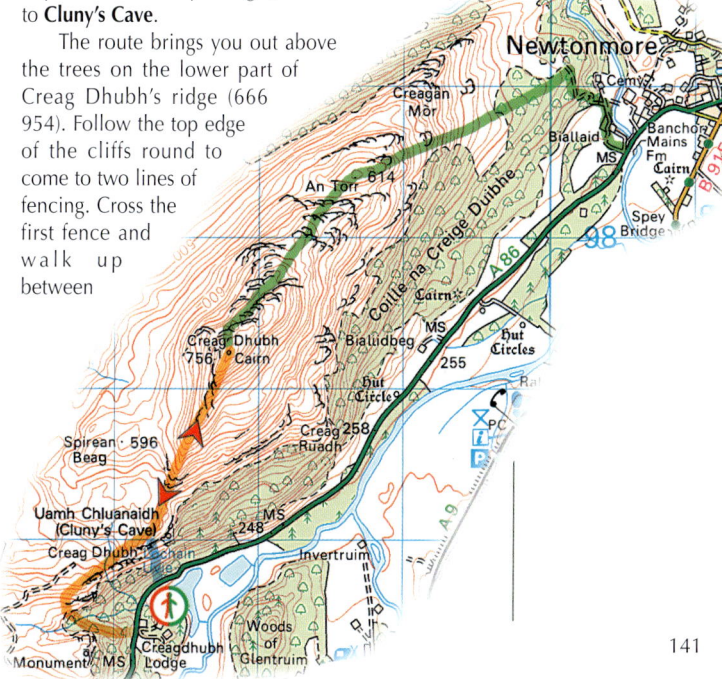

The route brings you out above the trees on the lower part of Creag Dhubh's ridge (666 954). Follow the top edge of the cliffs round to come to two lines of fencing. Cross the first fence and walk up between the two to reach a stone wall. The path climbs steeply for a brief distance from here, before levelling out with Lochain Uvie now below you to the right.

A stile (673 963) marks a distinct narrowing of the ridge and a much clearer route. Continue up, increasingly steeply, and across a second stile. As you near the summit the terrain levels, but becomes rockier as you pass over a couple of false tops to gain the summit of **Creag Dhubh** (756m) (678 972, 3km, 1hr30). Here there are great views over Badenoch and the Monadhliath mountains.

Return by the same route (6km, 2hr30).

Alternatives
Direct from the Lochan Uvie
An alternative, much rougher ascent of the southwest ridge, starts at the parking area at Lochan Uvie. Pass through the gate to come to two rock climbers' paths. Take the right path up through birch trees. On reaching a boulder field the path disappears. Head northeast across the boulders, watching out for the resident wild goats. Continue traversing northeast to reach a fence around a plantation then follow the fence line uphill. At the top of the plantation continue straight on up very steep, rough ground to join the ridge and the route described above. Return by the route described above (5km, 480m, shown in blue).

Looking down the ridge

The Northeast Ridge from Newtonmore

Creag Dhubh can also be climbed by way of its northeast ridge from Newtonmore. To do this, start on the A86 at Ballaid on the outskirts of the village. Follow the small road to the riding centre, passing behind it to take a track off to the left. Follow this through two gates and uphill, then leave it for a small path off to the left. This passes through some birch trees before climbing around a crag to An Torr and onto the ridge proper. Follow the ridge steeply up to the summit. You could either return by the same route (8km, 520m) or, ideally, arrange transport to allow you to complete a route over both ridges (7km, 520m, shown in green).

23 MORRONE (or MORVEN) (859m)

Morrone is from the Gaelic mor-shron, meaning 'big nose', or Morven from mor bheinn, 'big mountain'

Distance	12.5km
Time	3hr30–4hr
Ascent	580m
Difficulty	A short and easy circular route on good clear paths and tracks.
Maps	OS Landranger 43, OS Explorer 387
Access	For stalking information contact the Callater and Clunie hillphone on 013397 41997.
Getting there	Start at the tourist information centre in Braemar (150 913). There is a public car park next to it, or Braemar can be reached by bus from Aberdeen (Stagecoach www.stagecoachbus.com or Traveline Scotland 0871 200 22 33, www.travelinescotland.com).
Something else	Hang out in the pretty village of Braemar and visit Braemar Castle (013397 41219, www.braemarscotland.co.uk) or if that's not big enough, head a few miles down the road to Balmoral (013397 42534, www.balmoralcastle.com).

> A mountain with royal connections, Morrone stands guard over the village of Braemar.

Set in the heart of Royal Deeside, Morrone rises up from Braemar. Overlooking the River Dee, the village and the mountain passes that meet there, it has long stood watch as history has unfolded at its foot. It is a history with many royal links.

King Malcolm III is seen as the likely founder of Braemar, establishing a castle there around the time of his defeat of Macbeth in 1057, the defeat that helped put him on the throne. The village of Castleton of Braemar grew up around the castle. Malcolm is also credited with holding the first ever Highland Games at Braemar, possibly as a means of selecting soldiers for his army.

Almost 1000 years on, the Braemar Gathering is probably the most famous of the Highland Games, with a hill race up Morrone one of the big events, and it is still attended by royalty. Though outlawed for 30 years

In the Morrone Birkwoods

23 Morrone (or Morven)

following the Battle of Culloden, the Braemar Gathering restarted in the early 1800s, and was attended by Queen Victoria in 1848, following her purchase of Balmoral. Victoria bestowed royal patronage on the event and it has been regularly attended by the royal family ever since.

The Queen is the current patron of the Gathering, but an interesting tale lies with two of the vice-patrons, the Duke of Fife and Captain Farquharson of Invercauld. While now reconciled, there was once a long-running rivalry between the predecessors of the Duke of Fife, who owned the Mar Estate, and the Farquharsons of Invercauld. Braemar consisted of two halves – Auchendryne in the Mar Estate and Castleton in Invercauld. It was this split and rivalry that led to the building of two hotels in the village, the Fife Arms and the Invercauld Arms, and two village halls, both named after Queen Victoria.

Route

From the **tourist information centre** walk left along **Braemar**'s main street. Turn left to go up Chapel Street until the road ends by a car park and a pond. Here you are entering the **Morrone Birkwood** Special Area of Conservation, where the best British examples of downy birch and juniper woodland are to be found.

A private track continues from the end of the road. Go along this, ignoring a path to the right, then at a junction go left to head towards a house. Just before the house take a small path off to the right (141 907). This climbs through lovely woodland, taking you back to the track briefly before heading off to the left onto a path again.

Climb, ignoring the blue markers for a different circular walk, to arrive at a **viewpoint** (142 905). From here head left along a track, then almost immediately right onto a small path (signed to Morrone). This passes through a gate in the deer fence and continues all the way to the top of Morrone. It is a good path, though steep in places, with great views back over Braemar village and the River Dee valley.

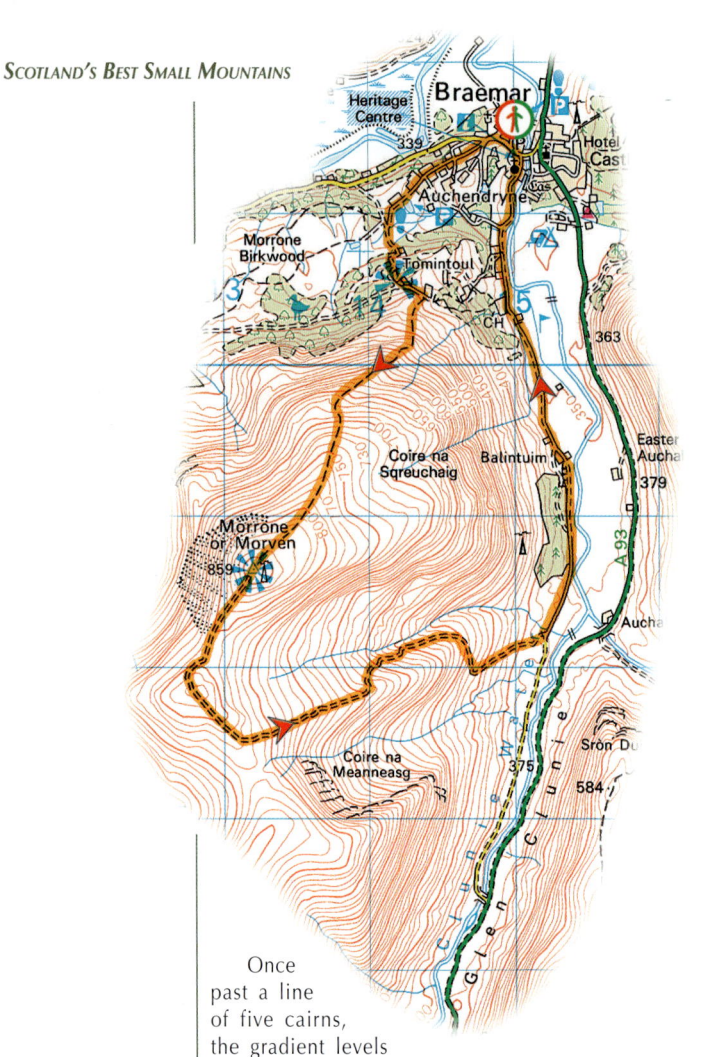

Scotland's Best Small Mountains

Once past a line of five cairns, the gradient levels out and it is a final short walk to the summit of **Morrone** (859m) (132 886, 4.5km, 1hr45). The summit is marred by a large telecommunications mast and a shed, but the views more than make up for it, with the peaks of the southern Cairngorms spread out to the northwest.

23 Morrone (or Morven)

Looking down on Braemar

Head southwest from the summit onto a wide stony track. This was built to allow the mast to be installed, and takes you all the way down the hill by way of a lower top to the southwest of Morrone. It ends at a single-track road in **Glen Clunie**.

Walk left along this pleasant road, with the pretty pools of **Clunie Water** to your right. This takes you north past the **golf course** and back into the centre of Braemar by the tourist information centre (12.5km, 3hr30 – 4hr).

Alternatives
Straight there and back
Rather than completing the circuit, you could return by the ascent route (9km, 530m).

Scotland's Best Small Mountains

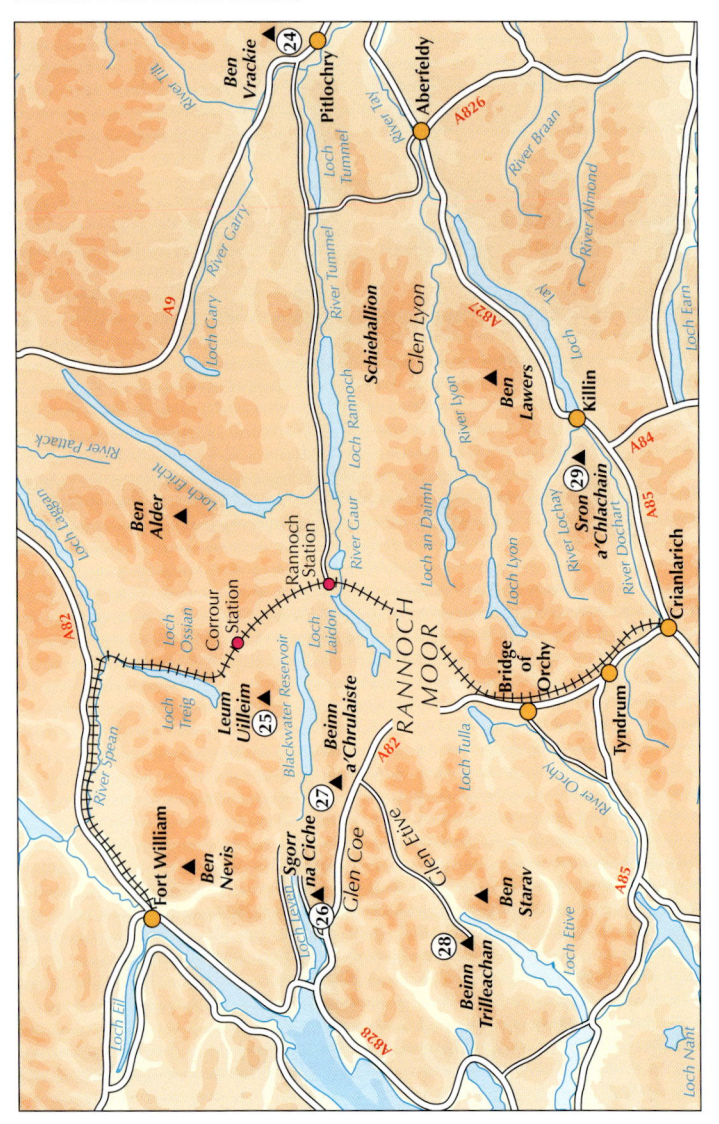

The Pap of Glencoe

GLENCOE AND CENTRAL SCOTLAND

24 BEN VRACKIE (841M)

'speckled hill'

Distance	9km (+4km to/from Pitlochry)
Time	3hr30
Ascent	700m
Difficulty	Straightforward and well-made paths take you all the way to the summit, though the last section is a bit steep and rocky.
Maps	OS Landranger 43 & 52, OS Explorer 386
Getting there	There is a dedicated car park behind the village of Moulin (944 597). Go left after the Moulin Inn, then turn, following the signs to Ben Vrackie. Alternatively, it is easy to reach Pitlochry by train or bus and walk the 2km to the start (Traveline Scotland 0871 200 22 33, www.travelinescotland.com).
Something else	Enjoy a real ale made on site while warming up in front of a roaring fire in the Moulin Inn (01796 472196, www.moulininn.co.uk).

Readily accessible, Ben Vrackie offers a great escape from the cities of Scotland's central belt. Its fine paths lead you to the top of one of the best viewpoints in the Southern Highlands, and the Moulin Inn offers a cosy fireside seat at the bottom.

Located in beautiful Highland Perthshire, Ben Vrackie dominates the skyline above Pitlochry. The route up it starts and ends in the pretty village of Moulin on the outskirts of Pitlochry.

There has been a settlement at Moulin as far back as the Bronze Age, with archaeologists dating ancient hut circles in the area from 3000BC. A hut circle refers to the remains of a prehistoric circular house, the walls of which would have been made by constructing a bank of earth and stone then building with wood on top. While the wood has long since disappeared, the shapes of the earth banks remain. There are more than 50 such remains on Moulin Moor.

In more recent times the village became famous for its inn. Opened in 1695, the Moulin Inn catered to villagers, drovers and those stopping off at the staging post in Moulin. When the railway line to Pitlochry was finished in the 1870s, it became a popular destination for tourists. People travelled from towns and cities to take in the so-called 'hydropathic airs' of Highland Perthshire. It is still in demand today, with its cosy fires and onsite brewery proving a popular place to end a walk up Ben Vrackie.

The start of the alternative route up Ben Vrackie is also worth a mention. Killiecrankie is famous for the beautiful wooded gorge through which the River Garry flows, and as the scene of an historic battle.

The Battle of Killiecrankie took place in 1689, between Viscount Dundee and his Jacobite army, and government troops sent to defeat them, led by General

Moulin Inn with Ben Vrackie behind

Mackay. In this, the first of the major battles of the Jacobite Rebellions, the government army was caught between their enemy and the River Garry. With nowhere to run, the government troops were defeated and the Jacobites won, but only at the expense of Dundee, who was killed during the fight.

Those government soldiers who did try to flee by jumping the River Garry were mainly killed or drowned, but one, Donald MacBean, remains famous today for managing to achieve the seemingly impossible. Soldier's Leap still marks the spot where he apparently jumped five and a half metres to safety, with only the loss of one shoe.

Route

Take the path from the **car park** up through very pleasant beech woodland. The path climbs steadily, meeting and crossing a forestry track. You reach a second forestry track, which you go left along before turning right to rejoin the path. Continuing uphill, the path sticks to the edge of the woodland with good views down over Pitlochry.

The slope lessens as you come up through an area of recent tree felling, to arrive at a deer fence and gate. Passing through the gate brings you out of the trees onto open hillside, crossing a small **burn** as you do.

The good, wide path takes you north then northeast across the heather, with a bench pleasingly located for surveying the river valley below. Ignore a smaller path off to the left to head between the lumpy tops of **Meall na h-Aodainn Moire** and **Creag Bhreac**. The path curves round the former to drop down slightly to **Loch a'Choire**.

Walk across the dam at the southeast end of Loch a'Choire and cross the small burn at the far end to gain the steeper slopes of **Ben Vrackie**. From here the path climbs over 300m in height, with zigzags and stone steps helping in places. It follows the line of a gully northeast before doubling-back at a gentler gradient to reach the summit (841m) (950 632, 2hr, 4.5km). From here there are fantastic views over neighbouring Beinn A'Ghlo to the north.

24 BEN VRACKIE

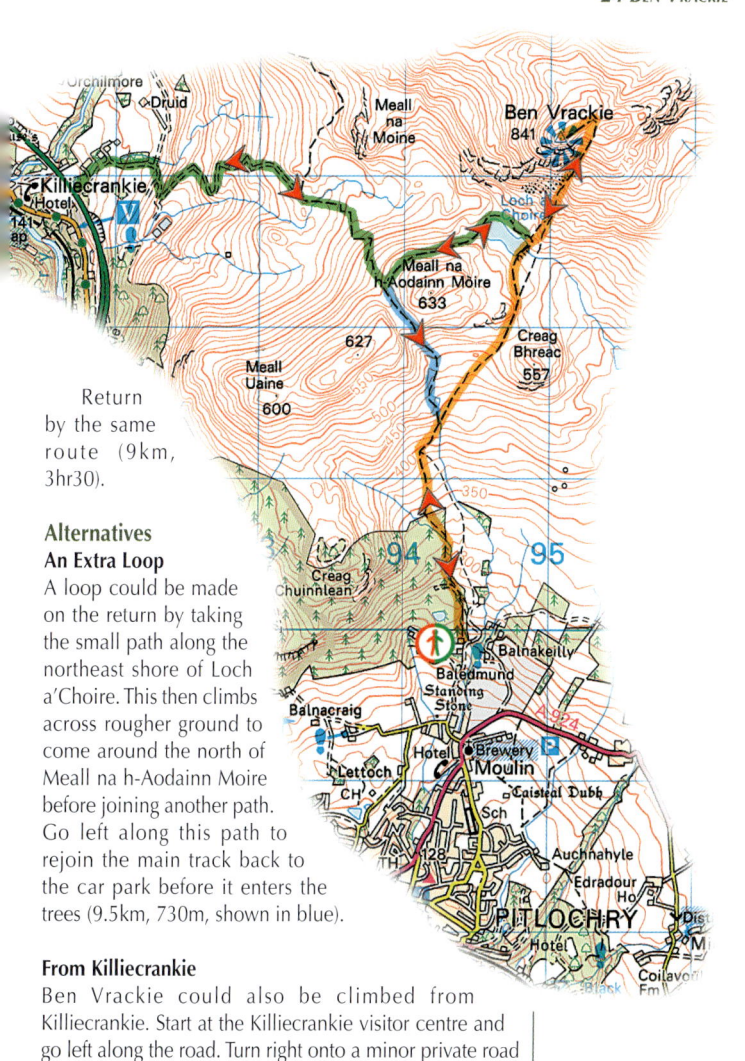

Return by the same route (9km, 3hr30).

Alternatives
An Extra Loop
A loop could be made on the return by taking the small path along the northeast shore of Loch a'Choire. This then climbs across rougher ground to come around the north of Meall na h-Aodainn Moire before joining another path. Go left along this path to rejoin the main track back to the car park before it enters the trees (9.5km, 730m, shown in blue).

From Killiecrankie
Ben Vrackie could also be climbed from Killiecrankie. Start at the Killiecrankie visitor centre and go left along the road. Turn right onto a minor private road to pass underneath the A9, then leave the road for a track that passes by waterworks on its way to the bealach. At the

153

Beinn A'Ghlo from the summit

bealach you take the path to the left that passes between Meall na Moine and Meall na h-Aodainn Moire, to reach Loch a'Choire and the main route described above. Return the same way (12km, 760m, shown in green).

25 LEUM UILLEIM (909m)

William's Leap, thought to have been named after William Caulfield, one of General Wade's military-road builders

Distance	11km
Time	3hr30–4hr
Ascent	580m
Difficulty	A short, easy route with some small paths and tracks, but also pathless rough and boggy ground. The broad shoulders are easy to follow, but could be tricky in cloud.
Maps	OS Landranger 41, OS Explorer 385
Access	Corrour Estate 01397 732 200, www.corrour.co.uk
Getting there	Start at Corrour station (355 664). There is no road access; trains to Corrour run on the West Highland line from Glasgow and Fort William (three times a day

25 LEUM UILLEIM

	from each – Scotrail 08457 550033, www.scotrail.co.uk or Traveline Scotland 0871 2002233, www.travelinescotland.com).
Something else	Take a walk to scenic Loch Ossian before marvelling in wonder that there is such a remote bar and restaurant.

> Proving that the West Highland line is not just for trainspotters, Leum Uilleim offers a great horseshoe of a walk set in acres of wilderness and only accessible by train – a chance to really get away from it all.

That Leum Uilleim, William's Leap, is now only accessible by train is quite ironic, considering it is thought to have been named after William Caulfield, a famous road builder.

William Caulfield succeeded General Wade as the military's chief road builder in 1740. From 1715 onwards, Wade and his successors, including Caulfield, were responsible for building over 250 miles of roads in Scotland. Linking the forts in Perth and Fort William, then north to Fort Augustus and Inverness, the roads were built to allow the quick movement of troops and artillery, with the intention of quelling any Jacobite uprisings. While William may have had a mountain named after him, it is Wade whose name remains synonymous with the roads.

But it is because William's 'leap' is now only easily accessible by rail that Leum Uilleim is so special. It is located on the beautiful West Highland line, voted one of the best train journeys in the world. The line running from Glasgow to Mallaig, also known as 'the Iron Road to the Isles', was built by the Victorians, and when it opened in 1894 was regarded as one of their greatest engineering feats.

Stepping off the train at Corrour station, you realise with great pleasure that with no roads to bring more

Leum Uilleim from Corrour station

people, the hills are going to be pretty much your own for the day. Set in the heart of 52,000 acres of wilderness, it shouldn't be a problem finding some peace and quiet. In fact most of your fellow passengers are likely be heading for the nearby Munros, or are there simply to look at the view. And it is a famous view.

If you've ever seen *Trainspotting*, the view of Leum Uilleim as you arrive may seem quite familiar. The film featured both the hill and the station, with tourists still making the trip just to see the famous backdrop. The actual walk up it, though, is well worth the extra effort.

The route over the horseshoe of ridges and twin tops makes a great circular walk. The gentle climb up the long southwest shoulder provides fantastic views over the Nevis range, and then, once on the summit, there is a 360° panorama taking in Rannoch Moor, Glen Coe, *Schiehallion* and Loch Ossian. A descent of Leum Uilleim's steep nose brings you back to the station where, with any luck, you'll have just enough time left to sample the delights of the bar/restaurant before you catch the train.

25 LEUM UILLEIM

Route

Starting at **Courror station**, cross the railway line to head west on the opposite side of the line to the café. Two tracks start here – go left, ignoring the right, signed to Fort William. Soon after, cut off to the right onto a small but clear path. This guides you across the bog to meet the burn, the **Allt Coire a'Bhric Beag**.

The path follows the burn's left-hand side before crossing it and heading up onto the shoulder of **An Diollaid**. The path all but disappears, but keep climbing, heading northwest.

This brings you onto the shoulder by a distinctively perched boulder at about 580m. From here, head left up the shoulder on an all-terrain-vehicle track that doesn't appear on the map. This track takes you southwest up the very long, gentle shoulder of **Tom an Eoin** and beyond, with views to the right over to the Nevis range.

When the track divides (323 650), take the left fork until it begins to descend. Here leave it to keep to the top of the shoulder and come to the cairn and rocky top of **Beinn a'Bhric** (876m).

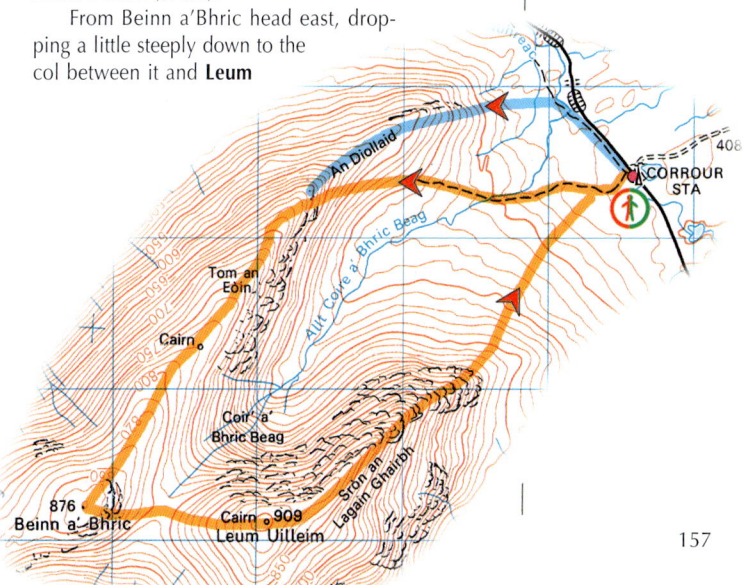

From Beinn a'Bhric head east, dropping a little steeply down to the col between it and **Leum**

Uilleim. Continue east climbing up the broad shoulder to gain just over 100m of height and the summit (909m) (330 641, 7km, 2hr15).

From the large cairn on the summit head northwest – the ridge here is narrow and gentle at first. A small path then takes you more steeply down the rocky lumpy shoulder of **Sron an Lagain Ghairbarbh**. As you near the bottom, head directly for the station, picking up bits of paths to help you across the boggy ground and rejoin the original track (11km, 3hr30–4hr).

Alternatives
The entire An Diollaid shoulder
An alternative route onto the shoulder is to cross the railway line, but this time take the right-hand track. This is very wet in places. Follow it for 650m until, just after a bridge, an all-terrain-vehicle track leaves it to the left (351 668). This is the unmarked track you join in the main route described above, and can be followed the full length of the shoulder from here, then completing the route as above (11.5km, 580m, shown in blue).

The view from Beinn a'Bhric

26 SGORR NA CICHE (PAP OF GLENCOE) (742m)

'Peak of the breast' or 'nipple', from cíche in Gaelic or pap in Scots

Distance	8km
Time	3hr30
Ascent	720m
Difficulty	A short route that follows a path to the summit. The path can be very muddy lower down, and the last section is steep and rocky, with some easy scrambling.
Maps	OS Landranger 41, OS Explorer 384
Getting there	Start at the Lochan car park on the east side of Glencoe (104 593), signed from the village centre. Buses pass through Glencoe on the Glasgow/Edinburgh to Fort William/Oban route (Traveline Scotland 0871 200 22 33, www.travelinescotland.com).
Something else	Visit the Clachaig pub, where a sign still states that hawkers and Campbells are not welcome; everyone else can benefit from real fires and regular live music (01855 811252, www.clachaig.com).

Made famous by breasts and battles, Sgorr na Ciche's distinctive shape dominates the entrance to Glencoe. This short route gives a flavour of the drama and fierceness that characterises both the landscape and its history.

Better known as the Pap of Glencoe, Sgorr na Ciche, translates as 'peak of the breast' or 'nipple', and looking at its distinctive shape it's easy to see why. The Pap is one of many hills in Scotland named after breasts by a Gaelic culture that lacked the taboos and hang-ups of the later more Presbyterian society of the Highlands. The Cioch in the Cuillins on Skye and the Paps of Jura are two notable examples.

The Pap of Glencoe and Loch Leven

Rising up from Loch Leven at the entrance to Glencoe, the Pap stands watch over one of the most dramatic glens in Scotland. The wild, forbidding landscape, composed of dark rocky peaks and perilous ridges, echoes the long and dramatic history of the glen. The event for which Glencoe is best known is the Massacre of Glencoe.

The Massacre of Glencoe took place in February 1692, against the backdrop of the accession to the throne of William of Orange and the subsequent Jacobite uprisings. Highland clans, loyal to James VII, William's challenger to the Scottish throne, were offered the chance of a pardon if they swore an oath to William. While the MacDonalds of Glencoe did swear the oath, they were viewed to have done so late and reluctantly. A plot was devised, allegedly with the consent of the King, to punish their apparent disloyalty. Under the command of a Campbell, a clan with whom the MacDonalds had a long history of conflict, 120 soldiers were billeted with the MacDonalds in Glencoe. The MacDonalds hosted them believing they were there to collect taxes, but their real

26 Sgorr na Ciche (Pap of Glencoe)

orders were to kill any MacDonald male under the age of 70.

The massacre began early one morning at Invercoe, at the foot of the Pap, and at other settlements in Glencoe. It is thought that a number of soldiers refused to participate, allowing some MacDonalds to flee, but all told 38 men were killed and many women and children died from exposure in the snow after their houses were burnt down.

Subsequent inquiries sought justice for the MacDonalds, but with little effect, and the long-running feud between the MacDonald and Campbell clans was greatly exacerbated.

Route

From the car park walk back down towards the road, and just before you reach it take a small, good path off to the left. It heads southeast, running parallel to the road, with some wooden sculptures along the way. Cross a forestry track to continue on the path until it returns to the road. Turn left along the road and then left again, just beyond the first house, to take a track through a gate and start climbing (it may be possible to park off the road nearer this point).

Climb steeply from the road and then take a path off to the right and across a wooden bridge. This path, rough in places, zigzags upwards and to the southeast before turning steeply northeast up the side of a gully. Some more zigzags, across peat bog, bring you to the col at 562m (125 589).

From the col a small path traverses northeast steeply up through rock and scree, requiring some scrambling in

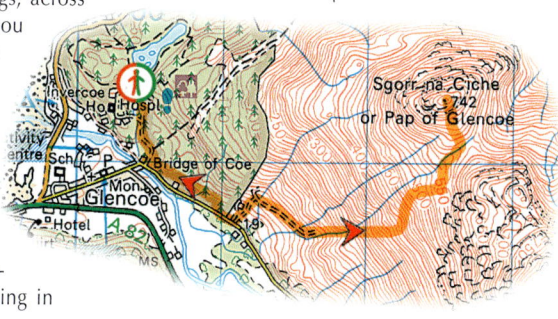

On the rocky summit

places, to arrive at the summit of **the Pap** from the north-east (742m) (125 594, 4km, 2hr).

Return via the same route (8km, 3hr30).

27 BEINN A'CHRULAISTE (857M)

'rocky hill', from the Gaelic crulaist

Distance	13km
Time	4hr
Ascent	670m
Difficulty	A short and relatively easy route, but a lack of paths on the hill itself calls for good navigation. The return is via the well-walked West Highland Way.
Maps	OS Landranger 41, OS Explorer 384
Getting there	Start at the Kings House Hotel (259 546). There are regular buses passing here on the Glasgow/Edinburgh to Fort William/Oban route (Traveline Scotland 0871 200 22 33, www.travelinescotland.com).

27 BEINN A'CHRULAISTE

Something else Do as many travellers before you have, and enjoy a pint in the Climbers' Bar of the Kings House (01855 851 259, www.kingy.com).

A gentle hill set amidst the rugged beauty of Glencoe. With the best view of Buachaille Etive Mor, Beinn a'Chrulaiste rises above the Kings House Hotel, a welcome resting place over the years for drovers, soldiers, labourers and walkers.

Rising up above the Kings House Hotel, where this route begins and ends, Beinn a'Chrulaiste provides a great viewpoint over the dramatic grandeur and rugged beauty of Glencoe. From its peak you can see right down through the Pass of Glencoe and across to a unique view of Buachaille Etive Mor, the glen's most famous peak.

This circuit of Beinn a'Chrulaiste takes in rights of way used by travellers for centuries. As you walk along you do so in the footsteps of clansmen, drovers, Jacobites, soldiers

Kings House with Beinn a'Chrulaiste behind

of the Crown and, more recently, walkers from around the world on what is now the West Highland Way.

The West Highland Way was Scotland's first long-distance footpath. Stretching from the outskirts of Glasgow to Fort William, it covers 152km and is walked by over 80,000 people a year. But the slopes of Beinn a'Chrulaiste were walked long before the West Highland Way came into being.

In the 1700s drovers brought cattle around the sides of Beinn a'Chrulaiste on their way to the Falkirk Trysts. They joined with many others to arrive at these huge markets, where there were as many as 150,000 cattle, sheep and horses. Altnafeadh, were the route meets the West Highland Way, is an old resting stop for the cattle.

From Altnafeadh to the Kings House Hotel you are walking on an old military road. Known as a Wade road, it was part of a network of roads built during the 1700s by General Wade. He saw a need for troops to be able to move around the Highlands more quickly, if Jacobite rebellions were to be quelled. The roads are his legacy, though while in command of the army in 1745 he failed to stop Jacobite forces marching on London. It was the Duke of Cumberland, who took over from him, who ultimately defeated the Jacobites at the Battle of Culloden.

The Kings House existed then too. It was used after the Battle of Culloden as a barracks for troops whose purpose was to capture any remaining Jacobites and ensure that no further uprisings occurred. Built in the 17th century, it is thought to be one of the oldest inns in Scotland, though its name comes from King George III, who stationed the troops there.

Route

Cross the bridge at the rear of the **Kings House Hotel** and follow the old tarmac road. Then, rather than following the signs for the West Highland Way, turn right onto the track signed to Rannoch. Follow this track until it crosses the **Allt a'Bhalaich**.

Leave the track here to walk up the east side of the Allt a'Bhalaich. A small path climbs gently alongside the lovely pools and falls of the river, passing some ruins. The path disappears in places, but if you keep to the riverbank you won't go wrong.

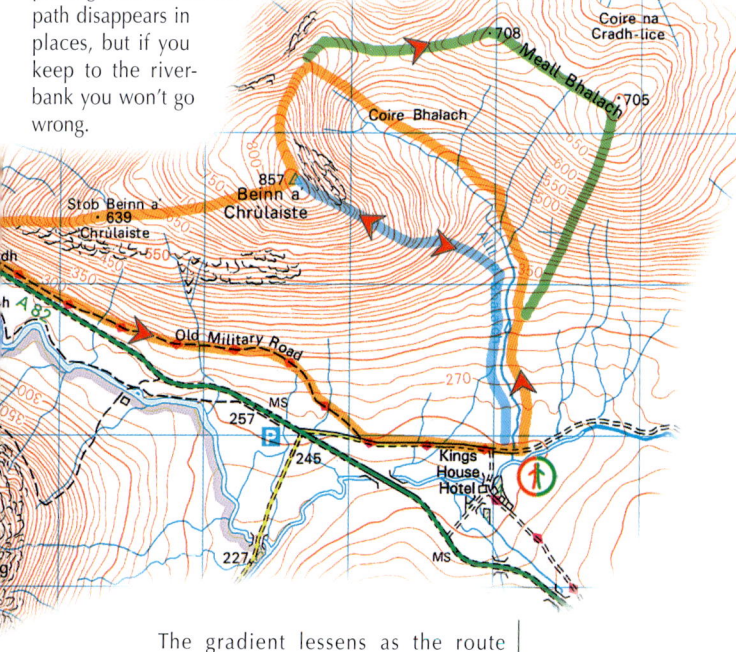

The gradient lessens as the route bends round to head northwest into **Coire Bhalach**. There is little path here, but continue northwest across rough ground to reach the northeast shoulder of **Beinn**

Looking back at Kings House and Creise

a'Chrulaiste. Climb more steeply now to gain the shoulder between Beinn a'Chrulaiste and neighbouring **Meall Bhalach**, at about 700m (246 574). From here you can see down to the Blackwater Reservoir and towards Kinlochleven.

Climb easily up the shoulder, heading west-south-west then south, to reach the summit (857m) (246 566, 5.5km, 2hr). The view over to the rocky face of Buachaille Etive Mor is stunning.

Continue by heading west to descend over rocky then grassy ground, avoiding bog, to the knobbly top of **Stob Beinn a'Chrulaiste** (639m), with views right down Glencoe. Keep descending west, more steeply now but with some sections of path, until you reach a fence. The buildings of **Altnafeadh** are now just below. Follow the fence down until it joins another, which you then follow down, doubling-back on yourself briefly to arrive at the **West Highland Way** by a gate and stile (225 561).

Follow the West Highland Way through **Glencoe** back towards the Kings House Hotel. When it meets a single-track road, go left along it to head back across the bridge to the start (13km, 4hr).

Alternatives
This route could easily reversed, or either option for ascent being used for both outward and return routes.

Ascent of the southeast ridge
A slightly shorter but steeper approach would be to ascend the southeast ridge. To do this, go up the west, rather than east, side of the Allt a'Bhalaich then leave the river to climb the steep and rocky ridge right to the summit (6km, 600m, shown in blue).

Taking in the Two Tops of Meall Bhalach
An ascent of Beinn a'Chrulaiste could also be extended to take in the two tops of Meall Bhalach. These tops and the shoulder connecting them to Beinn a'Chrulaiste are broad and mainly grassy, making for easy walking. For a longer day out, ascend Beinn a'Chrulaiste via Altnafeadh, reversing the main route above until you reach the shoulder above Coire Bhalach, then continue to traverse the two tops of Meall Bhalach before dropping down to rejoin the Allt a'Bhalaich (15km, 780m, shown in green).

28 BEINN TRILLEACHAN (839M)

'mountain of the oystercatchers'

Distance	10km
Time	5hr
Ascent	1100m
Difficulty	A reasonably challenging route due to the long climb up pathless rough ground. While there are steep drops to the east, the ridge itself is not narrow, but the descent from Trilleachan Slabs is steep and rocky.
Maps	OS Landranger 50, OS Explorer 377
Access	Forestry Commission, West Argyll Office 01546 602518
Getting there	Start at the car park just by the head of Loch Etive near the end of the road (111 453).

Scotland's Best Small Mountains

Something else	Wild camp beside one of the River Etive's beautiful pools (but make sure you avoid the midge season).

> Located in one of the most beautiful glens in Scotland, Beinn Trilleachan is home to some dramatic rock slabs and one of the finest views you'll come across.

Beinn Trilleachan is located in what is argued to be one of Scotland's most beautiful glens, Glen Etive. A journey down the glen starts at Buachaille Etive Mor in Glencoe, and follows the rapids and falls of the River Etive to the head of striking Loch Etive. It is from the banks of the loch that Beinn Trilleachan rises up to face the peak of Ben Starav on the opposite bank.

While a great hill walk, Beinn Trilleachan is perhaps better known to rock climbers, being home to the Etive

Taking a rest on the long ridge

Slabs, the vast sheets of smooth granite rock that make up the east face of the mountain. While the slabs lie at a supposedly easy angle of 40°, their smoothness makes the various, interestingly named routes up them challenging to say the least. Worrying to all but the most hardened rock climber will be the name 'Coffin Stone', a huge boulder that sits at the base of the slabs.

Walking up Beinn Trilleachan allows you to gain the top of the slabs in a less death-defying way, and still benefit from the magnificent views down Loch Etive.

The loch stretches for 30km from the foot of the mountain out to the sea at Connel, just north of Oban. While it is a sea-loch, the water level of Loch Etive is slightly higher than sea level. At low tide this results in water from Loch Etive pouring out into the Connel narrows, creating the stunning Falls of Lora.

Also at the far end of the loch, Deirdre of the Sorrows is said to be buried. One of the best-known figures in Celtic mythology, when Deirdre was born the druids predicted that kings and lords would go to war over her beauty. She was betrothed to Conchobar, the King of Ulster, at an early age, but after falling in love with Naoise, a young warrior, escaped from Ireland with him and his brothers to Glen Etive. After being tricked into returning to Ireland, the brothers were killed, and Deirdre is said to have either killed herself or died of a broken heart. The druids granted Deirdre her dying wish and buried her along with the brothers at Dun Mhic Uisneachan, near Benderloch.

Route

From the car park, cross the road and take a small muddy path off to the right, which follows the fence line of the **Glenetive Forest** plantation. This heads north-northwest up and onto the shoulder of **Beinn Trilleachan**.

At about 170m (107 461), as the gradient is levelling out, go left to leave the path and start the long climb up the shoulder. Heading southwest, ascend rough grassy ground quite steeply, avoiding some rocky outcrops.

You may well pass over the top of **Meall nan Gobhar**, the first top, without noticing, but you continue climbing southwest from there, with the rock outcrops becoming more numerous.

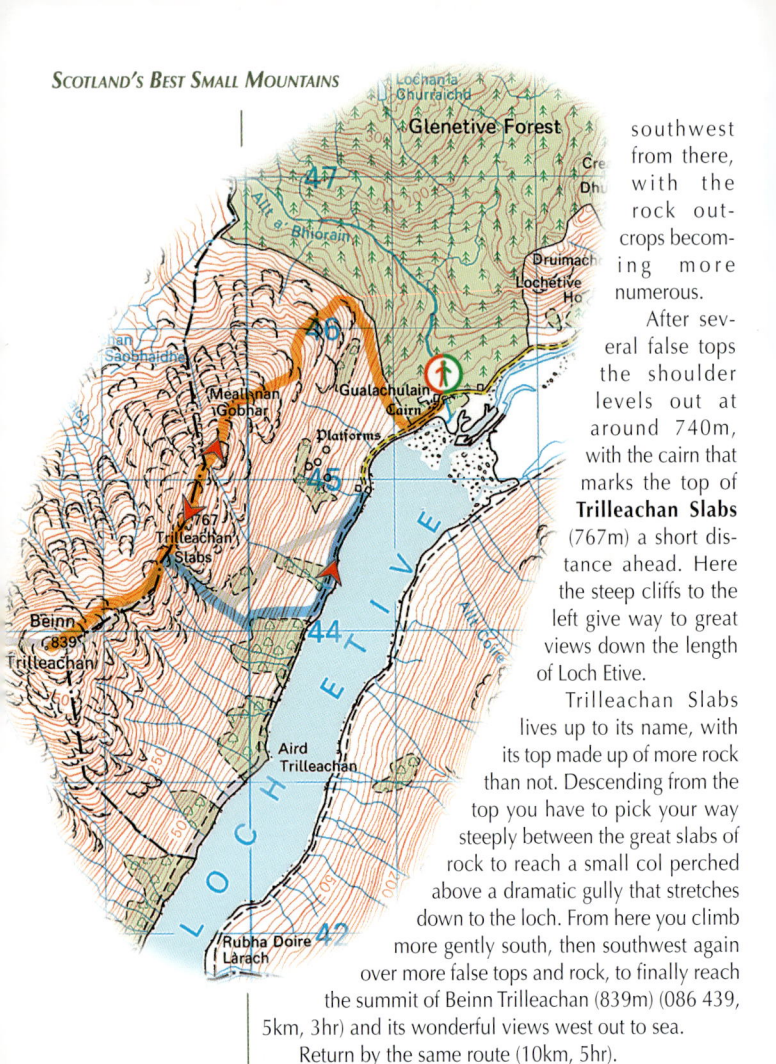

After several false tops the shoulder levels out at around 740m, with the cairn that marks the top of **Trilleachan Slabs** (767m) a short distance ahead. Here the steep cliffs to the left give way to great views down the length of Loch Etive.

Trilleachan Slabs lives up to its name, with its top made up of more rock than not. Descending from the top you have to pick your way steeply between the great slabs of rock to reach a small col perched above a dramatic gully that stretches down to the loch. From here you climb more gently south, then southwest again over more false tops and rock, to finally reach the summit of Beinn Trilleachan (839m) (086 439, 5km, 3hr) and its wonderful views west out to sea.

Return by the same route (10km, 5hr).

Alternatives
Steep Return via the Gully
The rocky nature of Beinn Trilleachan means that the only commonly used route by walkers is the one described

28 BEINN TRILLEACHAN

The Etive Slabs on the flank of Beinn Trilleachan

above. It is possible, however, to make a return from the col between Trilleachan Slabs and the summit by way of the long gully mentioned, although this is a very steep descent with big drops, and should only be considered by the highly competent and confident. It also makes an escape route if you need to get off the ridge quickly.

The top of the gully is at 700m (097 451) and deer paths zigzag down very steeply to reach the top of a ravine. This is crossed near the top, and then hard-going long grass and heather slopes lead you down to the trees and a fence below. Follow the fence left to cross a burn and come to a stile. Cross the stile then head down to the path visible below. This runs alongside Loch Etive back to the start (9km, 1010m, shown in blue).

29 SRON A'CHLACHAIN (521m)

'nose of the village'

Distance	6km
Time	2hr–2hr30
Ascent	460m
Difficulty	A very short route, the ascent all on a small path, but steep in places. The descent is over rougher ground.
Maps	OS Landranger 51, OS Explorer 378
Getting there	Start at the car park next to the village hall (573 331) in the centre of Killin. Buses run to Killin from Callander (Traveline Scotland 0871 200 22 33, www.travelinescotland.com).
Something else	Visit the Moirlanich Longhouse (0844 4932137, www.nts.org.uk/Property/80) or take a photo of the Falls of Dochart before a drink in the pub of the same name (01567 820270, www.falls-of-dochart-inn.co.uk).

A short circular route above one of Scotland's prettiest villages, Sron a'Chlachain offers great views over the hills and glens of the ancient Celtic land of Breadalbane.

Sron a'Chlachain is special because of its location high above the village of Killin. One of the few smaller peaks in the area, it commands breathtaking views of Ben Lawers and the Tarmachan ridge, down Loch Tay and over Killin itself.

Killin is one of Scotland's most picturesque villages, and steeped in legend and history. Located in the ancient Celtic Earldom of Breadalbane – the name comes from the Gaelic *braghaid albainn*, meaning 'high country of Scotland' – the name Killin is thought to come from a story about a Celtic hero called Fingal. Legend tells that

29 Sron a'Chlachain

Looking down Loch Tay from the first cairn

Fingal was buried in Killin after being beheaded during a fight with a local leader called Tailleachd over a beautiful fairy. *Cill fhinn*, pronounced Killin, is Gaelic for the burial place of Fingal.

Fingal's Stone sits just off the path at the start of the route up Sron a'Chlachain. An ascent of the hill, however, shows evidence in the landscape of more recent history.

Looking down on the village of Killin, the remains of a rail line to the banks of Loch Tay can be seen. From 1888 until 1939 this took people to a steamship that travelled the length of the loch.

Descending from the hill, the path follows what appears to be an old drovers' route to arrive at the Moirlanich Longhouse.

The Moirlanich Longhouse, now owned by the National Trust for Scotland, is a rare surviving example of the Scottish longhouse, a building in which a family and their livestock lived under one roof. This longhouse dates from the mid-19th century and is a cruck-frame construction, built from local timber, stone, earth and bracken.

Tenant farmers occupied the longhouse until the 1960s, and it is now a visitor centre giving a window into 19th-century life in Scotland.

Route

Starting outside the village hall, take the path to the rear of the car park, which runs through **Breadalbane Park**. This brings you to a metal gate signed 'Sron a'Chlachain hill path, 1 mile'. Just to the left of here is Fingal's Stone. Take the small path straight up across rough grazing towards woodland, which you enter by way of a stile. In this woodland are many beautiful mature oak trees.

Once out of the woods the path climbs quite steeply up through bracken. It divides in a couple of places, but the forks rejoin. It levels out, giving great views down over Loch Tay, then continues up in a series of quite steep stages. The last of these stages runs along the right-hand side of a stone wall to arrive at a cairn. This is the first of three cairns, the last of which marks the summit of **Sron a'Chlachain** (521m) (558 328, 2km, 1hr).

From the summit, continue to follow the wall as it drops down into, then up the other side of, a small gully, heading northeast then east. When the wall bends downhill, leave it to continue east to meet the top of a path (548 332). This appears to be an old drovers' path, and while overgrown, the many feet walking it over the years have left a distinctive grove on the hillside. It zigzags downhill and crosses a burn. At the

29 Sron a'Chlachain

The Longhouse

time of writing, a fence crosses the path just before the burn, so a suitable place should be found to pass over this to avoid any damage.

Continue downhill, passing through a gate then heading diagonally to reach a second gate, which opens onto the road directly opposite the **Moirlanich Longhouse**. Follow the road to the right to meet the **A827**, the main road through **Killin**, and head right along this back to the start (6km, 2hr–2hr30).

Alternatives
Straight there and back
For a shorter route, keeping to paths, descend by the same route as ascending (4km, 460m).

Taking in Meall Clachach
Extend the route by continuing to/from the summit of Meall Clachach (603m). This is a straightforward walk across broad boggy land east from Sron a'Chlachain (9km, 620m, shown in blue).

Scotland's Best Small Mountains

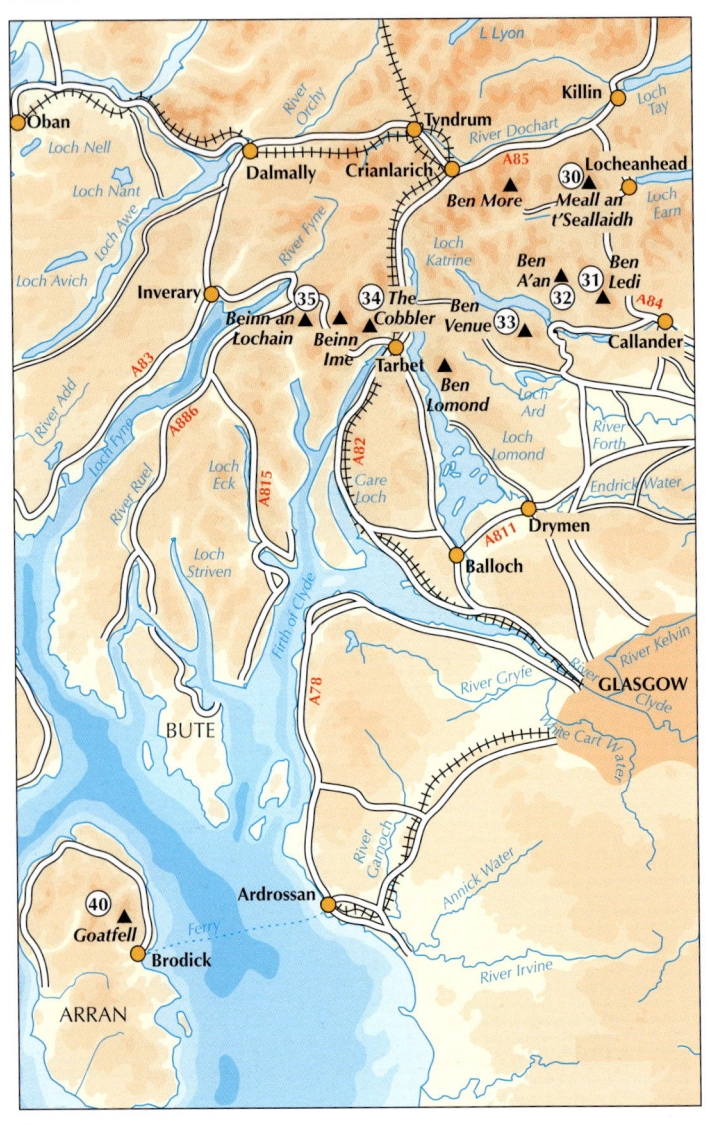

The rocky pinnacle that crowns the summit of The Cobbler

ARROCHAR AND THE TROSSACHS

30 MEALL AN T'SEALLAIDH (852m)

'mountain of the view'

Distance	20km
Time	6hr
Ascent	990m
Difficulty	This long route starts and ends on good tracks, but much of the walk is across rough, pathless ground, where good navigation skills are essential.
Maps	OS Landranger 51, OS Explorer 365
Access	Forestry Commission, Aberfoyle office 01877 382383
Getting there	Start by the graveyard in Balquhidder where Rob Roy is buried (536 209). Buses run from Stirling to the Kingshouse hotel (Traveline Scotland 0871 200 22 33, www.travelinescotland.com).
Something else	Pay your respects to Rob Roy, then enjoy afternoon tea at the Old Library Tea Room (01877 384622).

An adventure into the glens and passes of Rob Roy's outlaw country, on a peak that lives up to its name.

Forming part of the Braes of Balquhidder, Meall an t-Seallaidh rises up behind the pretty hamlet, its wooded glens and remote passes the scene of many a historic and fictional tale. The most famous of all being that of Rob Roy MacGregor, the legendary hero – or outlaw – who is buried in the graveyard at the mountain's foot.

Rob Roy, or Robert, MacGregor died in Balquhidder in 1734. If one takes a look at his life, it is perhaps surprising that he died in bed aged 63, for while he was a party to the Jacobite cause, he was also famous for raising and rustling cattle.

Rob Roy was branded an outlaw when he failed to repay a loan from the Duke of Montrose. Rob Roy

30 Meall an t'Seallaidh

Kirkton Glen with the ridge up to the right

claimed that the loan had been stolen, but the Duke took his land and cattle, starting a long feud between the pair. As an outlaw Rob Roy spent much of his life evading capture, the hills and glens of the Trossachs proving the perfect hideout for him and his men. There were few roads, and even Balquhidder translates from Gaelic to mean 'the distant farm'.

Opinions differ as to whether Rob Roy was simply a thief looking out for himself and his profit, or whether he had in fact suffered a great injustice and was more of a Robin Hood-like figure. What is clear is that he was a popular figure, as much today as then. This is in no small part due to fictional accounts of his life. In fact, it was a work of fiction that is said to have saved him.

Rob Roy had finally been captured and was imprisoned in London. While awaiting his fate, the novelist Daniel Defoe published *A Highland Rogue*, a fictionalised account of MacGregor's life. Some credit this as the reason that King George gave Rob Roy a pardon.

The story of Rob Roy MacGregor has gone on to be the inspiration for many more books and films, including *Rob Roy* by Sir Walter Scott.

Scotland's Best Small Mountains

Route

Starting by **Rob Roy's grave** in **Balquhidder**, take a track from an information panel up to the right of the graveyard. This takes you around the back of graveyard to meet a wide path signed 'To **Kirkton Glen** and Clan Maclaren Creag an Tuirc'.

Follow this path quite steeply uphill though conifers. As the gradient lessens ignore a small path off to the right, then, just afterwards, when the track divides, go left (the right fork takes you to the viewpoint of Creag an Tuirc). Here you are walking alongside a **river**, though you can only catch glimpses of it down in the gorge to the left.

Map continued on page 182

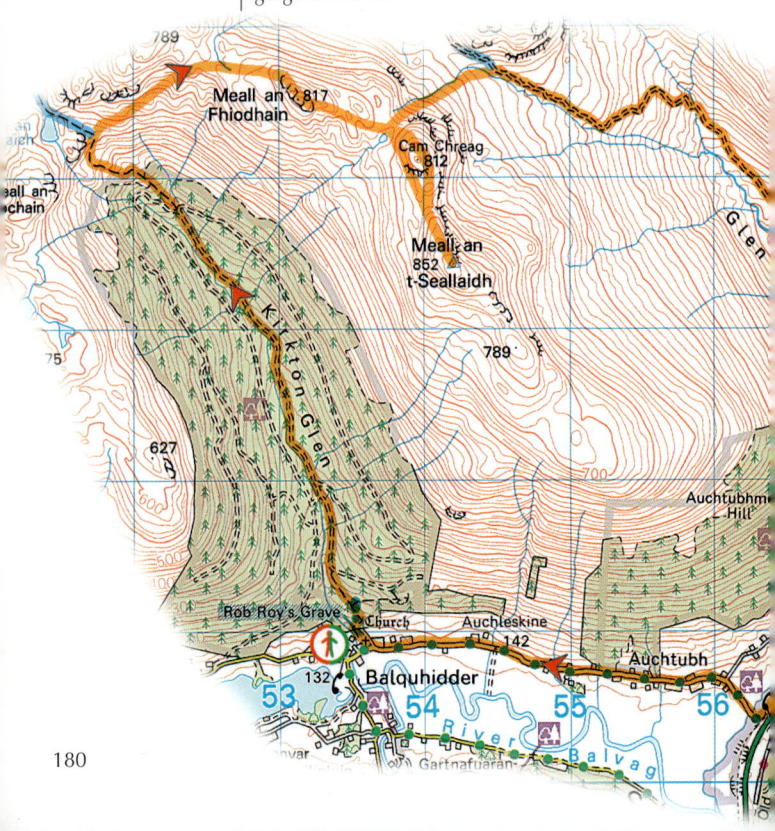

30 Meall an t'Seallaidh

Cross another track to stay by the river, continuing to do so when you cross a bend in a further track. Younger trees here allow for more open views as the track carries on along the level. The peaks of Meall an t'Seallaidh are up to your right.

At the intersection of tracks almost 3.5km from the start (523 237) a path leaves the track signed to Glen Drochaid. Take this little path up and out of the woods by way of a stile. Continue quite steeply, zigzagging in places, on the increasingly faint path, to come up towards the pass by an enormous boulder, known as 'Rob Roy's Putting Stone' (516 242).

From the 'putting stone' leave the path to head right and northeast across rough ground, traversing up to gain the broad shoulder between the **unnamed peak** (789m) and **Meall an Fhiodhain**. Sections of deer and sheep path make the going easier.

The shoulder is broad and hard to navigate in cloud, with lots of peat bogs to steer round. A line of old fence posts aids navigation, taking you to the top of Meall an Fhiodhain (817m). The peaks of Cam Chreag and Meall an t'Seallaidh lie ahead, with good views over to Ben Vorlich and Stuc a'Chroin.

Carry on along the shoulder, still following fence posts, to a small **lochan** just before Cam Chreag (737 242). Here you can either choose to climb the steep slope, still by the fence posts, to the top of **Cam Chreag** (812m), or skirt around it to its right. Either way, continue south from Cam Chreag up the grassy ridge to gain the summit of **Meall an t'Seallaidh** (852m) (542 234, 8.5km, 3hr).

From the summit retrace your steps to the lochan by Cam Chreag.

Head northeast from this point, down steep grassy slopes and then across rough heather, to reach the track visible below though not marked on the map (542 247). This track runs through the bealach between Meall an t'Seallaidh and **Creag Mac Ranaich**.

Follow the track right into **Glen Kendrum**. It fords the **Kendrum Burn**, then keeps to its left-hand side all the way down the glen. Pass through a gate to carry on along the top of the woods. When the track divides, follow it down to the right to join a **dismantled railway**. Go right along the railway, passing underneath an old railway

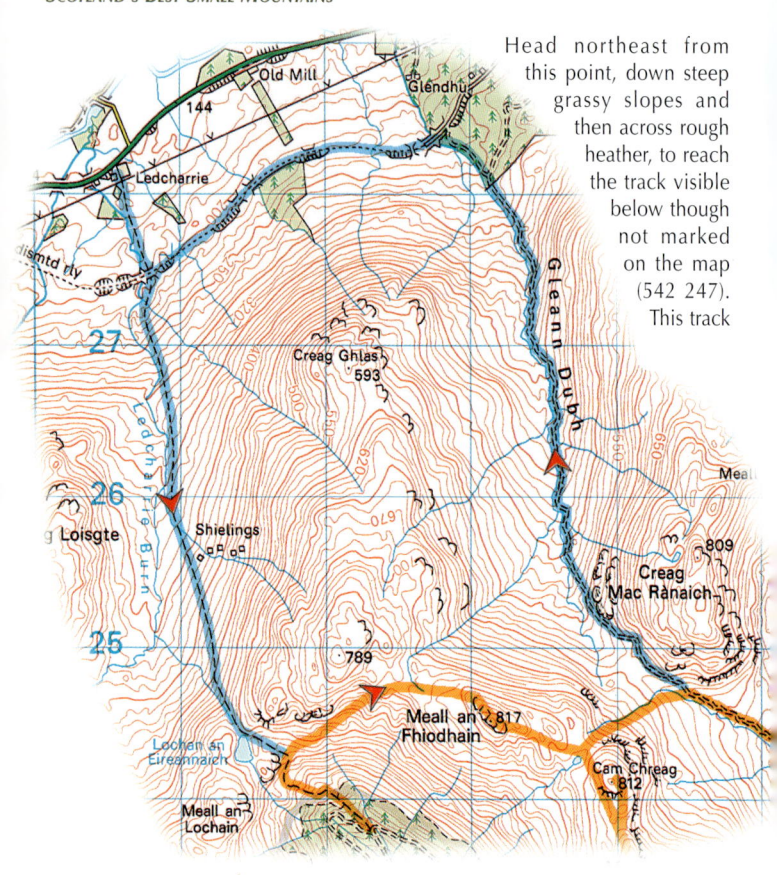

Map continued from page 180

30 Meall an t'Seallaidh

footbridge to walk along the level track through lovely mature mixed woodland.

The railway merges with a **cycle way** (National Cycle Route 7). Go right along it until it meets the road to Balquhidder. From here you just follow the single-track road to the right to return to the start (20km, 6hr).

Alternatives
There-and-back or Back-to-front
Either Kirkton Glen or Glen Kendrum could be used as a there-and-back route, or the circuit could be reversed.

Ascent from Ledcharrie
An alternative circuit of Meall an t'Seallaidh can be made from Ledcharrie to the north. Walk up the path by the Ledcharrie Burn to pass the Lochan an Eireannaich and reach Rob Roy's Putting Stone. From here follow the main route described above until you reach the track in the bealach between Creag Mac Ranaich and Meall an t'Seallaidh. Follow this track left down Gleann Dubh, making use of another section of the dismantled railway to head left back to the outward path (17km, 980m, shown in blue).

Rob Roy's Putting Stone

31 BEN LEDI (879M)

from either beinn an leothaid, 'mountain of the gentle slope', or beinn le dia 'mountain of God' (more likely)

Distance	9km
Time	4hr
Ascent	760m
Difficulty	Ben Ledi presents no real technical difficulties, and having broad shoulders, there is little exposure. The descent to Stank Glen can be hard to navigate in cloud, making it easy to miss the path, and care should be taken.
Maps	OS Landranger 57, OS Explorer 365
Access	The Forestry Commission owns much of the land on and around Ben Ledi and occasionally footpaths, particularly in Stank Glen, are closed for forestry work. It is worth checking with the Forestry Commission (01877 382383) or the National Park office in Callander (01389 722126).
Getting there	There is no public transport direct to Ben Ledi, but it is possible to cycle or walk to it along a cycle path from Callander. Parking is 5km north of Callander (586 092), reached by taking a turning to the left signposted to Strathyre Forest Holidays.
Something else	Take a look at the beautiful Falls of Leny before heading into Callander for some well deserved fish and chips at the Mhor Fish Shop (01877 330213, http://mhor.net).

A great circular route on 'the mountain of life and death'. Marking the start of the Southern Highlands, Ben Ledi offers wooded slopes and a rugged, barren top, all within a stone's throw of Scotland's central belt.

Ben Ledi stands prominently at the gateway to the Southern Highlands. Approaching from the south, it is a distinctive part of the skyline long before you near it, and gives stunning views over the surrounding countryside.

31 Ben Ledi

Ben Ledi

Perhaps it is this prominent position that was a factor in it becoming an important spiritual location.

Ben Ledi was the site of celebrations for the Celtic festival of Beltane. Beltane, which takes place on the eve of 1 May, is one of the quarter-days in the Celtic calendar and marks the start of summer, an event which was celebrated from as early at the 10th century until as late as the 1900s. Fires were lit on the hillside by people from the surrounding villages, including Callander and Balquhidder, to mark this passage into summer and to promote fertility.

If Ben Ledi was known for promoting fertility and life, it has also become associated with death. Lochan nan Corp, which means 'small loch of the dead', lies to the north of the summit towards Benvane. It was so named in the 19th century, after a funeral party travelling to a burial ground on the shores of Loch Lubnaig was drowned after falling through the ice covering the loch.

Scotland's Best Small Mountains

Route

The well-made path (with blue markers) leaves the **car park** and heads uphill into spruce trees. After 600m going quite steeply uphill, it crosses a forestry track to come out of the trees in an area that has been clear felled.

A further 800m on and you come to a stile just after crossing a small **burn** (which should present no difficulties even in winter). From here you get views down over Loch Lubnaig and to the hills to the north.

Cross the stile to continue up, heading southwest now on a rougher path. This brings you up and round on to the shoulder of Ben Ledi (571 087), described by Walter Scott in his poem 'The Lady of the Lake'. Follow the shoulder up northwest, with views now to Loch Venacher to the south and over Callander to the east. The path takes you over two smaller tops, the second with a cross, before gaining the

Map continued on page 188

main summit of **Ben Ledi** (879m) (562 097, 4km, 2hr20). ▸

To descend, follow the line of old fence posts north-west, looking over to nearest neighbour Benvane, then north on a less distinct path to come down to a col with a small cairn (558 110) (**Lochan nan Corp** is just beyond, to the north). Here a steep, and potentially muddy, path takes you down east into **Stank Glen** and to a fence. Cross the fence by a stile to regain a good path and continue downhill.

When this path divides shortly afterwards, go right to stay on the left side of the **burn**, both here and at a second divide. This takes you onto an older section of path and down into the trees. The path crosses and skirts a forestry track a few times, passing a beautiful waterfall to arrive at a minor road 1km north of the car park. Go onto the road and follow it back to the start (4hr, 9km).

Alternatives
The route could easily be reversed, or the same way followed for both ascent and descent.

From Bochastle Forestry Car Park
Bochastle Forestry car park is on the A821 (607 081), and is useful if the main car park is full. Take the small path from the car park to join a forestry track. Turn right along it, to walk through the planted slopes of

> The cross is in memory of a member of the mountain rescue team who died in a helicopter crash on Ben More.

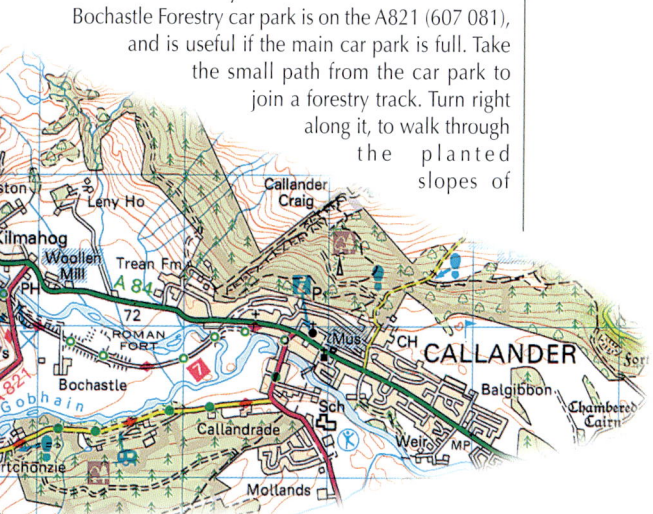

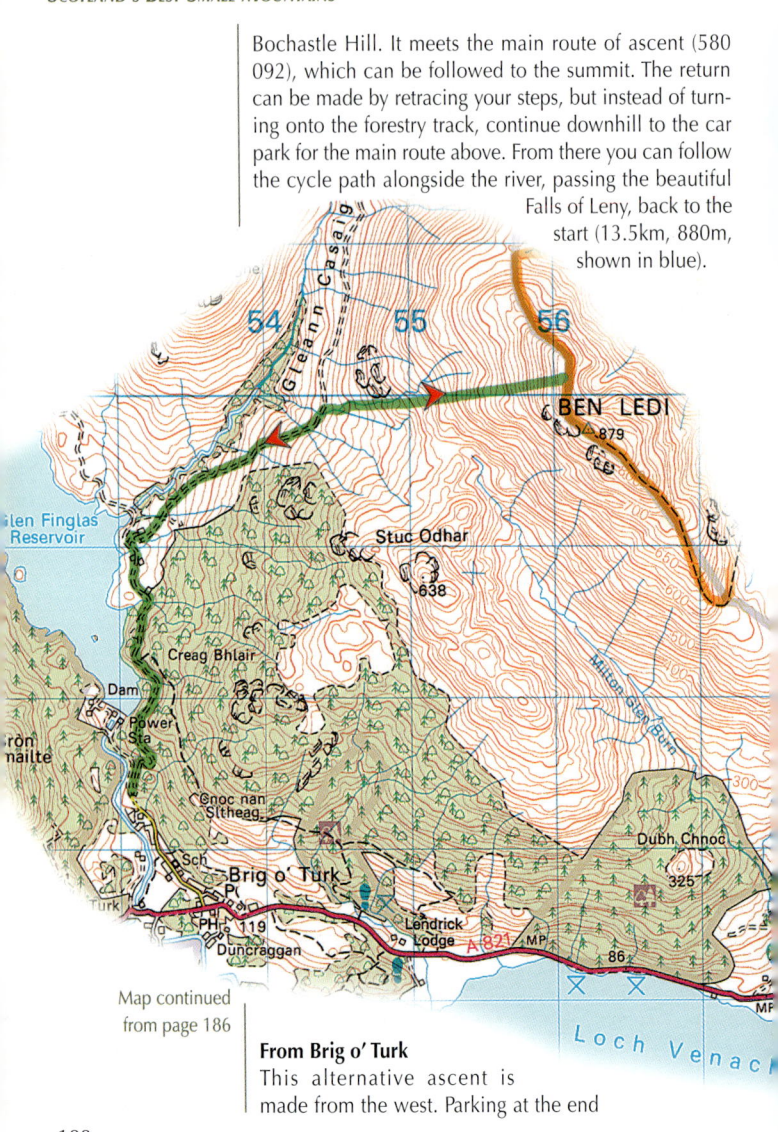

Bochastle Hill. It meets the main route of ascent (580 092), which can be followed to the summit. The return can be made by retracing your steps, but instead of turning onto the forestry track, continue downhill to the car park for the main route above. From there you can follow the cycle path alongside the river, passing the beautiful Falls of Leny, back to the start (13.5km, 880m, shown in blue).

From Brig o' Turk

This alternative ascent is made from the west. Parking at the end

31 Ben Ledi

Perfect place for a rest – waterfall in Stank Glen

of the public road to Glen Finglas Reservoir, follow the private road up to and alongside the east of the reservoir. When it divides, follow the track to the right into Gleann Casaig. Once past the forestry plantation, leave the track to climb east across heather slopes to gain the shoulder of Ben Ledi, just north of the summit. Return by the same route (12km, 880m, shown in green).

32 BEN A'AN (461m)

from either am binnean, meaning 'small pointed peak', or beannan, 'little mountain'

Distance	3.5km
Time	1hr30–2hr
Ascent	300m
Difficulty	A very short outing with good paths most of the way; the last section is steep and stepped in places.
Maps	OS Landranger 57, OS Explorer 365
Access	It is unlikely that there will be access issues (Forestry Commission office in Aberfoyle, 01877 382383).
Getting there	Start at the Ben A'an car park (509 070) on the A821. A post bus runs throughout the year from Callander and during the summer months the Trossachs Trundler runs buses from Stirling. (National Park website www.lochlomond-trossachs.org or Traveline Scotland 0871 200 22 33, www.travelinescotland.com).
Something else	Cruise down Loch Katrine on the steamship *Sir Walter Scott* (01877 332000, www.lochkatrine.com).

A short but prominent peak straight out of a romantic saga, it is with good reason that for centuries people have flocked to the beautiful countryside of the Trossachs, with Ben A'an at their heart.

Sir Walter Scott wrote 'While on the north, through middle air, Ben-an heaved high his forehead bare', and in doing so made the little peak of Ben A'an famous.

Sitting right at the centre of the Trossachs, Ben A'an is very much loved and walked in its own right, even though it is actually a lower top of lesser-known Meall Gainmheich (564m). Its beautiful oak- and birch-forested slopes give way to a prominent rocky peak with great views of the surrounding countryside.

32 Ben A'an

Crossing the burn on the way up

'The Trossachs' translates from the Gaelic *na troise-achan*, meaning 'crossing place', and once referred to the short stretch of land at the foot of Ben A'an where boats were dragged between Loch Achray and Loch Katrine. The Trossachs now refers to a larger area of forests, lochs and peaks – an area that inspired Sir Walter Scott's poem, 'The Lady of the Lake', from which the above quotation is taken.

Written in 1810, the poem is a romantic epic telling the tale of a feud between King James V and the Douglas clan, and of the love between Douglas's daughter Ellen and a young knight loyal to the king. For much of the tale, the protagonists take refuge on a small island on Loch Katrine. To this day there is an island on Loch Katrine called Ellen's Isle.

In writing the poem, Scott made the area hugely popular with tourists, including Queen Victoria, who made several visits. Today you can take a trip down Loch Katrine on the steamship *Sir Walter Scott*, which has been travelling the length of the loch telling the tale of ,the lady of the lake' for over a century.

Route

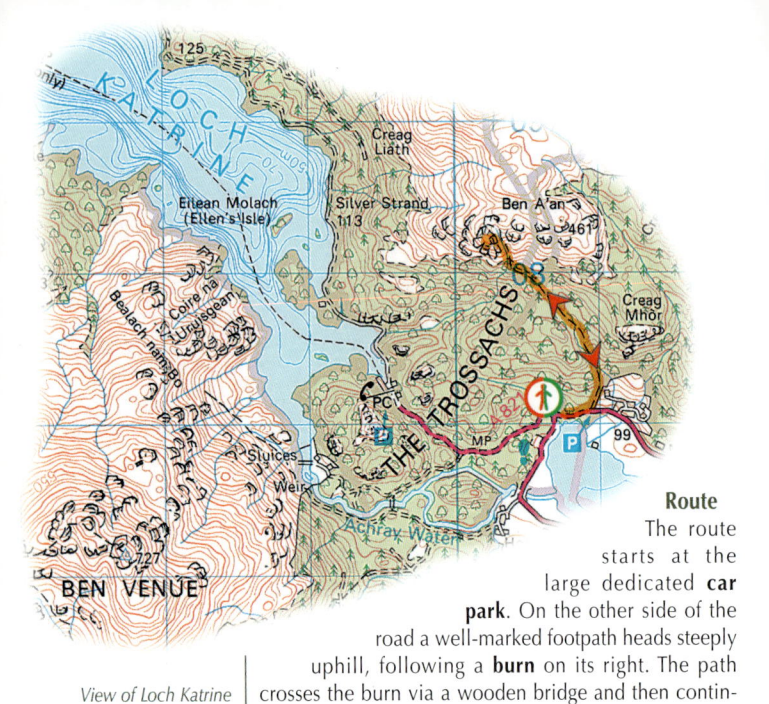

The route starts at the large dedicated **car park**. On the other side of the road a well-marked footpath heads steeply uphill, following a **burn** on its right. The path crosses the burn via a wooden bridge and then continues steeply for a short distance before levelling out. This

View of Loch Katrine from the summit

is a nice gentle section as you wind your way through conifers, crossing the burn again (this time via stepping-stones). When the path leaves the trees, the small but prominent peak of Ben A'an lies straight ahead. There are good views of Ben Venue to the left and of Loch Katrine down below.

The route takes you steeply up from here via a well-made path, with many steps, in the east gully. It climbs to just below the summit before becoming more gradual and bending round to reach the summit of **Ben A'an** from the rear (461m) (502 081,1.7km, 1hr). From the vantage point at the top you have a great view over the whole of the Trossachs, with Arrochar's Cobbler in the distance.

Return via the same route (3.5km, 1hr30–2hr).

33 BEN VENUE (727M)

'small mountain', from Gaelic beinn mheanbh

Distance	14km
Time	4hr30
Ascent	740m
Difficulty	Straightforward route following well-signed paths all the way to the summit. Top section muddy in places with a rocky summit.
Maps	OS Landranger 57, OS Explorer 365
Access	Forestry Commission office in Aberfoyle (01877 382383)
Getting there	Start at the Ben Venue car park (505 068) on the A821. A post bus runs throughout the year from Callander, and during the summer months the Trossachs Trundler runs buses from Stirling. (National Park website www.lochlomond-trossachs.org or Traveline Scotland 0871 200 22 33, www.travelinescotland.com).
Something else	Explore the rest of the Queen Elizabeth Forest Park from the David Marshall Lodge visitor centre, home to an osprey-viewing area, café and Go Ape adventure course (01877 382383, www.forestry.gov.uk).

> Ben Venue is the epitome of a small mountain. With forested slopes and a rocky peak, it sits in majestic countryside with some royal connections.

Standing proud at the heart of the Trossachs, queens, dukes and outlaws have all paid homage to the small but impressive peak of Ben Venue. Surrounded by Loch Katrine, Loch Achray and Loch Ard, its prominent position belies its 727m in height.

Ben Venue is part of the Queen Elizabeth Forest Park. The park, whose 41,500 acres stretch from Loch Lomond to Strathyre, was purchased by the state in 1928. In 1953 it was designated a National Forest Park to commemorate Queen Elizabeth II's coronation. In 2002 it became part of the Loch Lomond and Trossachs National Park, Scotland's first national park. But its royal connections do not end there.

Queen Victoria, possibly inspired by Sir Walter Scott's poem 'The Lady of the Lake', which is set in the

Ben Venue and Loch Katrine from Ben A'an

33 Ben Venue

Achray Water

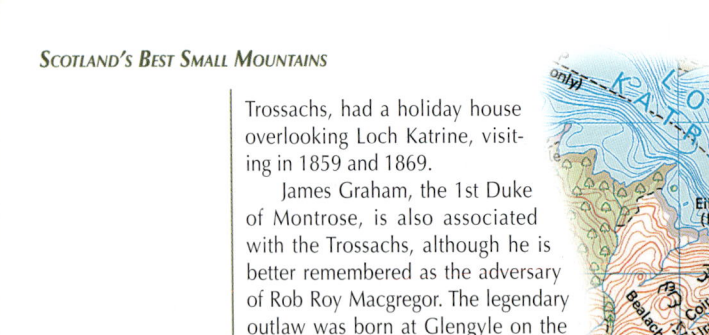

Scotland's Best Small Mountains

Trossachs, had a holiday house overlooking Loch Katrine, visiting in 1859 and 1869.

James Graham, the 1st Duke of Montrose, is also associated with the Trossachs, although he is better remembered as the adversary of Rob Roy Macgregor. The legendary outlaw was born at Glengyle on the banks of Loch Katrine in 1761. He and the Duke of Montrose had a near 30 year feud following a loan made by the duke to Rob Roy. The money was allegedly stolen, preventing Macgregor paying it back. The duke outlawed Macgregor and took his land, and Macgregor retaliated by

33 Ben Venue

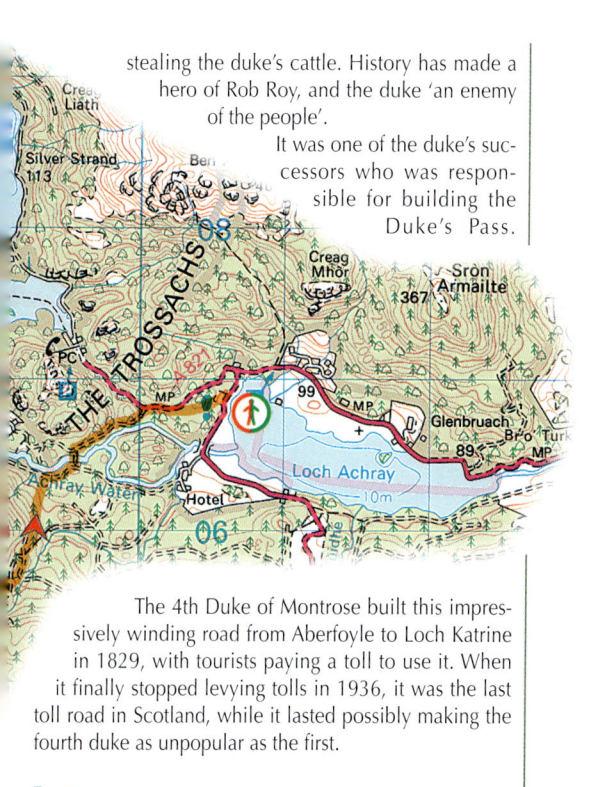

stealing the duke's cattle. History has made a hero of Rob Roy, and the duke 'an enemy of the people'.

It was one of the duke's successors who was responsible for building the Duke's Pass.

The 4th Duke of Montrose built this impressively winding road from Aberfoyle to Loch Katrine in 1829, with tourists paying a toll to use it. When it finally stopped levying tolls in 1936, it was the last toll road in Scotland, while it lasted possibly making the fourth duke as unpopular as the first.

Route

Leave the **car park** via a path to its rear, following blue waymarks. The path divides after going over a small lump – go left, crossing a boardwalk to reach the private road to Loch Katrine dam. Go left along the road, taking a small path off to the left at another blue waymark (495 065). This goes down to and across **Achray Water** by way of a new wooden bridge. This takes you to on to a series of paths that will lead you through **Gleann Riabhach**.

When you come to a signpost, go right on the wide track signed to Ben Venue, then left again onto a smaller path up through the trees. When this meets a track, continue right to reach another, more level track. Go left along this briefly before taking another small path off to the right (again signed). This path heads up through a fire break in denser plantation, crossing one final forestry track.

The path contours through the plantation, eventually leaving the trees behind to emerge onto open hillside (474 051). From here the path is more like a typical Scottish hill path, with boggy, rough sections. It climbs north-northwest into the corrie with a burn to the left. You gain the broad shelf of the corrie before a final, steeper climb to the col between **Creag a'Bhealaich** and **Ben Venue** at 580m.

Leaving the large cairn at the col, head right – northeast – up a steeper, rockier path, following the ridge line. This divides halfway up, the left fork heading first to the smaller of the two tops, the right fork directly to the highest. Either way can be taken to arrive at the summit (727m) (474063, 7km, 2hr30). From here there are great views down to Loch Katrine, over the other Trossach hills and across to the Arrochar Alps.

Return via the same route (14km, 4hr30).

Alternatives
From Loch Ard
This route from Loch Ard starts at the entrance to Ledard Farm on the B829. There is some parking on the opposite side of the road (459 022). Walk up the private road towards Ledard Farm. After 250m follow a sign to 'hill access', which takes you onto a small path and across a footbridge over the Ledard Burn. This path continues to follow the burn to pass between the peaks of Beinn Bhreac and Creag a'Bhealaich, joining with the above route at the col (469 060) (12km, 720m, shown in blue).

Traverse from Loch Ard to Loch Achray
If transport is available, complete a traverse of Ben Venue from Loch Ard to Loch Achray (13km, 760m).

34 THE COBBLER (BEN ARTHUR) (884M)

Probably originally named after the legendary King Arthur, the highest peak was named The Cobbler because it looked like a cobbler bent over his work. Today the whole hill is commonly known as The Cobbler.

Distance	12.5km
Time	4hr30
Ascent	1000m
Difficulty	A clear route on mainly good paths, with a steep rocky section involving some easy scrambling. The true summit is a rocky outcrop perched on the top and reached only by an airy scramble, but this can be omitted.
Maps	OS Landranger 56, OS Explorer 364
Access	The Cobbler is in the Loch Lomond and Trossachs National Park, contact the park visitor centre at Ardgarten for more information (08707 200 606, Easter to October) or the National Park Centre in Luss (01389 722120). It is also in the Forestry Commission's Ardgartan Forest (01877 382383).
Getting there	Start at the Succoth car park on the A83 just beyond Arrochar (295 048). It is possible to travel by train to Tarbet station and walk for 3km to the start. Alternatively there are buses that stop at the car park (Traveline Scotland 0871 200 22 33, www.travelinescotland.com).
Something else	Explore more of the Argyll Forest Park from the Ardgarten visitor centre (01877 382383, www.forestry.gov.uk) or head over for a picnic on the bonny, bonny banks of Loch Lomond.

Possibly the most famous of Scotland's small mountains, the distinctive jagged peaks of The Cobbler have been a popular destination for walkers and climbers for over a century.

Scotland's Best Small Mountains

The rocky pinnacle that crowns the summit

The Cobbler, while far from being the tallest of the Arrochar Alps, is easily the most famous. In fact you could go so far as to say that it's one of the most important and famous hills in Scotland, as it was the starting place for so many walkers and climbers.

Scotland's first ever climbing club, The Cobbler Club, was founded there in 1866, albeit with only three members. By the 1890s pioneers of the soon to be much larger Scottish Mountaineering Club made good use of The Cobbler's gullies and rock faces. But it was in the 1930s that The Cobbler really came into its own.

Faced with industrial depression and unemployment, shipyard and factory workers from Glasgow started to venture out into the hills, beginning the movement away from climbing being a pastime purely for the rich. Travelling by the recently opened railway, or by bus, bike and even on foot, many unemployed workers found their way to the rocky peaks of The Cobbler. With no money for accommodation, they often spent several days out on the hill, taking advantage of the shelter afforded by the Narnain Boulders. As the 1940s and 50s progressed, and more rock climbing routes were forged, The Cobbler became a training ground for many of Scotland's leading climbers.

Located in the Argyll Forest Park, now part of the Loch Lomond and Trossachs National Park, it remains one of the most popular hills for walkers.

Route

The path starts across the road from the **car park**, then zigzags up quite steeply to come to a track. You turn left along the track briefly, then right, back onto a path, to continue zigzagging uphill.

This brings you to the **Allt a'Bhalachain** by a small weir, and as you climb up the right-hand side of the burn, The Cobbler comes into view dramatically ahead.

The terrain levels as the good path heads towards and past the **Narnain Boulders**. The path divides 300m on (268 058). Take the left fork to cross the burn and start a steep ascent up the front of The

Cobbler. The path deteriorates here, becoming rocky and requiring some easy scrambling in places before it reaches the col between The Cobbler and its northern top.

Head left from the col up a small path to gain the broad summit of **The Cobbler** (884m) (259 058, 5.5km, 2hr30). The true top is the rocky outcrop perched precariously on the edge of the summit. Those with a head for heights and willingness to scramble can crawl through a hole in the rock and edge along an exposed ledge to climb onto its top, but this is definitely optional. The hole in the rock is called 'Argyll's eyeglass' after the Duke of Argyll, who apparently regularly climbed to this lofty viewpoint.

From the summit it is well worth returning to the col then climbing briefly again to gain the northern top. A path heads northeast from the col, circling round to the left to reach the top.

To return, retrace your steps to the col, then follow a clear path north to skirt round the northern top and come down to the path from Beinn Ime by the Allt

Rainbow and Beinn Ime from north top

a'Bhalachain. This good path descends by way of stone steps in places, and was built as a new, easier route to the summit. It is definitely easier on the knees going down than the route of ascent.

Once back alongside the burn, follow it back to where the path divides and retrace your outward route back to the start (12.5km, 4hr30).

Alternatives
There-and-back via the Narnain Boulders
For those who wish to avoid any scrambling, the return route from the summit can also be used as the ascent route by taking the right fork when the path divides after the Narnain Boulders.

From Glen Croe
To ascend from Glen Croe, follow the right-hand side of the burn from the A83 (243 060) up to the Bealach a'Mhaim. From the bealach follow the main path right to join the route of descent described above, or cut off southeast sooner to make a steep ascent straight to the col. While shorter, this route is steep and lacks the classic views of The Cobbler's peaks (7km, 740m, shown in blue).

The Cobbler's Southeastern Ridge
It should also be possible to make an ascent or descent of The Cobbler by way of its long southeastern ridge, so long as you avoid the south top itself, which is only for experienced rock climbers. A good circuit could be made by following the main route up as described above, then retracing your steps down into the corrie on the front of The Cobbler and round to the foot of the south top. From there a path leads you down the ridge. When it meets the forestry track, follow this left to rejoin your original route near the start (12km, 1050m, shown in green).

35 BEINN AN LOCHAIN (901m)

'hill of the little loch'

Distance	6km
Time	3hr
Ascent	680m
Difficulty	A very short route but not without its challenges. The lower ridge is rocky, with some easy scrambling to negotiate, the higher section is very steep with some exposure.
Maps	OS Landranger 56, OS Explorer 364
Access	Beinn an Lochain is in the Loch Lomond and Trossachs National Park (park visitor centre at Ardgarten 08707 200 606, Easter to October, or the National Park Centre in Luss 01389 722120).
Getting there	Start at the lay-by on the A83 just to the north of Loch Restil (234 088). There are buses from Arrochar and Tarbet station to Rest and be Thankful (Traveline Scotland 0871 200 22 33, www.travelinescotland.com).
Something else	Visit the Ardkinglas Estate, home to beautiful woodland gardens, a tree shop, café, and the famous Loch Fyne Oyster Restaurant (01499 600261, www.ardkinglas.com).

> A short scramble up a fine rocky ridge brings you to the top of Beinn an Lochain and a great vantage point over the Arrochar Alps and historic Glen Croe.

Beinn an Lochain is most famous for having once been classed as a Munro before later measurements showed that Hugh Munro's original listing was wrong. It should, however, be most famous for a great rocky ridge walk and its position rising above Glen Croe and Rest and be Thankful.

A scramble up Beinn an Lochain's northeast ridge takes you to its fine rocky summit, and views west to Loch

35 Beinn an Lochain

Beinn an Lochain from The Cobbler

Fyne and Argyll and east to the Arrochar Alps, including the distinctive jagged peaks of The Cobbler.

To reach Beinn an Lochain from the south you have to follow the road as it climbs steeply up through Glen Croe from Ardgarten on Loch Long. As you do so, spare a thought for those who had to make the climb before the advent of motorised transport. It is little wonder that the end of the climb was dubbed 'Rest and Be Thankful'.

In fact it was the makers of the original road that gave it this name back in the mid-1700s. They were government soldiers under the command of William Caulfield, one of General Wade's road engineers, building a military road from Dumbarton to Inveraray. On reaching the top they placed a stone there inscribed with the words 'Rest-and-be-Thankful' and the name stuck.

The original road, since replaced by what is now the A83, went on to be used for a variety of purposes. Throughout the 1950s and 60s the Royal Scottish

Scotland's Best Small Mountains

Automobile Club organised the Rest and be Thankful Hill Climb, with drivers being timed to see how quickly they could make an ascent of the old road. More recently it was used in the filming of *Restless Natives*.

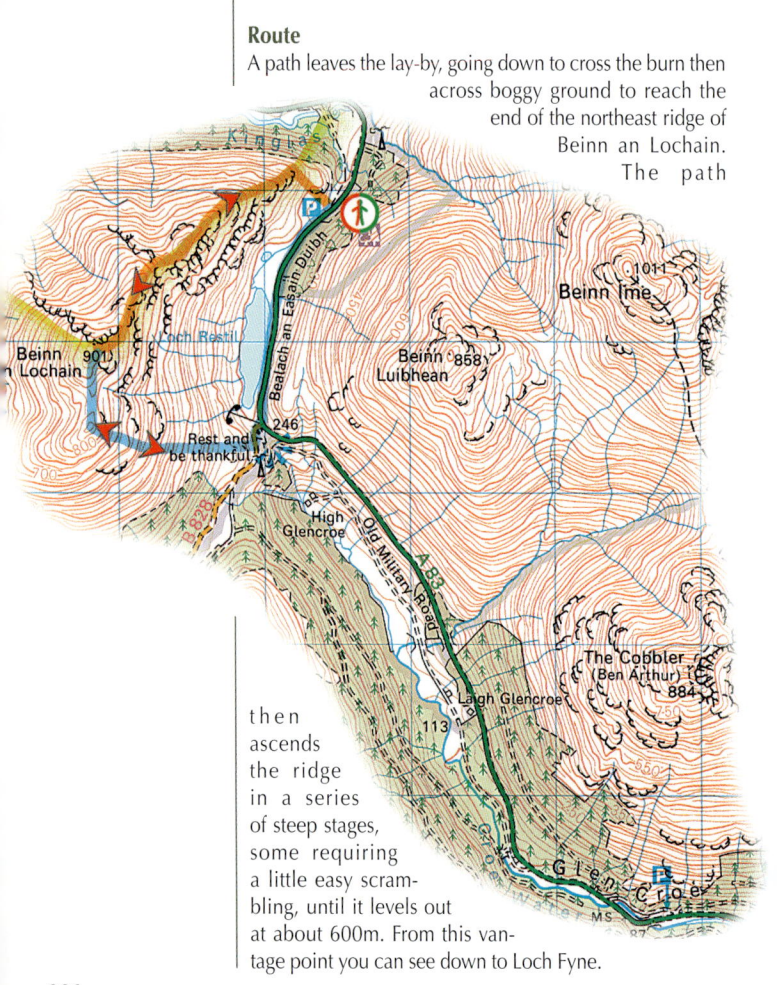

Route

A path leaves the lay-by, going down to cross the burn then across boggy ground to reach the end of the northeast ridge of Beinn an Lochain. The path then ascends the ridge in a series of steep stages, some requiring a little easy scrambling, until it levels out at about 600m. From this vantage point you can see down to Loch Fyne.

35 Beinn an Lochain

From here you drop slightly to an airy col before a longer, much steeper climb up, traversing to the right of rocky outcrops to gain more level, grassy terrain. The real top is now in view ahead, and is reached by way of a final steep climb. Keep to the left of the crags on the crest of the ridge to arrive at the large cairn that marks the summit of **Beinn an Lochain** (901m) (218 079, 3km, 1hr45). From here are great views east to Beinn Ime, The Cobbler and the other Arrochar peaks, and of the steep road up Glen Croe to Rest and be Thankful.

Return by the same route (6km, 3hr).

Dramatic cloud on the summit

Alternatives
Circuit via Rest and Be Thankful

From the summit a small path leads south past some small lochans, for which the hill is named, to Beinn an Lochain's lower second top. It is worth visiting this top its own right, but it is also possible to make a descent from here to the Rest and Be Thankful car park. However this is extremely steep, down rough slopes, and as such is much less appealing than the route described above. It is probably not advisable unless you are very keen to make a circular route (7km, 720m for circular route including road walk, shown in blue).

207

Scotland's Best Small Mountains

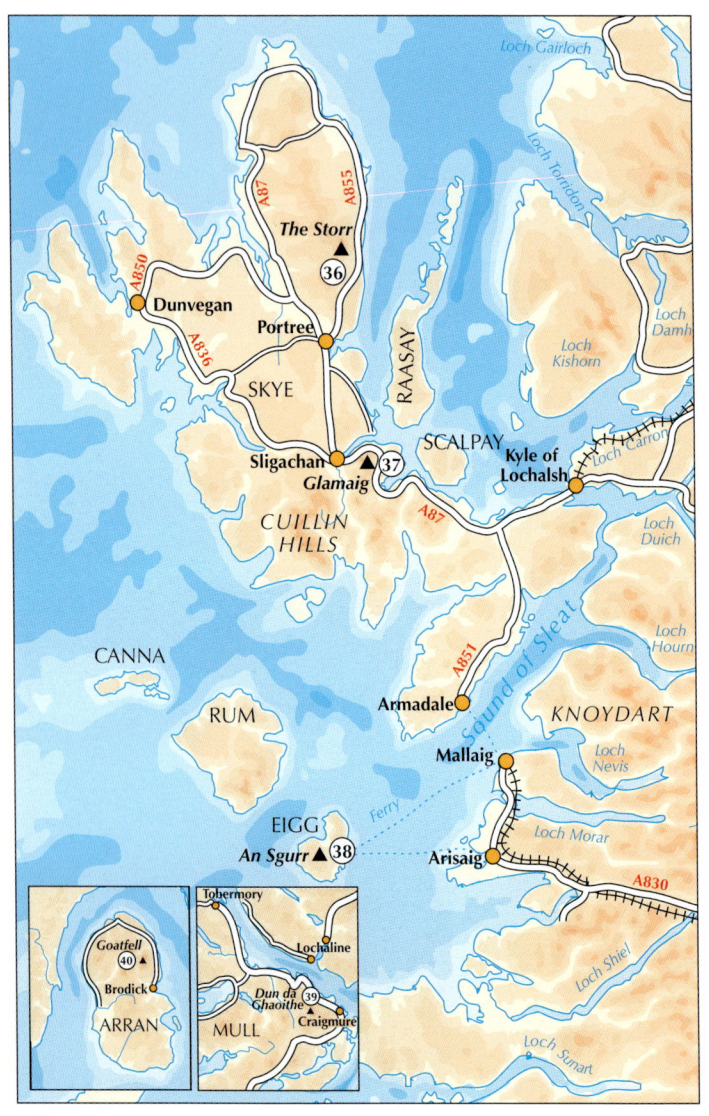

Duart Castle and the Sound of Mull

THE ISLANDS

36 THE STORR (719m)

'big' or 'prominent', from Norse

Distance	8.5km
Time	3hr30
Ascent	700m
Difficulty	The first section of this short route is on good paths. From the shoulder onwards there are no paths, but the walking is easy on short grass. The final section from the bealach is steep and rocky.
Maps	OS Landranger 23, OS Explorer 408
Getting there	Start at the car park at the end of Loch Leathan on the A855 from Portree (509 528). There are several buses a day to and from the car park from Portree (www.rapsons.com for timetables or Traveline Scotland 0871 200 22 33, www.travelinescotland.com).
Something else	Explore more of the amazing Trotternish Ridge with a walk to the Quirang or head into Portree for a cup of tea with a harbour view at Café Arriba (01478 611830, www.cafearriba.co.uk).

Step into a land that time forgot to mingle with giants and volcanoes, not to mention some breathtaking views on this great circuit.

A walk up the Storr is an adventure into the weird and wonderful landscape of Skye's Trotternish ridge. Climbing the Storr, the highest point on the ridge, is like visiting a land that time forgot, one with Jurassic rock formations and tales of giants – so much so that the 1975 film *The Land that Time Forgot* was actually filmed here.

The rock formations are volcanic, formed around 60 million years ago, leaving behind great pinnacles of rock, including the Old Man of Storr itself. Standing at 48m high, it gets its name from a folktale that tells of an

36 THE STORR

The Storr and the Old Man

old man and his wife being turned to stone by giants, ogres or fairies, depending on which version you hear. The Old Man is now in solitude, however, as 'his wife' subsequently fell over.

While you are unlikely to come across any dinosaurs or giants, you will meet with some amazing views. From the summit you can see as far as the Outer Hebrides to the west, the Torridon hills to the east and the mighty Cuillin ridge to the south. To the north you look over the grass and rock of the Trotternish ridge right to the very northern tip of Skye and the sea beyond.

Route

The well-made path leaves the **car park** heading northwest up through the woods to arrive at a fence with the Old Man of Storr straight ahead. Continue up the path from here, now on open hillside, taking the right fork when the path divides. This brings you up into the surreal rocky landscape and to the foot of **the Old Man of Storr**, where the path divides again. Go right, to traverse northeast below crags, heading up and between jutting outcrops of rock. A sign here advises against continuing (presumably because of the danger of rock falls), but the path does continue on to the col.

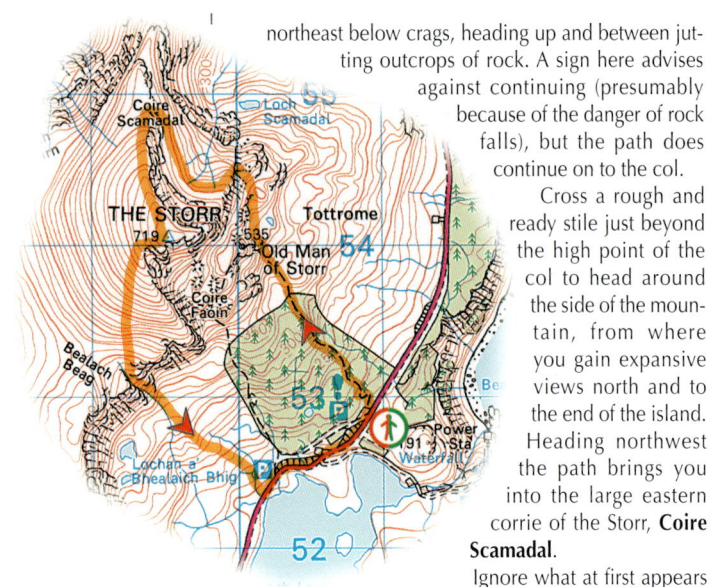

Cross a rough and ready stile just beyond the high point of the col to head around the side of the mountain, from where you gain expansive views north and to the end of the island. Heading northwest the path brings you into the large eastern corrie of the Storr, **Coire Scamadal**.

Ignore what at first appears to be a route steeply left up to the summit, and instead stay on the path as it contours around the bowl of Coire Scamadal beneath the crags. You can then easily gain the north shoulder, doubling-back on yourself to ascend its broad grassy slope to the summit of **the Storr** (719m) (495 540, 5km, 2hr).

At the top

From the top, head west then south down steep grassy slopes to the plateau and the watershed of the burn at **Bealach Beag**. Follow the burn down from the bealach (492 531) on a small rocky and, at first, steep path. Once away from the crags leave the burn and head east over gentle, open hillside to reach the road near the edge of woods. A gate a couple of hundred metres to the right from the edge of the woods gives you access to the road. From there, head left along the road to return to the car park (8.5km, 3hr30).

37 GLAMAIG (775M)

'greedy woman', from Gaelic glamag

Distance	13km
Time	5hr30
Ascent	1300m
Difficulty	The path is boggy in places, but easy enough up the shoulder to Beinn Dearg Mheadhonach, but from there onwards this route is characterised by very steep scree slopes.
Maps	OS Landranger 32, OS Explorer 411
Getting there	Start at the Sligachan Hotel by the old bridge (487 298). Buses run to Sligachan from Armadale, Portree and the Skye Bridge (www.rapsons.com for timetables or Traveline Scotland 0871 200 22 33, www.travelinescotland.com).
Something else	Camp at the foot of Glamaig and escape the midges to sample some of the 200 whiskies on offer at the Sligachan Hotel (01478 650204, www.sligachan.co.uk for campsite and hotel).

Scree-hopping on the Red Hills of Skye, Glamaig offers rocky ridges and the best Cuillin viewpoint, with just a bit of adrenalin mixed in, and that's without taking part in the famous hill race.

The classic view of Glamaig's Sgurr Mhairi

Glamaig and its neighbours form the Red Hills, or Red Cuillin, of Skye. Beinn Dearg Mhor and Beinn Dearg Mheadonach literally meaning 'big red hill' and 'middle red hill'. They are so named because the granite they are composed of can look red in certain lights. They are smaller and more rounded than their darker Cuillin neighbours, but that is not to say they are not challenging. Composed almost entirely of scree, and with some fine ridges of their own, they definitely offer an exhilarating day out.

Located right across Glen Sligachan from the Cuillin ridge, Glamaig is possibly the best viewpoint on Skye, and not only that – it's also Skye's most distinctive peak. Even when looking from the mainland, it's easy to spot its conical shape. But that is not the only reason it is famous.

In 1899, when a Gurka visiting Skye with a climbing party decided to run up and down Glamaig, little could he have imagined that he would have inspired a hill race almost a century later. Starting at the Sligachan Hotel,

Harkabir Thapa ran to the top of Sgurr Mhairi, Glamaig's highest peak, and back, in 75 minutes. The local landowner at the time, McLeod of McLeod, couldn't believe it, so Thapa did it again, this time apparently in 55 minutes, with some reports claiming he did it with bare feet!

In 1987, his run inspired the start of what is now an annual hill race up Glamaig. Hill runners from all over gather in July to race up and down the death-defying scree slopes. The record at the time of writing stands at 44 minutes and 41 seconds, set by Mark Rigby in 1997. He definitely wore shoes. The fastest descent from the top to the hotel stands at 13 minutes.

The hotel at which the runners assemble is a bit of an institution in its own right. The Sligachan Hotel has been standing in its present location since 1830, and has long been a favourite with walkers and climbers, not least because it has its own microbrewery.

Route

From the old bridge, take the path on the left bank of the **River Sligachan**, signed to Loch Coruisk and Glenbrittle. This soon divides and you take the left fork to walk up the right bank of the **Allt Daraich**. Leave this good path 200m on to pass through a gate, but stay with the Allt Daraich.

A smaller path takes you onto boggier ground and through a further gate, following a line of old fence posts. When the line of these posts bends to follow the river, head east-southeast. A small but very visible path runs from here up the end of the shoulder of **Druim na Ruiage**.

A short but steep climb brings you to the little point at 428m at the northwest end of the shoulder. From here the going is gentler as you ascend the broad grassy shoulder, with the twin peaks of Beinn Dearg Mheadhonach and Beinn Dearg Mhor ahead. The last section of the shoulder up to **Beinn Dearg Mheadhonach** is over steeper scree, but the zigzags of the path make the going easier.

At the summit of Beinn Dearg Mheadhonach (651m) there are fantastic views of Sgurr nan Gillean and Am Basteir at the end of the Cuillin ridge. From the top follow the ridge down to the **Bealach Mosgaraidh** before a longer, steeper ascent to the narrow top of **Beinn Dearg Mhor** (731m). Again, the zigzags of the path on smaller scree make this easier. From this airy position, the hillside drops straight to the sea at Loch Ainort.

The descent from Beinn Dearg Mhor starts gently, heading north. You then turn northwest to drop down to the **Bealach na Sgairde**. This is very steep, across quite large scree, requiring great care to be taken.

From the Bealach na Sgairde (which, appropriately, means 'the scree pass') it is almost 300m of ascent up more scree slopes to reach the summit of **Sgurr Mhairi**, Glamaig's highest peak (513 300, 775m, 4hr).

From the summit, retrace your steps to the Bealach na Sgairde, then down the side of the burn. Contour round the hillside on one of the small deer paths to gain the spur to the left of the burn. This makes for the easiest walking, and you can follow it down until the burn joins the Allt Daraich. At that point cross the Allt Daraich and follow its left bank back to the start, passing some very tempting pools on the way (13km, 5hr30).

37 GLAMAIG

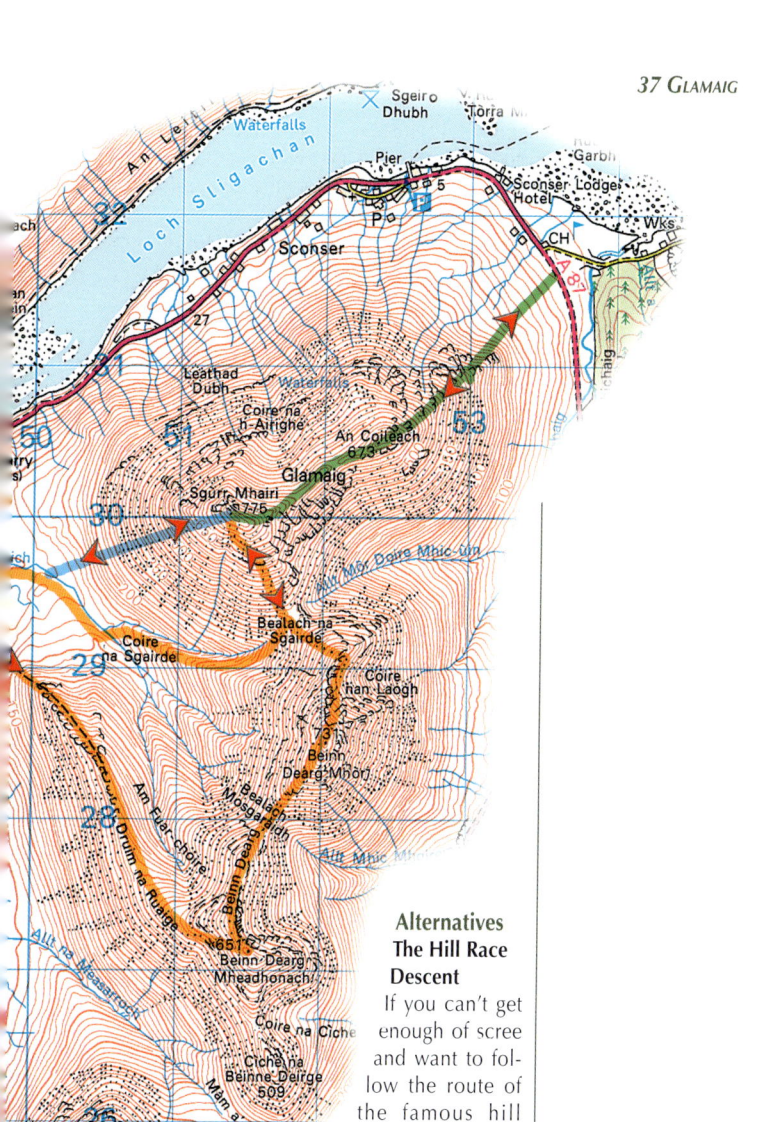

Alternatives
The Hill Race Descent

If you can't get enough of scree and want to follow the route of the famous hill race, then you could descend directly from Sgurr Mhairi, heading

217

Beinn Dearg Mhor and Sgurr Mhairi from Beinn Dearg Mheadhonach

west down the steep scree slopes to meet the river and the outward route below (11km, 1240m). This could also be used as a short, but punishing, ascent and descent of the peak (6km, 760m, shown in blue).

From the Northeast

An ascent of Sgurr Mhairi can also be made from the northeast, taking in the peak of An Coileach (673m) and the fine walk between the two. To do this, leave the A87 just before the junction with the road to Moll, picking your way between crags to climb to the northeast ridge (6km, 780m, shown in green).

38 AN SGURR (393m)

'the rocky peak'

Distance	8km
Time	3hr
Ascent	390m
Difficulty	This is a short route with a path all the way to the summit. It involves some exposure and a little scrambling on the ridge, but nothing too difficult.
Maps	OS Landranger 39, OS Explorer 397
Getting there	Start at the café/shop by the piers (484 838). Eigg is a wonderful destination to reach by public transport, with trains running to where the ferries leave. Caledonian MacBrayne run ferries to Eigg from Mallaig throughout the year (08000 66 5000 or www.calmac.co.uk. During the summer there are also ferries from Arisaig on the small wildlife boat *The Sheerwater* (01687 450224, www.arisaig.co.uk). For train/bus times to the ferries contact Traveline Scotland (0871 200 22 33, www.travelinescotland.com).
Something else	Take a walk to and into Massacre Cave then stock up on cake at the Eigg tearoom before the boat home (www.isleofeigg.net).

The volcanic rocky peak of An Sgurr on Eigg is instantly recognisable and a joy to climb. This is a short route to a lofty fortress, with insights into the island's turbulent past and promising green future.

The striking rocky point of An Sgurr, on Eigg, one of the Small Isles, is amongst the most prominent peaks on the whole west coast of Scotland. Its distinctive form is visible from most of the islands, and from many of the coastal hills on the mainland, making it a tantalising objective.

An Sgurr

Formed almost 60 million years ago by lava from a volcano on what is now the neighbouring island of Rum, An Sgurr is characterised by the dramatic columns of hard rock that give rise to its fortress-like appearance. In fact its summit was used as a fort in the past in times of danger. And a brief look at the history of Eigg suggests that there were plenty of times of danger.

Following Viking raiders and Norse settlers, Eigg was owned by the MacDonald clan, with islanders taking part in many battles and feuds with both the Crown and neighbouring clans. Most notable was the feud with the Macleods, which led to the death of the entire population of Eigg in the 16th century. The islanders hid in a cave on Eigg's shore when they saw a party of Macleods sailing towards the island. All 395 were killed when, on discovering the cave, the Macleods lit a fire at its entrance, suffocating the occupants. The cave, which is at the foot of An Sgurr, is now known as Massacre Cave.

Later, islanders suffered from the failed Jacobite uprisings and then the Clearances. And while the more recent history of Eigg has been less bloody, it has still been turbulent, with a succession of private owners clashing with locals.

This history of conflict ended in 1997 when the islanders managed to buy Eigg. The Eigg Heritage Trust, a partnership between islanders, the Highland Council and the Scottish Wildlife Trust, now owns the island, and today it is at the forefront of pioneering community and environmental work.

Route

From the café/shop take the road straight ahead (not the main road to the right). This soon becomes a track, taking you through the trees to a junction by the village hall. Here you continue straight on, following red waymark. The left fork would take you to Massacre Cave, which is well worth a detour on the return if time allows.

Pass through a gate to leave the trees, An Sgurr now straight ahead. The track takes you up to and past a house, where it goes through a gate to come onto another track. Go left along the track for a short distance to arrive at a cairn (473 840). From here a small but clear path heads off to the right, taking you all the way to the top.

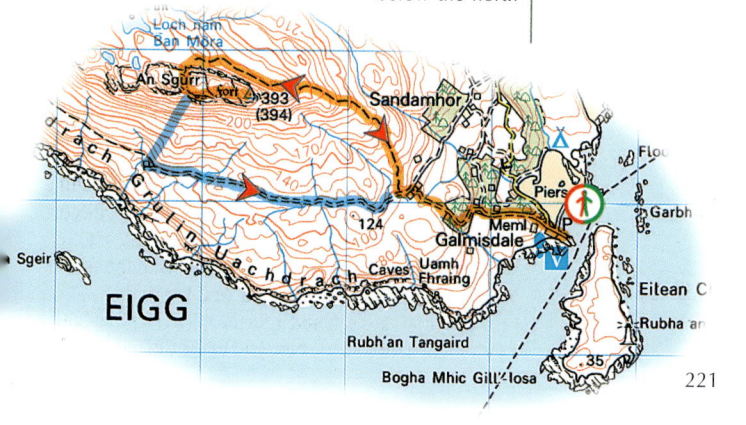

The path climbs steadily across peat and heather, with some boggy sections, towards An Sgurr. It then passes by the impenetrable east rock face to run along below the north side of the peak's ridge. After heading gently west, the path turns south and steepens to gain the ridge by way of a grassy gully.

Once on the ridge the path doubles-back, heading east up and over its rocky outcrops, with some easy scrambling, to gain the summit (393m) (463 847, 4km, 1hr45). With dramatic drops on all sides except the way you came, the airy summit of **An Sgurr** offers impressive views over the whole of Eigg, as well as the neighbouring Small Isles, Skye and the mainland.

Return by the same route (8km, 3hr).

Alternatives
Circular Route via Grulin
It is possible to complete a circular route of An Sgurr by retracing your steps down the ridge then heading north off it. This takes you down steep heather slopes to join the track that runs from the abandoned village of Grulin back to the cairn where you left the track originally. This descent lacks a path, however, and is over rough, steep ground (8.5km, 470m, shown in blue).

Eigg and the Sgurr with Rum behind at sunset

39 DUN DA GHAOITHE (766M)

*'fort of the two winds', dun being
Gaelic for 'fort' or 'castle'*

Distance	18km
Time	5hr30–6hr
Ascent	900m
Difficulty	The ascent up the track is easy though steep in places, then gives way to a pathless but straightforward ridge. The descent is steeper, across very rough ground in places, until the final good track and short road walk.
Maps	OS Landranger 49, OS Explorer 375
Getting there	Start at the tourist information centre in Craignure (717 371). Ferries run to Craignure from Oban (CalMac 08000 66 5000, www.calmac.co.uk). For train/bus times to Oban, Traveline Scotland 0871 200 22 33, www.travelinescotland.com.
Something else	Take the Mull Railway to Torosay Castle and gardens (01680 812421, www.torosay.com) or visit the impressive fortress of Duart Castle (01680 812309, www.duartcastle.com).

Spectacular sea views on a fine long ridge make this circular route on Mull's second highest peak well worthy of a day trip.

Known in Gaelic as Muile nam Mor-bheann, Mull, Scotland's fourth largest island, definitely lives up to this name, which translates to mean 'Mull of the big mountains'. Dun da Ghaoithe is Mull's second highest peak after Ben More. Rising up from Craignure Bay, its long ridge and deep corries make it seem far higher than its 766m.

Located on the southeast of Mull, a walk along the ridge of Dun da Ghaoithe offers a view out to sea in

Scotland's Best Small Mountains

The view west from the summit

almost every direction. The Sound of Mull passes by its foot, with a view northeast right up Loch Linnhe. The Firth of Lorne is to its south, and Loch Scridain gives way to the Atlantic to the west.

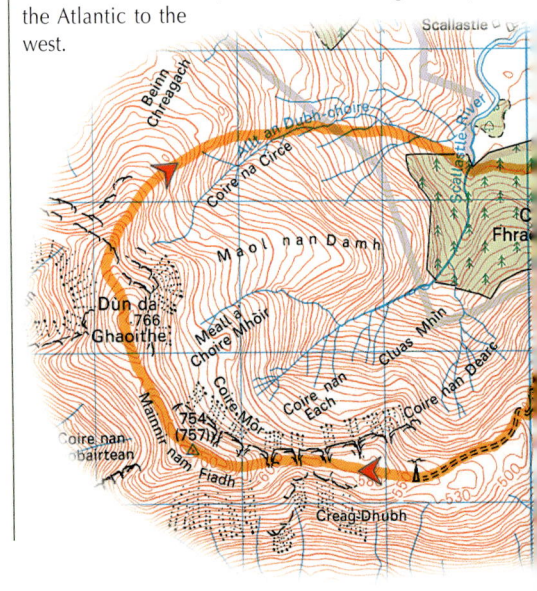

39 Dun da Ghaoithe

Starting at Craignure, the route up Dun da Ghaoithe passes by picturesque Torosay Castle, which you could actually travel to by way of the Mull railway. At only 2km in length and with scaled-down trains, it is Scotland's only island passenger railway. Torosay Castle is in fact a Victorian country home set in 12 acres of garden, both of which you can visit. Neighbouring Duart Castle is more of the real deal.

Owned by the Clan Maclean, Duart Castle is a 13th-century fortress. Located on Duart Point, it occupies a strategic position at the intersection of Loch Linnhe, the Sound of Mull and the Firth of Lorne, and has an enormous 30ft tall and 10ft thick wall. The Macleans had owned the castle, and much of Mull as well, for 300 years until 1691, when they surrendered it to the Duke of Argyll following the failed Jacobite uprising. The castle was then used as a garrison for government troops until 1751, before being abandoned.

The ruins of the castle were bought back and restored by Sir Fitzroy Maclean, the 26th chief of the Clan Maclean in 1910. It is now a visitor attraction and home to the clan chief once again.

Route

From the **tourist information centre** in Craignure, walk right along the road (the **A849**) on the pavement on the left-hand side. Once the pavement runs out, a small path goes off to the left through the Hedgehog Wood to **Torosay Castle**.

This signed path keeps you off the road and passes through lovely mixed woodland. It brings you out onto the main drive to the castle. Go right up the drive to rejoin the A849. Head left along it briefly, taking the first turning to the right to climb to **Upper Achnacroish**. Here the road ends and a track begins.

Follow the track as it climbs steeply in places up past the mast on **Maol nan Uan**, with great views back to the Sound of Mull and Duart Castle. The track ends at a second mast, but you continue straight on past it to climb a grassy slope and continue along the broad shoulder.

As you walk, heading roughly west, without a path, there are views out to sea on both sides. The shoulder, which begins broad and gentle, steepens and narrows as it climbs to the trig point and cairn that mark the top of **Mainnir nam Fiadh** (754m). It is an easy walk from here round to the main summit of **Dun da Ghaoithe** (766m) (672 362, 10km, 3hr30).

From the summit head northwest briefly to reach and descend by way of the **Beinn Chreagach** shoulder (the descent of Maol nan Damh is down very steep rock and not advisable). As you descend there are a couple of rocky outcrops, but these are easily avoided or negotiated, and the rock soon gives way to grass. Keep to the right of the shoulder, aiming east-northeast for where a fence crosses the **Allt an Dubh-choire** (687 375). Here cross the burn and pass through the gate immediately on the other side.

Follow the burn downhill, keeping well to its right, across very rough ground, making this the least pleasant section of the walk, but thankfully a short one. Once the terrain levels, follow a fence to your right to reach a gate (696 372). A path on the other side leads onto a wider path, where you turn left to come to a bridge over the **Scallastle River**.

Cross the bridge and follow the track on the other side as it takes you into the forestry plantation. Ignore a turning to your right and continue to reach the Scallastle Woodland car park (712 375). Here the Forestry Commission is working to replace the plantation conifers with native woodland. Turn right out of the car park to walk right along the A849 back to the start (18km, 5hr30–6hr).

Alternatives
An Easier Route
The easiest route up Dun da Ghaoithe is to park at Upper Achnacroish, at an old car park (723 348), and ascend and descend by the track route (14km, 800m). (The car park is private so ask for permission before leaving your car there.)

Dun da Ghaoithe and the Allt a Dubh-choire

40 GOATFELL (874m)

'goat hill', likely to be from the Norse 'geiter fjall'

Distance	11km
Time	4hr–4hr30
Ascent	920m
Difficulty	There are good clear paths for the entirety of this circular route, and the rockiest sections of ridge can be avoided, though there are steep slopes with some exposure.
Maps	OS Landranger 69, OS Explorer 361
Access	The Goatfell range is owned by the National Trust for Scotland and access is not affected by stalking. For stalking information outside National Trust land, call the North Arran hillphone on 01770 302363.
Getting there	Start on the A841 just beyond the road sign indicating you are entering Corrie (026 421). Regular local buses timed to meet the ferries to/from Brodick pass here (see www.stagecoachbus.com). Ferries from Brodick run from Ardrossan (Calmac 08000 66 5000, www.calmac.co.uk). For trains/buses to Ardrossan contact Traveline Scotland (0871 200 22 33, www.travelinescotland.com).
Something else	Explore Brodick Castle and its gardens (0844 4932152, www.nts.org.uk/Property/13) before sitting back with a local ale from the Arran Brewery (01770 302353, www.arranbrewery.com).

Follow in the footsteps of Vikings to scale the highest peak of a 'Scotland in miniature', with rocky ridges and great sea views the reward.

Arran has come to be known as a 'Scotland in miniature' due to its wild, mountainous north and gentle, populated south. It is in fact divided in two geologically by the Highland Boundary Fault, which traverses Scotland from Arran in the west to Stonehaven in the northeast.

Goatfell from Brodick pier

As Arran's highest peak, Goatfell commands stunning panoramic views of neighbouring mountains and islands, and across to the mainland. Goatfell was probably named by Vikings, presumably because it was home to wild goats, and the Viking influence can be seen elsewhere on the island. The site of Brodick Castle, for example, is thought to have been used by the Vikings in the 13th century, before they left Arran following the Battle of Largs in 1263.

The spirit of the Norsemen still appears to run strong in the area, with an Up-Helly-Aa held each year in Corrie at the foot of Goatfell. This festival involves a replica Viking longship being sailed from Sannox to Corrie before being set alight at the scene of a mock battle between the Vikings and the Picts.

Today, Brodick Castle and the Goatfell range are owned by the National Trust for Scotland. The 2200 hectares that make up the estate were donated to them in 1958 by Lady Jane Fforde, after being owned by the Dukes of Hamilton then Montrose for many years.

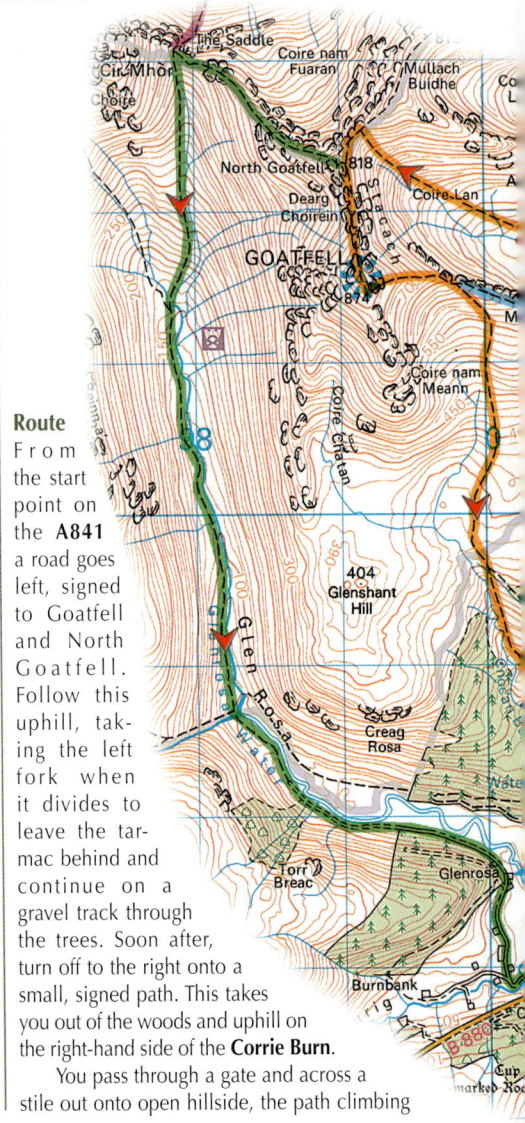

Route

From the start point on the **A841** a road goes left, signed to Goatfell and North Goatfell. Follow this uphill, taking the left fork when it divides to leave the tarmac behind and continue on a gravel track through the trees. Soon after, turn off to the right onto a small, signed path. This takes you out of the woods and uphill on the right-hand side of the **Corrie Burn**.

You pass through a gate and across a stile out onto open hillside, the path climbing

40 GOATFELL

Map continued on page 232

more steeply alongside a dramatic waterslide in the Corrie Burn. As the path levels out it divides (006 417), the left fork crossing the burn to gain the east ridge of Goatfell. You take the right fork, however, to head towards North Goatfell.

Scotland's Best Small Mountains

Map continued
from page 230

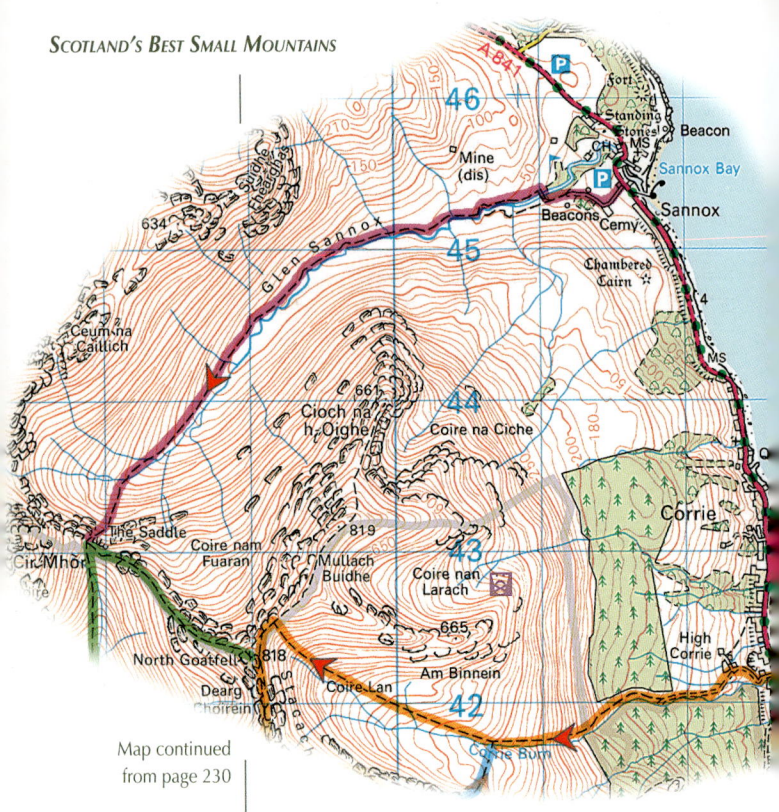

The path goes gently into **Coire-Lan**, becoming boggier and less well maintained, before climbing steeply up a better path to the col between **Mullach Buidhe** and North Goatfell. The views here of the pointed peaks and jagged ridges to the west are fantastic.

Follow the small path to the left to ascend to the summit of **North Goatfell** (818m). From here the crest of the **Stacach** ridge is narrow and very rocky, but can be avoided by taking a small path that runs to the left beneath it. This presents no real problems, and you soon arrive at the summit of **Goatfell** itself (874m) (991 415, 5.5km, 2hr30). From the summit on a clear day you can see the islands of Jura, Islay and Ghigha, over to the Firth of Clyde and, allegedly, on an exceptional day – Ireland!

The return is made by taking the prominent path down the east ridge, **Meall Breac**. This brings you steeply down, by way of steps in places, to the junction with the alternative ascent route mentioned above (998 414). Here you could take the left fork to return to your starting point. This route takes the right fork to continue downhill, the good path bringing you to and across the **Cnocan Burn**.

Once across the burn the path takes you down through lovely mature woodland, continuing straight on at a crossroads. Ignore smaller signed trails off to either side to arrive at a small road (008 378). Cross the road and continue on the main track to arrive at the Arran Brewery at **Cladach**, near Brodick Castle, the short track from which takes you back to the A841 and the finish.

There is a bus stop here for buses back to Brodick or your starting point, or it is a pleasant 3km walk into **Brodick** by way of a newly opened footpath (11km, 4hr–4hr30 without the walk back to Brodick).

Alternatives

While many people ascend and descend Goatfell by the main path from the Arran Brewery and Brodick Castle, there are many different options.

Return to High Corrie via Meall Breac

To return to your starting point at High Corrie, take the left fork on Meall Breac, the east ridge, as mentioned above, to return to the Corrie Burn and the outward footpath (9km, 880m, shown in blue).

Return via the Saddle and Glen Rosa

A circuit of Goatfell could be completed by ascending from the Arran Brewery at Cladach, following the path along the Stacach ridge to North Goatfell then dropping very steeply down the narrow rocky northwest ridge to The Saddle. From here you could descent south to walk the length of beautiful Glen Rosa back to the main road (16km, 1000m, shown in green).

On the Stacach ridge

From Sannox and via the Saddle

Follow the footpath up Glen Sannox to the Saddle, then ascend the steep and occasionally scrambly northwest ridge of North Goatfell before following the main route to the summit of Goatfell. Return the same way to avoid the need for transport, or by one of the Corrie Burn routes to make a circuit (same return route 14km, 1020m, Meall Breac, Corrie Burn return 11km, 860m, shown in pink).

APPENDIX A
Useful Contacts

Travel

Scotrail (Scotland's main train operator)
www.scotrail.co.uk

National Rail Enquiries
08457 48 49 50

Citylink (bus operator linking Scotland's cities and some ferry routes)
www.citylink.co.uk or 08705 50 50 50

Caledonian MacBrayne (operates most of the Scottish island ferries)
www.calmac.co.uk or 0800 066 5000

Traveline Scotland (details of public transport options in Scotland)
www.travelinescotland.com or 0871 200 22 33

Accommodation

Scottish Tourist Board
www.visitscotland.com or 0845 22 55 121

Scottish Youth Hostel Association
www.syha.org.uk or 0845 293 7373

Scottish Independent Hostels
www.hostel-scotland.co.uk

Weather

Mountain Weather Information Service
www.mwis.org.uk

SportScotland Avalanche Information Service
www.sais.gov.uk

Land and access

Forestry Commission
www.forestry.gov.uk

National Trust for Scotland (owns some estates and many of Scotland's historic visitor attractions)
www.nts.org.uk

John Muir Trust (owns some of Scotland's wild land)
www.jmt.org or 0131 554 0114

Scottish Outdoor Access Code
www.outdooraccess-scotland.com

Hill Phones network (for information on stalking and relevant contact numbers)
www.snh.org.uk/hillphones

Maps and more information
Ordnance Survey (for maps)
www.ordnancesurvey.co.uk or 08456 05 05 05

Harvey Maps
www.harveymaps.co.uk or 01786 841202

Scottish Natural Heritage (for more information on geology and wildlife in Scotland)
www.snh.org.uk

Historic Scotland (owns many of Scotland's historic visitor attractions)
www.historic-scotland.gov.uk or 0131 668 8600

APPENDIX B
Bibliography

Borthwick, A *Always a Little Further* (Diadem, 1993)

Dempster, A *The Grahams* (Mainstream Publishing Company, 1997)

Drummond, P *Scottish Hill Names* (Scottish Mountaineering Trust, 2007)

Haldane, ARB *The Drove Roads of Scotland* (Birlinn Limited, 2006)

Milne, R and Brown, H (ed) *The Corbetts* (Scottish Mountaineering Trust, 2002)

Murray, WH *Scotland's Mountains* (Scottish Mountaineering Trust, 1987)

Omand, D (ed) *The Argyll Book* (Birlinn, 2006)

Scottish Natural Heritage *Mountains* (2002)

Scottish Natural Heritage *North West Highlands* (2002)

Scottish Natural Heritage *Place Names in the North West Highlands* (2007)

APPENDIX C

Glossary of Gaelic Words for Common Mountain Features

Gaelic	English
abhainn	river
aird	promontory/headland
allt	burn
airigh	sheiling
bealach	pass
beinn	mountain
camas	bay
carn	rocky hill
choire/coire	corrie
coille	wood
creag	rock/cliff
eas	waterfall
eilean	island
gleann	glen
learg	slope
lochain	lochan/small loch
meall	lump/hill
sail	spur
sgorr/sgurr	pointed peak/hill
sron	shoulder/nose
toll	hollow
uamh	cave

APPENDIX D

Route Summary Table

Route	Mountain	Height	Overview	Distance	Time	Ascent	Difficulty	Page
Sutherland and the Far North								
1	**Ben Loyal**	765m	A royal hill in Scotland's far north, Ben Loyal is renowned for its queens, castles and treasure. Climbing far above the Kyle of Tongue, this route gives you an opportunity to conquer your own castle and gaze out over where the North Sea meets the Atlantic Ocean.	14km	5hr30	820m	A good walk in along tracks gives way to grassy slopes that are less challenging and steep than the rocky peaks of Ben Loyal might suggest.	26
2	**Quinag**	808m	Five tops, stunning scenery, several ridge walks and sea views make this an absolute epic, one of the best mountains in one of the wildest parts of Scotland.	13km	5hr30	1200m	This is a long, challenging route across rocky, narrow ridges, with some exposure and a lot of ups and downs.	30
3	**Suilven**	731m	Scottish mountains don't come any more iconic than Suilven. Instantly recognisable, this small but mighty peak rises up as if from nowhere to dramatic effect. A long, classic route with rewards a plenty.	23km	7hr	1170m	This is a long and demanding route. A good approach path gives way to boggier ground and a very steep, rocky ascent. The descent is equally steep, with a long walk out on boggy paths until the good path down the River Kirkaig.	34

SCOTLAND'S BEST SMALL MOUNTAINS

Route	Mountain	Height	Overview	Distance	Time	Ascent	Difficulty	Page
4	Cul Mor	849m	One of the highest peaks in Assynt, Cul Mor's rocky summit is a window to both beautiful views and to the history of the formation of the surrounding landscape.	12km	4hr30	760m	With a good path to start and end this is a relatively straightforward route, but does involve navigating across some rough, pathless ground, and a steep rocky final ascent up the ridge to the summit.	40
5	Stac Pollaidh	613m	Something of a national treasure, Stac Pollaidh is beloved by many. A circular route up to, and possibly along, its rocky pinnacles, offers a mini-adventure at the heart of the beautiful Inverpolly Estate.	5km	2hr – 2hr30	520m	The short circuit round the hill presents no difficulties, and while steep, nor does the ascent to the ridge. A traverse along the ridge however requires exposed scrambling, to grade 3 for the final summit, and anyone attempting it needs to remember they will have to return the way they climb.	45
6	Ben More Coigach and Sgurr an Fhidhleir	743m 705m	Rising dramatically out of the sea, the Ben More Coigach range dominates the Coigach peninsula while remaining fairly unknown to walkers. The great ridge walk combined with some of the best views in the world makes for a brilliant day out.	10km	4hr	900m	A short route with some steep slopes and exposed sections of ridge. Stretches without paths make for some rough walking and the need for good navigation in poor visibility.	48

APPENDIX D – ROUTE SUMMARY TABLE

Route	Mountain	Height	Overview	Distance	Time	Ascent	Difficulty	Page
Torridon and the northwest								
7	Beinn Ghobhlach	635m	Occupying a unique location on a remote peninsula, Beinn Ghobhlach offers a real chance to get away from it all. A wild and rugged walk with sea views and the potential for eagles soaring overhead.	12km	4hr30	760m	A remote rugged route that soon leaves all paths behind to climb rough heather then rocky slopes. Good navigation required.	56
8	Beinn Airigh Charr	791m	A long but simple walk into the heart of some of Scotland's most beautiful countryside. With stories of legendary shepherdesses, Arctic convoys and exotic plants, this a real gem of mountain, which longs to be explored.	25km	8hr	1100m	This is a long route but on good straightforward tracks and paths for the walks in and out, with a small but clear path to the col. No path on the tops and some steep slopes.	60
9	Baosbheinn	875m	A magical journey into the wilderness of a remote Torridon hill. This long and rugged route takes you back in time to the end of the last ice age to see the mountains it created in all their glory.	23km	8hr	1200m	Good track for the long walk in but then rough ground over open hillside with no paths to gain summit. Rocky, steep slopes with some small paths on main ridges.	65
10	Sgurr Dubh	782m	A wild excursion with an opportunity to take a trip into Scotland's geological past. Sgurr Dubh may be one of Torridon's least climbed peaks, but it offers some of the best views.	16.5km	6hr	830m	While there are sections with good stalking paths, much of this route is characterised by rough ground and confusing terrain. The final section involves several stiles over deer fence and a two-rope river crossing.	72

SCOTLAND'S BEST SMALL MOUNTAINS

Route	Mountain	Height	Overview	Distance	Time	Ascent	Difficulty	Page
11	**Beinn Damh**	903m	One of Glen Torridon's most distinctive peaks, this is a hill of two halves. Pleasant pony paths take you up past waterfalls and through lush forest in contrast to a striking, rocky ridge that reveals the full drama of the spectacular mountain scenery.	14km	5hr30	1180m	Most of this route is on very good paths, though the ridge itself is very rocky and becomes steep and narrow as it nears the summit.	77
Lochaber and the West								
12	**Sgurr Coire Choinnichean**	796m	A remote ridge walk located in the wonderful wilds of Knoydart, a peninsula sitting between heaven and hell. This route is only accessible by boat from Mallaig or by a long walk, and ends at the mainland's remotest pub.	13km	4hr30	900m	A shorter route, but one that takes in steep, pathless heathery slopes and a narrow rocky ridge.	84
13	**Streap**	909m	With a knife-edged ridge and several rugged tops en route, this long and challenging walk up Streap is enough to rival most Munros, and offers a great adventure.	17.5km	7hr	1400m	A long, challenging route across rugged ground with no paths, a lot of climbing, steep slopes and a very narrow rocky ridge to the summit.	88
14	**Rois-Bheinn** **An Stac** **Sgurr na Ba Glaise** **Druim Fiaclach**	882m 814m 874m 869m	Four peaks for the price of one make this a long and challenging circuit to rival any of its higher counterparts. Rugged ridges and superb views are the rewards for the adventurous.	18km	8hr	1600m	This is a long and demanding route. It starts on a boggy all-terrain-vehicle (ATV) track, but then there are virtually no established paths, making good navigation essential. Steep ground and rocky outcrops going up, then grassy/	94

APPENDIX D – ROUTE SUMMARY TABLE

Route	Mountain	Height	Overview	Distance	Time	Ascent	Difficulty	Page
							rocky ridges with some exposure, and descending across rough ground.	
15	Sgurr Dhomhnuill	888m	The shapely conical peak of Sgurr Dhomhnuill is the highest in Ardgour, and with dramatic drops on all sides it has great panoramic views. Not only that, but this is a mountain with many tales to tell, a place where natural and human history meet.	20km	6hr30	1150m	While this walk starts on a pleasant path, the rest of the route is pathless across rough ground. The ridges of Sgurr Dhomhnuill itself are very steep and rocky.	101
16	Beinn Resipol	845m	A traverse across the Ardnamurchan peninsula's highest peak, with some of the best views of the west coast. Not only that but Beinn Resipol is flanked by unique oak woodlands and steeped in local history too.	16km	5hr30	920m	This is a relatively straightforward day out on small, mainly clear but often muddy hill paths, with a pathless section across open hillside calling for good navigation; single-track road walk to finish.	107
17	Ben Hiant	528m	Hills, history, beaches and breathtaking views out on Britain's most westerly point, Ben Hiant is a route that has it all.	10.5km	4hr	620m	A compact route on small but mainly clear paths on hill and coast, but the pathless middle section needs good navigation. The walk starts and finishes on a single-track.	112

SCOTLAND'S BEST SMALL MOUNTAINS

Route	Mountain	Height	Overview	Distance	Time	Ascent	Difficulty	Page
The Great Glen to the Cairngorms								
18	Creagan a'Chaise	722m	Famous for a bloody battle, the rounded, heather-clad Hills of Cromdale offer great wild walking with wonderful views.	13.5km	4hr	580m	This is a gentle route up grass and heather slopes, but with few paths and broad shoulders, navigation can be very difficult in poor visibility.	120
19	Meall Fuar-mhonaidh	699m	Monster-spotting above the banks of Loch Ness. Whether or not you believe in Nessie, Meall Fuar-mhonaidh commands a great vantage point over Scotland's longest glen and largest loch. A short walk with a big character.	10km	3hr	525m	This is a short route on clear paths. The section along the shoulder can be boggy in places.	125
20	Meall a'Bhuachille	810m	A great circular walk atop broad shoulders and over four tops, accompanied along the way by fairies, rogues and great views of the Cairngorms.	16km	5hr30	750m	Good paths and broad shoulders make this a relatively easy route, although care should be taken on the tops in poor visibility.	129
21	Creag Dhubh (Argyll Stone)	848m	A ruined castle on an island in a picturesque loch, beautiful native Scots pine forest and a wild and windswept rocky summit, Creag Dhubh has much to recommend it. This is a good circular route through a real mixture of landscapes.	16km	5hr30	650m	This reasonably long route follows good paths in the forest, but involves a long stretch on open hillside without paths that calls for good navigation.	134

APPENDIX D – ROUTE SUMMARY TABLE

Route	Mountain	Height	Overview	Distance	Time	Ascent	Difficulty	Page
22	**Creag Dhubh (Newtonmore)**	756m	A battle cry, a mountain hideout and a rock-climbers' paradise, Creag Dhubh also offers a great short walk with fantastic views of Badenoch.	6km	2hr30	500m	This is a short but challenging route. The lower slopes require good route-finding, with the path disappearing for short sections in the woods. The upper slopes are steep and rocky with some sharp drops.	139
23	**Morrone (or Morven)**	859m	A mountain with royal connections, Morrone stands guard over the village of Braemar.	12.5km	3hr30 –4hr	580m	A short and easy circular route on good clear paths and tracks.	143
Glencoe and Central Scotland								
24	**Ben Vrackie**	841m	Readily accessible, Ben Vrackie offers a great escape from the cities of Scotland's central belt. Its fine paths lead you to the top of one of the best viewpoints in the Southern Highlands, and the Moulin Inn offers a cosy fireside seat at the bottom.	9km	3hr30	700m	Straightforward and well-made paths take you all the way to the summit, though the last section is a bit steep and rocky.	150
25	**Leum Uilleim**	909m	Proving that the West Highland line is not just for trainspotters, Leum Uilleim offers a great horseshoe of a walk set in acres of wilderness and only accessible by train – a real chance to get away from it all.	11km	3hr30 –4hr	580m	A short, easy route with some small paths and tracks, but also pathless rough and boggy ground. The broad shoulders are easy to follow, but could be tricky in cloud.	154

SCOTLAND'S BEST SMALL MOUNTAINS

Route	Mountain	Height	Overview	Distance	Time	Ascent	Difficulty	Page
26	Sgorr na Ciche (Pap of Glencoe)	742m	Made famous by breasts and battles, Sgorr na Ciche's distinctive shape dominates the entrance to Glencoe. This short route gives a flavour of the drama and fierceness that characterises both the landscape and history of this glen.	8km	3hr30	720m	A short route that follows a path to the summit. The path can be very muddy lower down, and the last section is steep and rocky with some easy scrambling.	159
27	Beinn a'Chrulaiste	857m	A gentle hill set amid the rugged beauty of Glencoe, with the best view of Buachaille Etive Mor, Beinn a'Chrulaiste rises above the Kings House Hotel, a welcome resting place over the years for drovers, soldiers, labourers and walkers alike.	13km	4hr	670m	A short and relatively easy route, but a lack of paths on the hill itself calls for good navigation. The return is via the well-walked West Highland Way.	162
28	Beinn Trilleachan	839m	Located in one of the most beautiful glens in Scotland, Beinn Trilleachan is home to some dramatic rock slabs and one of the finest views you'll come across anywhere.	10km	5hr	1100m	A reasonably challenging route due to the long climb up pathless rough ground. While there are steep drops to the east, the ridge itself is not narrow, but the descent from Trilleachan Slabs is steep and rocky.	167
29	Sron a'Chlachain	521m	A short circular route above one of Scotland's prettiest villages, Sron a'Chlachain offers great views over the hills and glens of the ancient Celtic land of Breadalbane.	6km	2hr – 2hr30	460m	A very short route, the ascent all on a small path, but steep in places. The descent is over rougher ground.	172

Appendix D – Route Summary Table

Route	Mountain	Height	Overview	Distance	Time	Ascent	Difficulty	Page
Arrochar and the Trossachs								
30	**Meall an t'Seallaidh**	852m	An adventure into the glens and passes of Rob Roy's outlaw countryside, on a peak that lives up to its name – 'mountain of the view'.	20km	6hr	990m	This long route starts and ends on good tracks, but much of the walk is across rough, pathless ground where the need for good navigation is essential.	178
31	**Ben Ledi**	879m	A great circular route on 'the mountain of life and death'. Marking the start of the southern highlands, Ben Ledi offers wooded slopes and a rugged, barren top, all within a stone's throw of Scotland's central belt.	9km	4hr	760m	Ben Ledi presents no real technical difficulty, and with its broad shoulders there is little exposure. The descent to Stank Glen can be hard to navigate in cloud, however, making it easy to miss the path, so care should be taken.	184
32	**Ben A'n or A'an (Binnein)**	461m	A short but prominent peak straight out of a romantic saga, it is with good reason that for centuries people have flocked to the beautiful countryside of the Trossachs, and Ben A'an at its heart.	3.5km	1hr30 – 2hr	300m	A very short outing with good paths most of the way; the last section is steep and stepped in places.	190
33	**Ben Venue**	727m	Ben Venue is the epitome of a small mountain. With forested slopes and a rocky peak, it sits in majestic countryside with some royal connections.	14km	4hr30	740m	Straightforward route following well-signed paths all the way to the summit. Top section muddy in places with rocky summit.	193

247

SCOTLAND'S BEST SMALL MOUNTAINS

Route	Mountain	Height	Overview	Distance	Time	Ascent	Difficulty	Page
34	**The Cobbler (Ben Arthur)**	884m	Possibly the most famous of Scotland's small mountains, the distinctive jagged peaks of The Cobbler have been a popular destination for walkers and climbers for over a century.	12.5km	4hr30	1000m	A clear route on mainly good paths, with a steep rocky section involving some easy scrambling. The true summit is a rocky outcrop perched on the top and reached only by an airy scramble, though this can be omitted.	199
35	**Beinn an Lochain**	901m	A short scramble up a fine rocky ridge brings you to the top of Beinn an Lochain and a great vantage point over the Arrochar Alps and historic Glen Croe.	6km	3hr	680m	A very short route, but not without its challenges. The lower ridge is rocky, with some easy scrambling to negotiate; the higher section is very steep with some exposure.	204
The Islands								
36	**The Storr (Skye)**	719m	Step into 'a land that time forgot' to mingle with giants and volcanoes not to mention some breathtaking views on this great circuit.	8.5km	3hr30	700m	The first section of this short route is on good paths. From the shoulder on there are no paths but the walking is easy on short grass. The final section from the bealach is steep and rocky.	210

APPENDIX D – ROUTE SUMMARY TABLE

Route	Mountain	Height	Overview	Distance	Time	Ascent	Difficulty	Page
37	Glamaig (Skye)	775m	Scree-hopping on the Red Hills of Skye, Glamaig offers rocky ridges and the best Cuillin viewpoint, with just a bit of adrenalin mixed in, and that's without taking part in the famous hill race.	13km	5hr30	1300m	The path is boggy in places but easy enough up the shoulder to Beinn Dearg Mheadhonach, but from there on this route is characterised by very steep scree slopes.	213
38	An Sgurr (Eigg)	393m	The volcanic rocky peak of An Sgurr on Eigg is instantly recognisable and a joy to climb. This is a short route to a lofty fortress, with insights into the islands turbulent past and promising green future.	8km	3hr	390m	A short route with a path all the way to the summit, but it does involve some exposure and a little scrambling on the ridge, but nothing difficult.	219
39	Dun da Ghaoithe (Mull)	766m	Spectacular sea views on a long fine ridge make this circular route on Mull's second highest peak well worthy of a day trip.	18km	5hr30 – 6hr	900m	The ascent up the track is easy though steep in places, then gives way to a pathless but straightforward ridge. The descent is steeper, across very rough ground in places until the final good track, and short road walk.	223
40	Goatfell (Arran)	874m	Follow in the footsteps of Vikings to scale the highest peak of a Scotland in miniature, with rocky ridges and great sea views the reward.	11km	4hr – 4hr30	920m	There are good clear paths for the entirety of this circular route, and the rockiest sections of ridge can be avoided, though there are steep slopes with some exposure.	228

NOTES

NOTES

THE GREAT OUTDOORS
tgo

The UK's leading monthly magazine for the independent hilllwalker and backpacker. With thought provoking articles, varied and exhilarating routes, expert gear reviews and outstanding photography, TGO's writers are at the heart of the walking world providing the essentials to inspire your next adventure.

To subscribe today call

0141 302 7718

or visit **www.tgomagazine.co.uk**

Get ready for take off

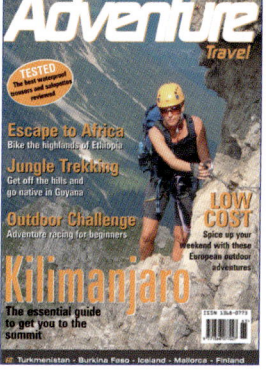

Adventure Travel helps you to go outdoors, over there.

More ideas, information, advice and entertaining features on overseas trekking, walking and backpacking than any other magazine – guaranteed.

Available from good newsagents or by subscription – 6 issues £15.

Adventure Travel Magazine T: 01789 488166.

LISTING OF CICERONE GUIDES

BRITISH ISLES CHALLENGES, COLLECTIONS AND ACTIVITIES
The End to End Trail
The Mountains of England and Wales
  Vol 1: Wales
  Vol 2: England
The National Trails
The Relative Hills of Britain
The Ridges of England, Wales and Ireland
The UK Trailwalker's Handbook
Three Peaks, Ten Tors

NORTHERN ENGLAND TRAILS
A Northern Coast to Coast Walk
Backpacker's Britain: Northern England
Hadrian's Wall Path
The Dales Way
The Pennine Way
The Spirit of Hadrian's Wall

LAKE DISTRICT
An Atlas of the English Lakes
Coniston Copper Mines
Great Mountain Days in the Lake District
Lake District Winter Climbs
Roads and Tracks of the Lake District
Rocky Rambler's Wild Walks
Scrambles in the Lake District
  North
  South
Short Walks in Lakeland
  Book 1: South Lakeland
  Book 2: North Lakeland
  Book 3: West Lakeland
The Central Fells
The Cumbria Coastal Way
The Cumbria Way and the Allerdale Ramble
The Lake District Anglers' Guide
The Mid-Western Fells
The Near Eastern Fells
The Southern Fells
The Tarns of Lakeland
  Vol 1: West
  Vol 2: East
Tour of the Lake District

NORTH WEST ENGLAND AND THE ISLE OF MAN
A Walker's Guide to the Lancaster Canal
Historic Walks in Cheshire
Isle of Man Coastal Path
The Isle of Man
The Ribble Way
Walking in Lancashire
Walking in the Forest of Bowland and Pendle
Walking on the West Pennine Moors
Walks in Lancashire Witch Country
Walks in Ribble Country
Walks in Silverdale and Arnside
Walks in The Forest of Bowland

NORTH EAST ENGLAND, YORKSHIRE DALES AND PENNINES
A Canoeist's Guide to the North East
Historic Walks in North Yorkshire
South Pennine Walks
The Cleveland Way and the Yorkshire Wolds Way
The North York Moors
The Reivers Way
The Teesdale Way
The Yorkshire Dales Angler's Guide
The Yorkshire Dales:
  North and East
  South and West
Walking in County Durham
Walking in Northumberland
Walking in the North Pennines
Walking in the Wolds
Walks in Dales Country
Walks in the Yorkshire Dales
Walks on the North York Moors
  Books 1 & 2

DERBYSHIRE, PEAK DISTRICT AND MIDLANDS
High Peak Walks
Historic Walks in Derbyshire
The Star Family Walks
Walking in Derbyshire
White Peak Walks:
  The Northern Dales
  The Southern Dales

SOUTHERN ENGLAND
A Walker's Guide to the Isle of Wight
London: The Definitive Walking Guide
The Cotswold Way
The Greater Ridgeway
The Lea Valley Walk
The North Downs Way
The South Downs Way
The South West Coast Path
The Thames Path
Walking in Bedfordshire
Walking in Berkshire
Walking in Buckinghamshire
Walking in Kent
Walking in Sussex
Walking in the Isles of Scilly
Walking in the Thames Valley
Walking on Dartmoor

WALES AND WELSH BORDERS
Backpacker's Britain: Wales
Glyndwr's Way
Great Mountain Days in Snowdonia
Hillwalking in Snowdonia
Hillwalking in Wales
  Vols 1 & 2
Offa's Dyke Path
Ridges of Snowdonia
Scrambles in Snowdonia
The Ascent of Snowdon
The Lleyn Peninsula Coastal Path
The Pembrokeshire Coastal Path
The Shropshire Hills
The Spirit Paths of Wales
Walking in Pembrokeshire
Walking on the Brecon Beacons
Welsh Winter Climbs

SCOTLAND
Backpacker's Britain:
  Central and Southern Scottish Highlands
  Northern Scotland
Ben Nevis and Glen Coe
Border Pubs and Inns
North to the Cape
Scotland's Best Small Mountains
Scotland's Far West
Scotland's Mountain Ridges
Scrambles in Lochaber
The Border Country
The Central Highlands
The Great Glen Way
The Isle of Skye
The Pentland Hills: A Walker's Guide
The Scottish Glens
  2 The Atholl Glens
  3 The Glens of Rannoch
  4 The Glens of Trossach
  5 The Glens of Argyll
  6 The Great Glen
The Southern Upland Way
The West Highland Way
Walking in Scotland's Far North
Walking in the Cairngorms
Walking in the Hebrides
Walking in the Ochils, Campsie Fells and Lomond Hills
Walking in Torridon
Walking Loch Lomond and the Trossachs
Walking on Harris and Lewis
Walking on Jura, Islay and Colonsay
Walking on the Isle of Arran
Walking on the Orkney and Shetland Isles
Walking the Galloway Hills
Walking the Lowther Hills
Walking the Munros
  Vol 1: Southern, Central and Western Highlands
  Vol 2: Northern Highlands and the Cairngorms
Winter Climbs – Ben Nevis and Glencoe
Winter Climbs in the Cairngorms

UK CYCLING
Border Country Cycle Routes
Lands End to John O'Groats Cycle Guide
Rural Rides No 2: East Surrey
South Lakeland Cycle Rides
The Lancashire Cycleway

ALPS – CROSS BORDER ROUTES
100 Hut Walks in the Alps
Across the Eastern Alps: E5
Alpine Points of View
Alpine Ski Mountaineering
  Vol 1: Western Alps
  Vol 2: Central and Eastern Alps
Chamonix to Zermatt
Snowshoeing
Tour of Mont Blanc
Tour of Monte Rosa
Tour of the Matterhorn
Walking in the Alps
Walks and Treks in the Maritime Alps

FRANCE
Écrins National Park
GR20: Corsica
Mont Blanc Walks
The Cathar Way
The GR5 Trail
The Robert Louis Stevenson Trail
Tour of the Oisans: The GR54
Tour of the Queyras
Tour of the Vanoise
Trekking in the Vosges and Jura
Vanoise Ski Touring
Walking in Provence
Walking in the Cathar Region
Walking in the Cevennes
Walking in the Dordogne
Walking in the Haute Savoie
  North
  South
Walking in the Languedoc
Walking in the Tarentaise & Beaufortain Alps
Walking on Corsica
Walking the French Gorges
Walks in Volcano Country

PYRENEES AND FRANCE/SPAIN CROSS-BORDER ROUTES
Rock Climbs In The Pyrenees
The GR10 Trail
The Mountains of Andorra
The Pyrenean Haute Route
The Way of St James
  France
  Spain
Through the Spanish Pyrenees: GR11
Walks and Climbs in the Pyrenees

SPAIN & PORTUGAL
Costa Blanca Walks
  Vol 1: West
  Vol 2: East
The Mountains of Central Spain
Trekking through Mallorca
Via de la Plata
Walking in Madeira
Walking in Mallorca
Walking in the Algarve
Walking in the Canary Islands:
  Vol 2: East
Walking in the Cordillera Cantabrica
Walking in the Sierra Nevada
Walking the GR7 in Andalucia
Walks and Climbs in the Picos de Europa

SWITZERLAND
Alpine Pass Route
Central Switzerland
The Bernese Alps
Tour of the Jungfrau Region
Walking in the Valais
Walking in Ticino
Walks in the Engadine

GERMANY
Germany's Romantic Road
King Ludwig Way
Walking in the Bavarian Alps
Walking in the Harz Mountains
Walking in the Salzkammergut
Walking the River Rhine Trail

EASTERN EUROPE
The High Tatras
The Mountains of Romania
Walking in Bulgaria's National Parks
Walking in Hungary

SCANDINAVIA
Walking in Norway

SLOVENIA, CROATIA AND MONTENEGRO
The Julian Alps of Slovenia
The Mountains of Montenegro
Trekking in Slovenia
Walking in Croatia

ITALY
Central Apennines of Italy
Gran Paradiso
Italian Rock
Italy's Sibillini National Park
Shorter Walks in the Dolomites
Through the Italian Alps
Trekking in the Apennines
Treks in the Dolomites
Via Ferratas of the Italian Dolomites:
  Vols 1 & 2
Walking in Sicily
Walking in the Central Italian Alps
Walking in the Dolomites
Walking in Tuscany
Walking on the Amalfi Coast

MEDITERRANEAN
Jordan – Walks, Treks, Caves, Climbs and Canyons
The Ala Dag
The High Mountains of Crete
The Mountains of Greece
Treks & Climbs in Wadi Rum, Jordan
Walking in Malta
Western Crete

HIMALAYA
Annapurna: A Trekker's Guide
Bhutan
Everest: A Trekker's Guide
Garhwal & Kumaon: A Trekker's and Visitor's Guide
Kangchenjunga: A Trekker's Guide
Langtang with Gosainkund & Helambu: A Trekker's Guide
Manaslu: A Trekker's Guide
The Mount Kailash Trek

NORTH AMERICA
British Columbia
The Grand Canyon

SOUTH AMERICA
Aconcagua and the Southern Andes

AFRICA
Climbing in the Moroccan Anti-Atlas
Kilimanjaro: A Complete Trekker's Guide
Trekking in the Atlas Mountains
Walking in the Drakensberg

IRELAND
Irish Coastal Walks
The Irish Coast to Coast Walk
The Mountains of Ireland

EUROPEAN CYCLING
Cycle Touring in France
Cycle Touring in Ireland
Cycle Touring in Spain
Cycle Touring in Switzerland
Cycling in the French Alps
Cycling the Canal du Midi
Cycling the River Loire
The Danube Cycleway
The Grand Traverse of the Massif Central
The Way of St James

INTERNATIONAL CHALLENGES, COLLECTIONS AND ACTIVITIES
Canyoning
Europe's High Points

AUSTRIA
Klettersteig – Scrambles in the Northern Limestone Alps
Trekking in Austria's Hohe Tauern
Trekking in the Stubai Alps
Trekking in the Zillertal Alps
Walking in Austria

TECHNIQUES
Indoor Climbing
Map and Compass
Mountain Weather
Moveable Feasts
Outdoor Photography
Rock Climbing
Snow and Ice Techniques
Sport Climbing
The Book of the Bivvy
The Hillwalker's Guide to Mountaineering
The Hillwalker's Manual

MINI GUIDES
Avalanche!
Navigating with a GPS
Navigation
Pocket First Aid and Wilderness Medicine
Snow

For full and up-to-date information on our ever-expanding list of guides, please visit our website:
www.cicerone.co.uk.

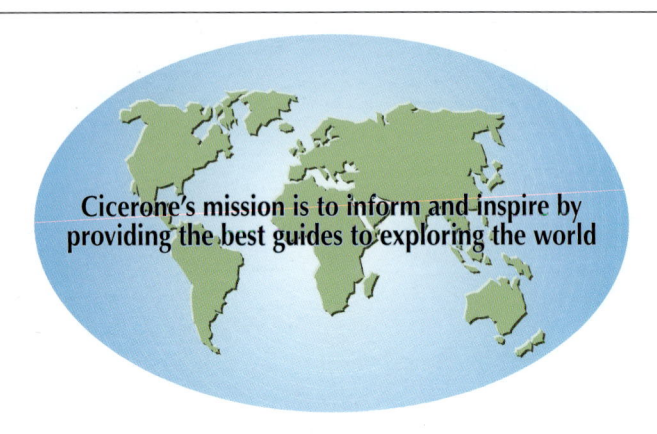

Cicerone's mission is to inform and inspire by providing the best guides to exploring the world

Since its foundation 40 years ago, Cicerone has specialised in publishing guidebooks and has built a reputation for quality and reliability. It now publishes nearly 300 guides to the major destinations for outdoor enthusiasts, including Europe, UK and the rest of the world.

Written by leading and committed specialists, Cicerone guides are recognised as the most authoritative. They are full of information, maps and illustrations so that the user can plan and complete a successful and safe trip or expedition – be it a long face climb, a walk over Lakeland fells, an alpine cycling tour, a Himalayan trek or a ramble in the countryside.

With a thorough introduction to assist planning, clear diagrams, maps and colour photographs to illustrate the terrain and route, and accurate and detailed text, Cicerone guides are designed for ease of use and access to the information.

If the facts on the ground change, or there is any aspect of a guide that you think we can improve, we are always delighted to hear from you.

Cicerone Press
2 Police Square Milnthorpe Cumbria LA7 7PY
Tel: 015395 62069 Fax: 015395 63417
info@cicerone.co.uk www.cicerone.co.uk

CICERONE